JILTED

JILTED

VI KEELAND

BRAMBLE

TOR PUBLISHING GROUP
NEW YORK

JILTED

A Bramble Book
Published by Tom Doherty Associates / Tor Publishing Group
120 Broadway
New York, NY 10271

www.torpublishinggroup.com

Bramble™ is a trademark of Macmillan Publishing Group, LLC.

The Library of Congress Cataloging-in-Publication Data
is available upon request.

ISBN 978-1-250-35985-8 (trade paperback)
ISBN 978-1-250-35986-5 (ebook)

Our books may be purchased in bulk for promotional, educational, or business use. Please contact your local bookseller or the Macmillan Corporate and Premium Sales Department at 1-800-221-7945, extension 5442, or by email at MacmillanSpecialMarkets@macmillan.com.

First Edition: 2025

Printed in the United States of America

0 9 8 7 6 5 4 3 2 1

For all the ladies who have had
their hearts broken standing at the altar.
Fuck him. Someone who deserves you is coming soon.

1

SLOANE

"Oh dear Lord." Elijah blinked up at me. "You're joking, right?"

I snort-laughed and raised my hand to get my brother Will's attention. "Nope. This is what we're stuck with."

My brother walked over. He wiped his hands on a bar towel and slung it over his shoulder. "What do you want now, Peaty?"

I rolled my eyes. "I'll take another margarita, and Elijah here will have . . ." I looked over and waited for my best friend and work partner in crime to fill in the blank. But he was too busy drooling over Will. I shook my head. "He'll have a margarita, too. But frosty ones this time, not on the rocks."

"*Frosty.*" Will huffed. "Two *pains in the asses* coming right up."

Elijah pushed up from his seat and leaned over the bar to watch Will walk away. "Are you *sure* he's not gay?"

"He screwed half my female friends in high school, married his college sweetheart, and has a daughter." I motioned toward my brother. "Besides, how can you even think that? He's wearing a *brown* shirt, *black* pants, and green *Crocs.*"

Elijah's nose wrinkled. "That is pretty bad. But I could overlook it with that jawline."

I chuckled.

"Why does he call you Peaty, anyway?"

"Because he's annoying. When I was little, I used to get really nervous when the teacher would call on me in class. I developed a habit of repeating the question back before answering, which somehow soothed me. Will and my other brother, Travis, found out and started calling me *Repeat.* It morphed into Peaty over the years."

"Hot and funny. Exactly my type. What a shame." Elijah scooped a few cashews from the small bowl on the bar and tossed one into the air, his mouth open. The nut smacked his cheek and fell to the floor.

"Do you think maybe we're being pranked?" I motioned to the papers spread out on the bar—our last-minute assignment for this evening. "How can a bride really pick these dresses?"

"Dresses? What about the *fascinators*? We're not in England, and this isn't a garden wedding. I think maybe you're right and someone is screwing with us."

I looked at the time on my phone. "Damn. It's already four. We have to get on the road soon or we're going to be late. Tell Will I went to the back to change when he comes with our drinks. I'm going to pull a Superman in the supply closet. It's bigger than the bathroom, and I don't want to accidentally dip my dress in toilet water like I did last month."

"Okay. But when it's my turn to get dressed, don't tell him I'm back there." Elijah winked. "I want him to walk in on me naked."

I slipped on one of the standard LBDs I always wore to the weddings we covered and paired it with sparkly silver stilettos. After, I fixed my makeup and sprayed my hair upside down in an attempt to give it some volume. When I came out, Elijah's head was bent back in laughter, while Will stood on the other side of the bar with a devious smile.

This can't be good. "Whatever he told you"—I tossed my duffle bag on the barstool—"it's a complete lie. Don't believe him."

Elijah laughed. "So when you were seven, you didn't give out wedding invitations to everyone you knew so they could come watch you marry the family dog? And the dog didn't spend the entire ceremony trying to hump your back?"

I scowled at Will. "That only happened because this jerk pretended to wish me luck and rubbed peanut butter on the back of my dress. Buddy was obsessed with peanut butter. If someone opened a jar, he'd hump a couch pillow."

Elijah continued to cackle. Too bad that incident hadn't soured me on my obsession with weddings. It could have saved a lot of heartache, and maybe right now I'd be a *real* journalist instead of a writer for *Bride* magazine.

"Go get changed, Elijah." I pointed to my brother. "And *you*, go back to being flattered by attention from seventeen-year-old girls who flirt with you so you'll accept their cousin's ID that says they're twenty-nine."

"Jeez," Will said. "Someone's cranky."

"Cranky? *Why would I be cranky?* Because I'm going to yet *another* wedding I don't feel like going to on a Saturday night?"

"You're on your period, aren't you?"

My eyes flared wide. "Go away, Will."

My brother meant no harm. This was who we were—busting chops was our love language. But I *was* a little cranky this afternoon. Or maybe I'd been that way for the last six months. I used to love my job. Getting dressed up and going to extravagant weddings and writing about them for a living? Dishing out advice to my more than 1.5 million bride-to-be followers on social media? It was my dream job, one I'd wished for even before I was old enough to plan an elegant backyard wedding with two-year-old Buddy the dog. I'd been *obsessed* with weddings since I was a little girl. Maybe even addicted—wedding movies, wedding dresses, wedding venues— heck, I'd had the readings for my future ceremony picked out since I was ten. My parents lived a fairy-tale life, and I *believed* I would get my own happily ever after. I lived for it. *Dumb.* I know that now. But the day I'd gotten engaged had been the happiest day of my life. Then my big day came and . . . I was left standing alone at the altar. *Jilted.*

And after that, my love of all things wedding turned sour. Like milk left out on a ninety-degree day, it curdled. Not to mention, the very next day, my original groom had died—Buddy. He'd been twenty-one, an age most dogs don't even get close to, so it wasn't a surprise, but seriously? The day after I'd been left at the altar?

Elijah came out from the back room, looking as dapper as usual. While I preferred to wear a simple black dress and blend in when we were working, that wasn't his style—not by a mile. This week, he wore a navy plaid suit, which had tapered pants with a break two inches above the ankle, and burgundy velvet shoes. Anything simpler wouldn't coordinate with his platinum-blond hair and Korean heritage. Few men could pull off the style, but Elijah's confidence could make anything work. I swallowed back bitterness and forced a smile. "You're going to outshine the groom in that getup."

He smiled. "Don't I always?"

Two hours later, we walked into the bridal suite at Chateau L'Amour. Elijah stopped abruptly. "Last chance," he said. "Please tell me someone is screwing with us and they're really filming a period-piece movie or something here."

I grimaced as I spotted one of the bridesmaids. The woman looked like she'd just stepped out of *Gone with the Wind* with a giant hoopskirt. It was even worse in person than in the photos we'd received in advance for designer credits. "Maybe she's one of those champagne greeters. You know, where they wear a big, full skirt that holds a hundred glasses of champagne."

"Do you *see* any champagne?"

"No, but . . . let's be optimistic." Just as I finished that sentence, two more women walked in, wearing identical dresses.

Elijah elbowed me. "Guess they have *three* champagne greeters."

I sighed. *Great.* It was hard enough for me to write glowing articles about tasteful weddings these days. "We'll have to focus on the bride."

He chuckled. "Who do you think picked out those monstrosities? I'll bet you these ladies look like they stepped out of *Vogue* compared to her."

He had a point. "Doesn't matter how bad it is; we have to remember, this assignment came from *Hayes* himself. So it needs to look stunning in the magazine. And Ted Hayes Jr. is apparently in the wedding party, so make sure you get a good picture of the big boss's son."

Elijah and I had originally been assigned another wedding this evening, but that bride had to have emergency surgery, so the event had been postponed. Instead, the CEO of the conglomerate that owned our magazine had stepped in with a replacement. Apparently the groom was a friend of his family or something. So my write-up and Elijah's photos needed to be glowing.

Elijah nodded. "Damn. Yeah, okay."

A woman wearing a black vest and a frazzled smile walked over. She looked down at the equipment bag Elijah carried. "Are you the videographer team?"

I shook my head. "We're with *Bride* magazine. We're covering the wedding for an upcoming spread."

"Oh." She frowned. "The videographer should've been here already. The bride is . . . impatient." She extended a hand. "I'm Claire, one of the two bridal attendants. If you need anything, just let me know."

"Would you mind pointing us to the bridal suite?"

"Of course. Follow me. I'll show you the way."

When we entered, a half-dozen bridesmaids floated around in a posh room, but I didn't see the guest of honor. "Is the bride around?" I asked. "I'd like to introduce myself and make sure it's okay to snap some pre-wedding photos of the ladies getting ready."

"She's—"

"Are you freaking kidding me?" a woman shrieked from the other room. "This *cannot* be happening to *me!*"

Claire leaned in and whispered. "That's the bride now."

The way she was screaming, I thought the worst. "Did . . . the groom call off the wedding?"

Claire shook her head. "No, she probably broke a nail."

Wonderful.

A door at the back of the room flew open, and Bridezilla marched out. Her hair and makeup were done and a sparkling tiara sat atop her head, but from the neck down she was still in pajamas. "Who's going next?" She looked around the room and pointed to a bridesmaid. "*You!* Take off your dress and go get sprayed."

"Sprayed?" I whispered to the attendant. "What's going on?"

"The maid of honor flew in last night. She lives in Florida. Apparently, Piper had a fit when she saw her because her friend looks *too tan.* She thinks it will make the rest of the bridal party look sickly in the pictures. The ladies in the wedding party all received texts late last night to show up two hours early today. Piper hired a person to come give them all spray tans. Said it was mandatory."

I felt my eyes widen. "You're joking?"

"Nope." The bridal attendant offered a weary smile. "I have to go find a place to get ice chips. She doesn't like cubes. Excuse me for a few minutes. Good luck with the bride."

Elijah and I looked at each other.

"Self-serve cocktail hour?" he said.

"You read my mind, friend."

We slipped out of the suite and made our way to the lobby to find the maître d'. "Hello. I'm Sloane Carrick, a writer for *Bride* magazine, and this is my associate, Elijah Kim. He's a photographer. Has anyone let you know we'll be covering today's wedding for the magazine?"

The maître d' stood taller and smiled. "Yes, we're thrilled to have you here at the Chateau. I'm Leonard Frommer. What can I do to get you settled in?"

"We were hoping to shoot some photos of wherever the cocktail hour will take place, before anyone arrives."

"Of course. Right this way."

Leonard escorted us down a long hall that connected two buildings. As we crossed over from one to the next, a man stepped out of a hidden hallway, walking in the opposite direction. I stopped myself from crashing into him, but barely, and the abrupt halt on these tall heels caused me to wobble.

The man grabbed my shoulders, saving me from falling. "*Whoa.*"

"Shoot. Sorry. I didn't see you."

The man did a quick sweep over my face and smiled. "I definitely *see* you."

Holy eyes. Are those things real? I blinked a few times. The color was unlike anything I'd ever seen. Azure, maybe? Like the color of the Caribbean Sea from a plane, but these babies were offset by the thickest black lashes. I was so distracted by their beauty, I didn't even break my stare to see what the rest of him looked like.

"Sloane . . ." Elijah slowed and looked back at me. "You coming?"

"Yeah, sorry." I gazed into those blue eyes once more. "Sorry again."

In a complete daze, I walked around the man and continued behind Elijah. After a few steps, I couldn't help myself, I looked back. The guy hadn't moved. He just stood watching me with a crooked smile. Unfortunately, ten feet later we made a right turn, so the show ended. I caught up to Elijah. "Did you see that guy's eyes?"

"No. Why?"

I shook my head. I'd sworn off men six months ago and wasn't going to let a pretty set of peepers get me off track. "Forget it. Not important."

At the end of the hall, a set of double doors opened to a beautiful solarium. Soaring glass ceilings and tropical plants made it feel like we were outside, yet we were in comfy air-conditioning. The maître d' gave us a quick tour and left us to shoot some photos on our own. As soon as the door shut behind him, Elijah and I made a beeline to one of the bars set up all around the room.

Elijah stepped behind it and took out two glasses. "Ma'am? What can I get for you? Just so you know, we'll be serving orange-stained bridesmaids for an appetizer and pickled bride for dinner. So you might want to order accordingly."

I laughed. "I'll take a shot of tequila."

"Excellent choice. Coming right up."

I glanced around the beautiful room. Cream linens and massive, deep-purple flower arrangements covered each table. Hydrangeas, like I'd chosen for my wedding, too.

Elijah poured a shot and slid it over to my side of the rolling bar. "Stop doing that."

"What?"

"Thinking about your wedding."

I sighed. "I wish it were that easy."

"You'll get your day. And it'll be with someone who deserves you next time. Josh was too boring and ordinary anyway."

I smiled sadly. "Thank you for saying that."

"And he won't have a needle dick. You deserve an ankle spanker."

In the weeks after my wedding, I'd drowned my sorrows in

tequila. Too much alcohol was like truth serum for me, and I now regretted a lot of things I'd told people—I'd shared some of the things Josh had said to me with my protective, police-officer oldest brother, Travis, for one. But I didn't regret getting drunk with Elijah and telling him Josh had a skinny dick. Childish, I know. Yet it made me smile every time he brought it up.

Elijah knocked back two shots to my one. He was better at holding his liquor than me. After, he snapped some photos of the beautiful cocktail-hour room and we headed back to Bridezilla. She seemed even more frantic and hateful than when we'd stepped out fifteen minutes ago, except the alcohol made me care less. When she stopped berating whoever she was on the phone with, I figured I'd get the introductions out of the way.

"Hi. Excuse me. I'm Sloane Carrick from *Bride* magazine, and this is—"

She cut me off. "What size are you?"

"Umm . . . A six usually, I guess. Why?"

Her eyes lit up. "Oh, thank God! I need you to go get dressed."

I looked down. "I . . . am dressed?"

"Not in *that* boring thing. In a bridesmaid's dress."

2

~

SLOANE

"I cannot believe I'm doing this."

Grinning from ear to ear, Elijah snapped another pic of me. "I'm going to have blackmail ammunition for years to come."

I scowled. "Stop taking my picture. It's bad enough Bridezilla talked me into wearing this thing. I don't want evidence of it anywhere."

"Evidence? Sweetheart, the whole world is going to see you in that once the photos are published in the magazine."

My eyes widened. "Absolutely not. We are *not* going to be publishing a full bridal-party picture."

"How can we not?"

"We've done it before. Not intentionally, but the Waddington wedding we covered—the one in East Hampton at the winery with the big metal sculpture out front? We published photos of the bridal party and groomsmen separately."

"Yes, but wouldn't you still be in the bridal-party photos?"

"Not when you're in control of the photos. Make sure you get some without me."

I looked at my reflection in the mirror. How the hell had this happened? One minute the bride was bitching because one of her bridesmaids couldn't make it—the audacity of the woman whose mother had a massive heart attack this morning and was now on life support. *"Doesn't she know I can't have an uneven number of bridesmaids and groomsmen?"* the bride had shrieked. *"It will* ruin *the wedding!"*

I had never met a more self-absorbed person in my life. This was supposed to be one of her closest friends, and she'd had a family crisis, but it didn't even register. I know brides get caught up in things. Heck, I had when I was planning my wedding. I'd lost sleep over my future mother-in-law buying a dress that didn't coordinate with my colors. But really, who the hell cared what the woman wore, as long as she was happy with it? Still, something about putting on a white dress built for a fantasy makes us want the *whole* fantasy—down to every last stupid detail.

God . . . I stepped closer to the mirror and examined the thing on my head. I'd always loved fascinators, thought they were so elegant and classy. But this deep-purple sculpture sticking up from my hair? Maybe, *maybe* a runway model who was nine feet tall could pull it off if she had on a super-plain dress and the hat was the focal point of the outfit. But that was not the case here. I looked down at the dress and shook my head. *So, so bad.* And I couldn't even think about how this shade of purple clashed with my auburn hair.

My eyes shifted from my reflection to the man standing behind me. Elijah was still grinning like a loon.

"She's not even fucking British!" I lamented.

He chuckled. "That's the least of your problems, babe."

I *really, really* didn't want to leave the bridal suite like this. But the next thing I knew, the door whooshed open. Bridezilla didn't even have the courtesy to knock after she'd sent me in here to change.

"Oh thank God!" she said again. "Caroline is a little more petite than you, so it fit nicer, but it's better than nothing. Could you possibly try to stuff your boobs in a little more? They look like they want to spill out."

My eyes bulged. Bridezilla didn't even notice. Then again, I was so consumed with this hideous farce of an outfit that I didn't immediately realize that she herself had finally gotten dressed. You know the saying, *every bride is beautiful*? Well, whoever said that was just being kind. It's not true—not when they're five-foot-nothing and wearing eight layers of tulle. It looked like Piper was trying to smuggle a full class of five-year-old ballerinas through airport security. Though at least she didn't have to wear this awful fascinator.

Bridezilla grabbed my arm. "What is that stuck to the back of your arm? A nicotine patch?" She held up both hands, shaking them. "That needs to come off."

"It's an *insulin pump*. I'm diabetic."

"Oh. I guess it has to stay, then?"

"Why yes, it does. I'm funny about keeping upright and not passing out." This woman was unbelievable. I stared at her in shock. How could someone have such terrible manners? She noticed and mistook my flabbergasted expression for one of awe.

Piper did a twirl. "Gorgeous, right?" she said. "It's one of a kind."

"I'll say," Elijah mumbled behind me.

"It's . . . special." I smiled.

Claire, the bridal attendant, knocked on the open door. Her eyes widened when she saw me.

"I was somehow persuaded into filling in for one of the bridesmaids," I offered.

"Yes," Piper said. "It wasn't a hard sell after I mentioned my daddy is best friends with the owner of the magazine she works for."

I was not a violent person, but I felt like punching this woman. Claire looked at me sympathetically before turning to the bride. "All of the ladies are done with their spray tans. We have about thirty minutes until the ceremony starts, if you want to begin with pictures. The photographer is waiting."

I'd almost forgotten about the spray tans—thankfully my brothers and I had inherited a bar from my Irish father but gotten our ability to tan easily from my Italian mother, so I'd been excused from the mandatory skin painting.

Piper's eyes dropped to my boobs and she sighed. "We'll have to reorder the girls so you're at the end, farthest from me. I don't want to look flat."

"Claire, you are my new best friend."

I didn't normally drink much at work events, but when Claire passed me a shot of tequila—my second in an hour—there was no way in hell I could refuse it. The clear liquid knocked back smooth, sliding gracefully down my esophagus and igniting a warm sensation in my belly. The pre-wedding bridesmaid photoshoot had been painful. Piper had barked orders, but luckily, Bridezilla had needed a bathroom break. When she left, I made sure Elijah snapped a bunch of candids of the ladies standing around and laughing without me, because one of *those* would be what we used in the magazine.

I couldn't wait to get out of this costume. Not only was it hideous, it was hot as hell, and the fascinator had been secured with a mound of bobby pins that were pulling my hair. At least it wouldn't be too long now. Once the ceremony was over, we'd move on to full bridal-party pictures, and then I could get changed. Maybe I'd get drunk tonight. Lord knows I'd already put in my pound of flesh for the magazine today.

The maître d' walked out to the lawn where we'd been taking pictures and told everyone it was time for the ceremony to start. I followed at the rear of the group as we shuffled down another long hallway, feeling even more uncomfortable without Elijah. But he'd had to go set up to take pictures of the bride coming down the aisle.

When we arrived outside the chapel, a gaggle of groomsmen was already lined up and waiting. It was one thing to look ridiculous when everyone around you also looked that way, but entirely another when you had to go out in public. My eyes jumped from one tuxedo-clad man to the next. A few were nice looking, and most seemed about my age. But when I got to the last man in line, I nearly gasped. It was the gorgeous, azure-eyed guy from earlier. I stood a little taller, momentarily forgetting what the heck I was wearing. Kelly, the friendliest of the bridesmaids, turned to me. "Let me introduce you to everyone."

"Okay."

She steered me down the line of groomsmen. The first guy was Matthew, the second was Harding. The third she introduced as Ted, so I made a little more effort for him. Maybe if the opportunity presented itself, I'd chat him up a little. It never hurt to be friendly to the big boss's family. Eventually, we got to the end of the line and stopped in front of the azure eyes. My enthusiasm for the event perked up a whole lot more.

"And this is Wilder. Your partner for the ceremony." She wagged a finger at him. *"Be nice."*

He smirked. "I'm always nice, love."

Ooh . . . Those eyes came with a British accent.

Bridezilla beckoned for Kelly, so she excused herself, leaving me and the azure eyes alone.

The groomsman, whose name was apparently Wilder, gave me the once-over. His eyes dropped down to take in my dress, then raised to the top of my head, where the fascinator that looked more like mangled horns sat protruding from my skull.

"You had on a different dress earlier. So the accident must've happened recently then?"

"Accident?"

He smirked and motioned to the fascinator. "I'm assuming there's a giant wound under there, since you thought it was a good idea to put *that* dress on instead."

3

SLOANE

"Are you joking?" My hands flew to my hips. "Who insults some-one they just met like that?"

"Actually I was." He grinned. "Joking, I mean."

"Well, it wasn't very funny. Do you think I want to be wearing this . . . this . . ." My arms flailed around. *"Costume?"*

The maître d' walked over. His eyes flashed down the hall and back. I suspected he was looking for the bride. "Is everything alright over here?" he whispered.

"Fine."

He gestured to the door. "People are waiting for the ceremony to start. The walls are thin."

I took a deep breath and nodded. "Of course. Sorry."

My eyes slanted to the guy standing next to me, my partner, it seemed. He still wore a shit-eating grin and looked pretty proud of himself. But while I continued to scowl, I took a moment to check out the rest of his face, since I hadn't been able to move past his eyes earlier. Square jaw, defined cheekbones, flawless tanned skin—I wasn't sure if Bridezilla made the men get spray tans, but his coloring was too golden bronze to have come from anything other than genetics. Not to mention, he was tall—a weakness of mine—with broad shoulders and . . . I inhaled. *Damn, the fucker smells good, too.*

I'd been so busy checking him out, I hadn't realized he'd watched me do it. When my eyes met his again, he raised a brow. "Like what you see?"

Ugh. *Cocky and rude.* I plastered on a fake smile. "Yes, what a shame something so pleasant doesn't come with a matching personality."

Instead of being insulted, his smile widened. If he enjoyed being offended, maybe we were going to get along after all, because I was even more cranky now.

Wilder extended his hand. "Where did you come from, Sloane?"

For some silly reason, I hesitated to put my hand in his. Though the reason became obvious when I did. My body jolted to life. *Oh Lord. For six months I haven't felt a thing, and this guy floats my boat?* Between the way he looked and his cocky grin, I was certain he made heaps of boats float.

Heaps? Did I really just think *heaps?* What, was I suddenly British now, too?

Wilder lifted my hand to his lips and kissed it. This time the jolt fanned out a little lower . . . I cleared my throat. "I'm filling in for a bridesmaid who had an emergency."

"Must be my lucky day then."

"Yes, lucky for you, the mother of a dear friend of the bride is currently on life support."

"Are you always this sassy?"

"Only when the first thing out of the other person's mouth is an insult."

He again lifted his eyes to my head. "Is that your natural hair color?"

Hair not hehr. "How come only some of the things you say sound British?"

"Because I'm American. Well, technically I have dual citizenship. But I've lived in London for the last decade."

He still had my hand in his. I pointed my eyes down to it. "Are you going to let go?"

He smiled and laced his fingers with mine. "Maybe later. I wouldn't want you to run away again, like you did earlier."

"I wasn't running away. I had somewhere to be."

"And now . . ." He squeezed our joined fingers. "You're here. So I'll hold on to this."

As cocky and rude as he was, there was something oddly endearing about him. I wasn't sure what it could be. Maybe it was just the hint of an accent that did it.

"Are you friends with the bride or groom?" I asked.

"The hole in my head would have to be bigger than the one in yours for me to be friends with Piper. Aiden is a mate of mine from college. I don't know how he tolerates her."

"How do you know I'm not friends with Piper?"

"Because you obviously have good taste. You find me attractive."

I burst out laughing. "Full of yourself much?"

"Perhaps. But I call 'em like I see 'em."

"You're much more attractive when you don't speak." I wiggled my hand from his grasp and looked around. "Wonder if they have any hand sanitizer around here."

Just then, music started playing from behind the doors, silencing our game of insults. A few minutes later, I walked down the aisle on the arm of Azure Eyes. As we took the mandatory stuttered steps, I looked around the beautiful room—filled with flowers and people dressed to the nines—and wondered, *What the hell ever made me love weddings so much? How I could have thought this staged ruse was magical?*

Halfway down the aisle, my eyes met Elijah's. His brows nearly hit his hairline when he noticed the man next to me. His surprise gave way to a smirk, and he gave me a secret thumbs-up. Only apparently it wasn't so secret.

Wilder leaned over and whispered, "Your friend approves."

I spoke through a sugary smile. "Bite me."

He chuckled. "Later for that, love."

"Would you like to dance?"

Two long hours later, I was back in my black dress, sitting at a table with a bunch of strangers. I looked up to find Wilder's sparkling eyes.

"No, thanks." I looked away.

Undeterred, he took Elijah's empty seat next to me. "Do you suck at dancing?"

I shook my head. "Does anything positive ever come out of your mouth? In the sum total of five minutes we've conversed, you've insulted the way I looked in a dress, asked me if I dyed my hair, and now you want to know if I suck at dancing?"

"I didn't insult the way you looked in the dress. I said *the dress* was horrible, which it was. *You* would look good in anything."

I cupped my ear. "Was that . . . a compliment?"

"I would've given you another if you'd let me. I asked about your hair color because it's beautiful."

"But only beautiful if it's natural?"

He smiled. "Is the guy you're with your boyfriend?"

"What business is that of yours?"

"I have a lot of bad habits, but hitting on women who are in a relationship isn't one of them."

I arched a brow. "So this is you hitting on me? I think you might need a lesson on what women want."

"*That* I definitely do not need." He took my hand, stood, and dragged me to my feet. "Dance with me, beautiful."

God, was I so big a sucker that one *beautiful* was going to erase all the insults? *No. No, I'm not.* No matter how much my body lit up from being close to the guy. "I'm going to pass."

"Let me buy you a drink?"

"The drinks are free."

"Two then?"

I couldn't help but laugh. "One drink. But only because my date disappeared a half hour ago with a man who is prettier than me, so I'm bored."

"Good to know." He again laced his fingers with mine and led us to one of the bars.

"What would you like to drink?"

"Just water, thanks."

"Why not something with alcohol?"

"Because I'm technically working."

Wilder's brows drew together. "Working?"

"I'm covering the wedding for a magazine."

"Which one?"

"*Bride.*"

"Oh."

"Don't worry, I probably won't mention the rude groomsman in my article. I tend to focus on the bride and groom. Or at least on the details of the wedding like the flowers, venue, and dresses."

He paused. "You're going to write about the dresses?"

I laughed. "You're right. On second thought, maybe the rude groomsman would be better."

"What do you normally drink, when you're not working?"

"Tequila."

"Have you ever tried a siesta?"

"Two parts tequila, half part each Campari, grapefruit juice, lime, and simple syrup."

He nodded. "Is it your go-to or something?"

I shook my head. "No, I'm more of a tequila-soda drinker than a sweet-drink girl. I prefer my sugar in the form of cupcakes or cookies. But my family owns a bar. I worked there all through high school and college, and somehow I'm still there a few days a week."

Wilder nodded. He turned to the bartender and ordered a gin and tonic and a tequila soda.

I took it when he passed the glass to me. "That's not what I asked for."

"I know."

"So why is it in my hand then?"

"I decided you're done with work for today."

"Is that right? *You* decided?"

He sipped his drink. "Yep."

"And what gives you that right? To decide anything for me?"

"I think you deserve it after being bullied into wearing a dress you didn't want to wear and tolerating me as a partner."

"How do you know Piper bullied me?"

"She does it to everyone. How do you think she got my poor buddy Aiden to the altar?"

"Why does your friend let her bully him?"

Wilder shrugged. "Hell if I know. I guess he's into that sort of thing—a woman who bosses him around all the time."

"And you're not?"

His eyes caught with mine, and the corners of his lips twisted up. "I'm okay with a bossy woman. But there are definitely times I prefer to do the bossing."

I think he might've been right about that hole in my head, because his tone made my body feel a little flushed. There was no doubt what he'd been referring to, at least not in my dirty mind. Needing to cool off, I sucked back some of my drink—a little too much since I'd forgotten he'd ordered me tequila. The mix was more tequila than soda, too. A few more sips and it reactivated the buzz I'd caught earlier.

"So what made you move to London?" I asked.

"My father's from here, but my mother's originally from Cambridge. They're divorced. She got sick when I was in my last year of college, and she moved back to be near her family in England. I have a half brother there, so after she passed away, I took a job in London to be closer to him. Been there ever since."

"I'm sorry."

He nodded and looked away. "Tell me about this job of yours that requires you to dress up in hideous gowns and tolerate someone like Piper."

I smiled. "It doesn't require it. But Piper's family is close with the head of the company that owns the magazine I work for, so I thought I should be amenable when she demanded it. I usually just attend the event and write about it for the magazine. We cover one wedding a month with a six-page story. Elijah, the guy with me, is the photographer. We're sort of a team. I also run the magazine's social media and YouTube channel, so our jobs go hand in hand."

"I guess you should be lucky she didn't paint you orange."

I covered my smile with my hand. "They *did* look orange when they went outside for the pictures, didn't they?"

"With those purple dresses, it was like ten Violet Beauregardes who ate Oompa Loompas."

I laughed. "Your honesty is amusing when it's not directed at me."

His eyes dropped to my lips. "I like it when you smile."

My guard was slipping down too fast for my liking, so I rounded the conversation back to work. "Sometimes I use a quote from a guest in my write-up. Would you like to give me one?"

He smiled. "That's probably not a good idea if your boss is a friend of the bride's family."

"True."

"Is your boss a jerk or something that you felt like you had to go the extra mile for the bride?"

"No, at least not that I know of. He's more of my boss's boss's boss. I don't really know him, other than to find him a little intimidating because of who he is and the way he talks. He's very direct."

Wilder smiled. "I know the type." He held out a hand. "Dance with me?"

The tequila had gone to my head, so I figured *why not*? I gulped back the rest of my glass and set it on the bar. "Fuck it. Okay."

He chuckled. "Don't sound so excited."

Wilder led me out to the dance floor. He took one of my hands in his, wrapped the other around my waist, and tugged me close. I looked up at him.

"What?"

"The polite thing to do when you dance with someone you barely know is to leave room for Jesus."

His lip twitched. "What?"

"I went to an all-girls Catholic school. A few times a year we had these dances where we could invite boys, and that's what the chaperones would say if they noticed our bodies touching—leave room for Jesus."

He smiled. "Well, I'm cutting Jesus out of this one. You feel too good to leave an inch."

That might be the first thing we'd agreed on. Wilder's body felt pretty damn amazing. Not surprisingly, he knew how to dance. The way he held me was bold, and his steps kept perfect time with the music, leaving my brain to think about *other things* he'd probably be good at. He had me in such a tight clutch, I had to crane my neck to pull back enough to look at him while I spoke. "When do you fly back to England?"

"The day after tomorrow. Will you miss me?"

"About as much as you'll miss me."

He smiled. "So heaps then."

Heaps.

He twirled us around. "Tell me, Sloane. What would you be doing tonight if you weren't here working?"

"I'd probably be helping my brothers at the bar."

"Not out with a boyfriend?"

I frowned. "Not anymore."

"It sounds like there's a story there."

"Isn't there always?"

"I suppose."

I didn't want to share *that* story, so I pushed the question back at him. "What would you be doing?"

"Lately? Scouring the streets looking for my little brother who sneaks out."

I hadn't expected him to say *that*. But it made me smile. "I have two older brothers. They came looking for me a few times."

His face was hopeful. "You learned your lesson?"

"I learned I didn't get caught as easily if I snuck my boyfriend in, rather than sneaking out to meet them."

Wilder frowned. "Great."

I laughed. "How old is your brother?"

"Fifteen going on twenty-five."

"I have a fourteen-year-old niece. I get it."

Elijah came onto the dance floor. "Hey. Do you have the—" He did a double take when he got a close-up look at Wilder. "Wow. Now I get what you meant about those eyes."

Wilder smirked. "Discussing my appearance with your friend, are you?"

I ignored his comment and spoke to Elijah. "What were you going to ask me?"

"Oh. Do you have the coat check ticket they gave you when they stored my camera equipment?"

"It's in my purse. Why?"

"I need something out of my bag." I noticed the cute guy he'd been talking to earlier waiting anxiously at the edge of the dance floor. I was a little afraid to ask what he needed.

"I'll grab it for you." I pulled away from Wilder, but he firmed his grip.

"Is your purse on the table?" he asked.

"Yes."

Wilder lifted his chin to Elijah. "Grab it yourself, will you, mate?"

Elijah's eyes sparkled. "No problem." He wiggled his fingers and rushed off in a hurry.

"What do you think you're doing?" I asked Wilder.

"Dancing."

"You can't tell someone it's okay to go in my purse."

"Is it filled with secrets?"

"No. But that's not the point."

He shrugged. "Okay. So what is the point?"

"You just—that's rude. It's *my* purse."

Wilder looked me in the eyes. "I wasn't ready to let go of you."

I was annoyed, yet oddly flattered. And tipsy now, too. And . . . I really liked the way it felt when he held me. Which meant I needed to put some distance between us—make room for Jesus *and my sanity.* I shook my head, wiggling out of his hold. "I need another drink."

"I'll go with you."

"I don't need an escort."

"A drinking buddy?"

I hesitated.

"Do you know anyone else here except for me and the lovely bride?"

"No, but—"

Wilder released his hold around my waist, only to slip his hand into mine and tug. "Come on. One drink. I'll be on my best behavior."

I hadn't been sure it was a good idea to have one drink with this man.

Which meant two was a terrible idea.

And that third we had, that was the one that landed me in the coat closet . . .

4

WILDER

"Thanks, mate. You're a lifesaver."

The waiter counted out the cash I'd handed him. "No problem. You ever want to pay three hundred bucks for a cupcake again, I'm your guy." He stuffed a few of the bills into his front pocket. "Oh, and if you happen to run into the chef who made these, you paid two hundred for them, not three."

I chuckled and shook my head—the same head that I was pretty sure I needed to get checked after what I'd just shelled out for a freaking cupcake. Though it was still warm, and smelled pretty delicious, too. *I should've negotiated a little extra for being fresh out of the oven.*

I glanced across the room to Sloane's table. Her seat was empty, as was her friend's, so I took a lap around the ballroom. There was no sign of her anywhere, but I did find Elijah.

"Hey. Have you seen Sloane around?"

"She's looking for the woman who works the coat check. No one was there. I told her I'd meet her out front in a few minutes. I want to say goodbye to someone before we get out of here."

"A waiter that sort of looks like Jared Leto?"

Elijah's eyes lit up. "He *does* look like him, doesn't he?"

I thumbed behind me. "Just went into the kitchen a minute ago. Door's over there."

"Thanks."

He started to walk away, but I reached out and stopped him. "Think you can take your time saying goodbye and give me a few extra minutes with Sloane?"

Elijah grinned. "Absolutely. Go get 'er, cowboy."

I hurried to the coat check room. When I got there, the door was cracked open. I found Sloane inside alone, riffling through coats. Her back was to me, so I slipped in and quietly shut the door behind me. She turned when she heard the metal clank, and her eyes widened before dropping to the cupcake I was holding.

"Oh my God." She lifted her hand and covered her smile. "I cannot believe you found one."

"You said the only thing that could make you kiss me was a cupcake."

"That was because I assumed there weren't any to be found."

I grinned. "Well then you underestimated how bad I want that kiss." I held the cupcake up. "I believe the deal was a kiss for a cupcake with chocolate frosting. What do I get for one that's still warm?"

Her tongue peeked out and ran along her top lip. "It's really still warm?"

"Fresh out of the oven."

"But . . . but . . . we're in the coat closet."

"I know." I grinned and took a few steps toward her. "That's a bonus. I won't have to share the moment with spectators."

Sloane had tried to cover up her reactions to my small touches all night—when I held her close to dance, when I *accidentally* brushed my nose along her cheek . . . But now, with just the two of us in a confined space, she had nowhere to hide. Her cheeks flushed, and her chest heaved up and down. Seeing the effect I had on her was such a damn turn-on. It was a good thing I wasn't going in search of someone to make me a cupcake now, or I might've emptied my bank account to get one.

I took another step closer and held out the cupcake. "Taste?"

She stared at it for a few heartbeats. It looked like she was debating her next move, and I hoped that move wasn't her bolting past me and running out of here. For some reason, I really wanted her to enjoy the cupcake, even if I didn't wind up getting that kiss. I would've spent the money just to watch her eat it. Eventually, she leaned forward, stuck out her tongue, and licked a long, seductive line of frosting from the top. As she took the cream into her mouth, her eyes closed, and she made a noise that was a cross between a groan of happiness and one of pain.

Jesus Christ. At this rate, I wasn't going to be able to hide what was happening in my pants when I walked out of here. *If* I could even walk out of here. I couldn't take it anymore. I needed to touch her. So I tossed the cupcake over my shoulder and closed the distance between us. Wrapping my hands around her cheeks, I pulled her to me and planted my lips over hers. She made that sexy groaning sound again, and I swear, it shot straight down to my balls. Slow went out the window after that. I reached around and grabbed her ass, lifting as I backed her up against the wall. I nipped at her bottom lip, begging for her to open. Our tongues eagerly collided, and the hint of sweet frosting mixed with her was the most delicious thing I'd ever tasted. Though *a taste* wasn't nearly enough. I wanted to devour every inch of her silky skin and leave marks where everyone could see. I felt like a teenager with a raging hard-on, unable to control myself. We groped and grabbed, nipped and sucked for a long time.

Until Sloane suddenly pulled back. It was so abrupt, I thought I'd done something wrong. At least until I followed her wide-eyed line of sight over my shoulder and realized we were *no longer alone.* Someone had come into the coat closet. And that someone was the mother of the bride, and she did *not* look too happy.

5

SLOANE

"Oh my God," I mumbled under my breath. "*Please, please* tell me I didn't do that."

"Do what?"

I jumped. "You scared the crap out of me."

Elijah leaned against my office doorway. "Sorry, I thought you were talking to me." His brows furrowed. "Who the hell were you talking to?"

"Come in, come in." I waved impatiently. "Shut the door behind you."

I lifted my phone and used two fingers to zoom in on the Instagram photo for a better look. Confirming what I'd thought I'd seen, I shut my eyes and blew out a deep breath. "I posted a nip-slip pic."

"A what?"

"A photo with a nipple that slipped out!"

"Of you?"

"I wish! It's one of the bridesmaids from Saturday night. I took a few photos for the magazine's Insta. I'd completely forgotten I did it until I got the message from Bill."

"The boss noticed it?"

"I'm not sure, but he messaged and said he was coming down in a little while to talk to me with the big boss. I thought it was about the coat closet, which would be bad enough. But then I saw the magazine's Instagram had gained a lot of followers, so I took a closer look. I don't even remember posting anything." I turned the phone around and held it out to Elijah.

His eyes widened. "That's a whole-ass nipple. How did you miss that thing?"

I dropped my head into my hands. "I was drunk. I made out with that guy in the coat closet and then—"

"*Whoa!* Back up. What guy in the coat closet?"

"Wilder. The guy with the ridiculous blue eyes."

"Him?" Elijah's lips curved to a dirty grin. "*Nice!*"

"No, it's not nice! It was a stupid thing to do. One minute we were having drinks, the next we were eating cupcakes."

"Cupcakes? I didn't see any cupcakes?"

"I don't even know where Wilder got them. After they cut the cake, he asked me if I wanted a piece. I said I preferred cupcakes to cake, and a little while later, we were eating cupcakes in the coat closet. Then we were making out. The mother of the bride walked in on us—and she's *friends* with Ted Hayes, the CEO of Hayes Media, the guy who owns the company that owns this magazine!" I pulled my hair at the roots. "Now I don't know if they're on their way down to fire me for that or the nipple pic."

"Give me your phone," Elijah said. "Let's get rid of the evidence."

"It's the internet. Nothing is ever really gone!"

"We can at least limit the damage. It will look better if we get sued."

My eyes grew wide. "Sued! Oh my God. You think the woman is going to sue us?"

"Damn . . ." Elijah said as he pressed buttons on my phone. "This thing has eight hundred thousand likes. Do you usually get that many?"

"*No!*"

"Oh." He frowned. "Sorry. Maybe no one's noticed."

"Why do you think it has eight hundred thousand likes? I haven't been able to get more than ten thousand the last few months. My stats have been awful since I lost my mojo."

"I didn't mean *no one, no one*. I meant Bill or Hayes."

"Then why are they on their way down here?" I yelled. "The CEO doesn't stop by to chitchat with me on Monday mornings!"

"Well, at least there's one good thing."

"What could possibly be good right now?"

"You're not going to have to wait long to find out." Elijah lifted his chin toward the hall. "Because here they come now . . ."

"Fuck." I opened my desk drawer and tossed my phone inside, as if hiding it would help.

Bill, the managing editor of *Bride* magazine, knocked and peeked his head in the door. I forced a smile and waved him in. "Hey, Bill."

"Morning, Sloane." He entered and stepped aside for the gentleman behind him—the one in the expensive three-piece suit. "Have you met Mr. Hayes yet?"

I shook my head. "No, I haven't had the pleasure."

"Ted Hayes." The CEO stepped forward, extending his hand. "Nice to meet you, Sloane."

This guy is polite when he fires someone. We exchanged a firm handshake, and I stayed standing after.

Elijah excused himself, slinking out as fast as he could. Over his shoulder, he gave me a look that said *Sorry I didn't stay and join you in front of the firing squad.*

Yeah. Thanks for the support, buddy.

"So how was the wedding this weekend? How was Piper?" Mr. Hayes asked.

"Oh, it was very nice. The bride was, uh, sweet."

Mr. Hayes busted out laughing. "Really? Because she's usually a spoiled brat. Or maybe you're just being kind because you know I'm friends with her parents?"

I smiled. "The wedding venue was lovely."

He nodded. "That's more like it. And my son? I hope he was hospitable?"

I hadn't gotten to talk to him aside from the introductions, because I'd stupidly been preoccupied with a certain blue-eyed jackass. So I gave a generic answer.

"Yes, Ted was very nice. I can see the resemblance."

Mr. Hayes snickered. "He's usually a bigger ass than Piper, especially when he's around all those douchebags from Harvard. Went to state school myself, got a fine education. But you know how it goes. You do for your kids—and make them into the very people we thought were assholes growing up."

I liked this guy. "I went to state school, too."

He nodded. "Anyway, Bill here tells me the social media posts from the wedding are blowing up."

Fuck. "Um, yes. They're definitely getting a lot of attention."

"Good, good. So how would you like to cover twelve more? Actually, eleven, since you already attended the first one. We'll make a series. Twelve dumbass Harvard boys from the same fraternity got engaged last year. Must've been something in the water. But making it into a series was my son's idea, actually. When he came over yesterday and suggested it, I thought it might be a bit much—seeing the same people every month in the magazine. A lot of the boys are in all of the wedding parties. But after talking to Bill and hearing about the way social media took a shine to the first wedding, I'm thinking maybe it could work. Though I wanted to hear firsthand from the woman in the trenches. Tell me, what do you think, Sloane?"

Ugh. I couldn't imagine dealing with that crew for a full year. I didn't get to know the other ladies too well, but if they tolerated Piper, there had to be something wrong with them. And the guys—well, I knew for certain at least one was a Harvard douche, as Mr. Hayes said. But . . . how could I say no when his son had suggested it? Plus, if he didn't know social media was blowing up because I'd posted a nip slip, I wasn't about to tell him. So I had no choice but to suck it up.

I plastered on my best smile. "I think that's a great idea. The readers will love it. I'm sure they'll look forward to the layout every month, a chance to revisit the group. People love a series of anything nowadays."

Hayes nodded, looking pleased. "Very good then. My son is popping in tonight before he flies home. I'll have him stop by your office and give you the names and contacts. Will you be here about six?"

I had my gym clothes in my desk drawer, hoping to hit my favorite six o'clock hot yoga class, but it was what it was. "I will be."

"Great. Nice meeting you, Sloane. And keep up the good work."

"Nice meeting you, too, Mr. Hayes."

An hour after they left my office, Elijah slunk back in. "You're still here. That's a good thing . . ."

I sighed. "I'm not so sure. I think I might've been happier getting fired. Hayes has decided we should do a *series* on the friends from the wedding Saturday night. Apparently a dozen Harvard guys from the same fraternity got engaged, and he wants us to cover *all* their weddings this year. Oh, and he also thinks readers love the crew because of all the social-media attention the pictures are getting."

"He doesn't know about the nipple?"

I shook my head. "Apparently not."

Elijah shrugged. "Well, there's at least a bright side to it."

"Really? What? Because I'm not seeing it at the moment. My life is about to be that old movie *Groundhog Day*—wake up, be reminded of being left at the altar all day long at work, yoga, dinner, sleep, repeat. The highlight of my week will be helping my brothers out at Carrick's a few nights."

Elijah unzipped the leather portfolio he always had stuffed with proofs. He slipped out a few pages of contact sheets and dropped them on the desk. "This, for one."

I looked down. The photos were all thumbnail sized, so I lifted the pages for a closer inspection. "Oh my God. Did you color enhance these?"

"Nope. Those are all him, girl."

Jesus. If it were possible, Wilder's eyes were even better in photos. They were mesmerizing. Colored contacts didn't make eyes shine that bright. My gaze went hazy as I thought back to Saturday night, to our kiss in the coat room . . . First kisses were *not* like that. They were awkward head turns, clashing teeth, tongues that needed to find their way. But with Wilder, there was no hesitancy. Once our lips touched, we kissed as if we wanted to eat each other alive. The entire drive home, my body had felt the aftershocks. Between my legs had throbbed as hard as my raging heartbeat. Too bad he was an asshole. I blinked myself back to reality with that thought.

"He's good-looking, but he knows it."

Elijah sat back in his chair. "Can't say I blame him. It's kind of hard not to notice. You guys had some crazy chemistry zinging between you. Are you going to see him again?"

"Are you nuts? No. The alcohol went to my head the other night, that's all. Besides, he lives in London."

"If he was part of the first wedding party, maybe he'll be at these other weddings we have to cover."

"God, I hope not."

"Might be a fun way to get back on the horse, so to speak."

"Think I'll pass and stay celibate."

I looked at the time on my phone. Almost seven thirty. Hayes had said his son would be here about six. How long did I have to hang around and wait for this guy? Now I was going to miss not only the six o'clock hot yoga but the 7:45 Pilates class I used as my backup. If this appointment hadn't been with the son of the CEO, I'd be long gone by now. People not respecting other people's time was a pet peeve of mine.

I got up from my desk and stretched, moving the book I was reading with me as I shifted left to right, then went to the kitchen to fill my water bottle. The office had long cleared out—even the cleaning people had come and gone—so the sound of my heels click-clacking on the tile echoed off the walls. While I was filling my bottle, I continued to read my book until my phone chimed with a text from my brother. He wanted me to cover for him at the bar Friday night. I dictated a voice text as I walked back to my office, but I stopped abruptly when I saw a man standing in the hall.

"*What the . . .*" My water bottle clanked to the floor, along with my book, while my heart picked up to a gallop.

"What are you doing here?"

"Hello, Cupcake." Wilder smiled. "I'm looking for you, of course."

"Why?"

He bent and picked up the items I'd dropped. "Because you ran out on me the other night before I could get your number."

I swallowed and started walking again, forgetting he still had my things. "I didn't plan on giving it to you anyway."

He narrowed his eyes, as if getting turned down wasn't something he was used to. "Why not?"

"Because I don't like you very much."

He grinned. "You seemed to like me a lot in the coat closet."

"That was an accident."

His brows jumped. "An accident? You accidentally sucked face with me?"

"I remember it differently. *You* were the one who sucked face with *me*."

"You didn't mind."

I brushed past him and walked into my office. He followed, setting my water bottle on the corner of my desk and holding the book out to me. Though he pulled it back to read the cover. "*Finding Your Inner Self*? Are you reading this crap?"

I plucked my book from his hand. "None of your business."

He shrugged. "I like you the way you are just fine."

"Look, Wilder. I'm flattered, but I'm also not interested. Yes, the kiss was nice. But you're not my type. Besides, you said you live in England."

"Nice? The kiss was more than nice. I think a writer could do better than that."

Heart-stopping, breath-stealing, fireworks-worthy—even a simple *amazing* would be better, but I didn't want to encourage this guy. Though, my dumb body seemed to have a mind of its own. My eyes dropped to his lips, and my chest heaved. Wilder didn't miss any of it, either. When I looked up, he smirked, which only made me scowl.

"It's not happening." I walked around to the other side of my desk, happy to put a little space between us. The breathing room must've let me think straight for the first time, because it dawned on me that he was here, inside my office. "How did you get into the building? The doors lock at six. You need a passcode to get in after that."

Wilder tilted his head, studying me, and smiled. "My father gave me his code."

"Your father?"

He nodded.

Why the hell does he look so amused? "Who is your father? Does he work here?"

"He does indeed."

Great. Just great. Now I'd dug myself a giant hole—posting a nipple photo of the big boss's friend's daughter and making out with some other employee's kid.

"Who's your father?"

"Ted."

I flipped through my mental employee Rolodex, but came up blank. "Ted who?"

"Ted Hayes."

My jaw dropped open. "But . . . the other guy is named Ted, the nice one from the wedding party."

"Believe it or not, there are more than two men named Ted in the world. In fact, there are four in my family."

"But you're Wilder."

"Theodore Wilder Hayes, the fourth. My grandfather is Theo, my dad is Ted. My father insisted I carry on the name, but my mother always hated it and called me Wilder instead." He shook his head. "No one calls me Theodore or Ted."

I closed my eyes. *This cannot be happening.* Maybe I was day-dreaming. That happened sometimes. Usually I was on a sailboat in the Caribbean or sipping Chianti in Italy in my daydreams, but it was possible. I mean, that kiss with Wilder was pretty great. *Yeah, that's it. He's not really here.* I pressed my eyes shut for a few more seconds, attempting to manifest it to happen. But when I opened them, all I could see was Wilder's goofy smile.

The one on his very full lips.

Under his Romanesque nose.

Both of which were perfect, but you didn't notice either of them because of the eyes above.

I took a deep, cleansing breath in, exhaling out anxiety. "This doesn't change anything," I told him.

Wilder shoved his hands into his pockets. "Of course not."

"I'm still not going out with you."

"Alright, but I *will* see you again very soon. And when I do, we'll both be dressed up, and we'll share a meal. Call it what you want."

"What are you talking about?"

He took a piece of paper from his pocket, offering it to me. "All the weddings where we'll be seeing each other. My father asked me to deliver you a list."

6

〜〜

WILDER

"Fuck it," I mumbled to myself and closed the PDF.

Wednesday afternoon, back at my flat in London, I was supposed to be reading a thirty-two-page contract—one of the dozens of things I should've been doing today since I'd been out of the office for a week. But instead, I clicked back over to the email Dad's assistant had sent this morning. This time, when the photos opened, I saved them to my hard drive, telling myself I might need them someday. For what? I had no stinking idea. But rather than trying to come up with an excuse other than *I'm obsessed with a certain woman who tasted like cupcake,* I used the time in a more productive manner: obsessing.

Sloane Carrick was a goddamn knockout—auburn hair, warm skin, green eyes, and a banging body, even under that hideous purple dress she'd had on. She might've run into me in that hallway, but I was the one who'd had the air knocked from my lungs. I flipped through the photos, looking for one where she wasn't dressed like Barney, and stopped when I reached a closeup of her face. She was hamming it up, looking right at the camera, holding a shot glass in one hand and giving the finger with the other. Her fiery attitude made my dick twitch in my pants. I liked the photo so much that I tagged it with a little heart, so it would join the folder of my favorites.

Eventually, I tore my eyes from Sloane's face and flipped through another hundred photos. The ones she wasn't in, I glossed over. The ones of the bride, I couldn't flip past fast enough. Toward the end of the collection, I paused at a group photo. It had been taken from above, so it took me a few seconds to figure out what I was looking at. The photographer must've been standing on a balcony or a second-floor deck, and the bridal party stood on the grass below, holding their flowers up in the air. It was an artsy shot, but my gaze snagged on Sloane's cleavage, and I zoomed in for a better look. Two creamy mounds filled my screen just as my little brother, Lucas, wandered into my office. He parked himself on a chair and leaned forward to check out my monitor.

"Nice rack," he said.

"Don't be disrespectful, you little shit."

I did realize the hypocrisy, as I sat at my computer ogling a woman, one door lock away from jacking off to these damn photos. But hey, I was the adult here, and it was my responsibility to teach my little brother some manners. I clicked the X in the top left corner and closed out of the photos.

"Who you wanking off to?" he asked.

"I'm not wanking off to anyone. I was doing some work."

"What is it you do again? Because that's what I'm going to college for."

I shook my head. Me helping raise a fifteen-year-old hadn't been on my or Lucas's Christmas list, yet here we were. I leaned back in my chair, giving him my full attention. "How was school? What are you up to this afternoon?"

"Wesley is coming over. We're figuring out what I'm going to do for my date tonight."

I side-eyed him. "Come again?"

Lucas kicked his feet up onto my desk. "I have a date tonight."

I smacked his sneakers off. "Who said you could start dating?"

"Dad and Brenda."

I wasn't sure that was true, but it wouldn't surprise me if it was. Lucas and I had different fathers, and his made mine look like father of the year. I'd never understood what Mom had seen in Lorenzo, Lucas's dad, other than he'd once played guitar in a rock band. The guy was a bum, if you asked me, and now he was Lucas's sole parent. My brother spent more time at my place than his home, especially now that Lorenzo had remarried. Brenda was younger than me. She was also a hippie who didn't believe in rules or punishments, which had been one thing when Lucas was nine and ten, but now he'd learned to manipulate the situation.

"I think you're too young to go out with girls."

"How old were you when you started?" he countered.

My inner soundtrack played a big *whomp whomp*. Apparently hypocrisy was a large part of raising kids. But I wasn't about to share that I'd been getting head at fourteen, and the best fifteenth-birthday present I'd received was seventeen-year-old Stacey Donovan letting me bury myself inside her. I was starting to realize there was a fine line between earning a teenager's trust with honesty and steering them in the right direction. I decided to shift the focus back to him.

"What's this bird's name you want to go out with?"

"Kate."

"Okay. Tell me why you want to take Kate out?"

Lucas shrugged. "I don't know. Everyone's doing it."

I pointed. "Wrong answer. I don't give two shits what everyone else is doing, and you shouldn't, either. A man should act with purpose. If you want to take this Kate out, it should be because you like her, and you should be able to state the reasons *why* you like her—not that other blokes are all into girls."

Lucas frowned. "You're really annoying."

"I'll tell you what, I'll meet you halfway. This Kate can come over here, *if* I speak to her parent first and it's okay with them. But you're hanging out in the living room, not going up to your room or doing dodgy shit. And you keep your hands to yourself."

He seemed to consider that for a moment, but then lifted his chin to my computer monitor. "Who was the woman on your screen when I walked in?"

"Someone I met at a friend's wedding in New York last weekend. Her name is Sloane. Why?"

He grinned and cupped his hands at his chest—the universal sign language for boobs. "I figured out why I like Kate. I think it's the same reason you like Sloane."

I chuckled and shook my head. "Get the hell out of my office, you knucklehead."

Lucas disappeared, so I forced myself to call up the contract I was supposed to be reading. But two paragraphs in, I found myself scrolling over to my photo library again. I managed to stop before clicking into the folder, but after few more pages of the boring contract, I somehow wound up on the Hayes Media website. Dad owned a shit ton of magazines and newspapers, and I knew the corporate website had links to all the different lines of business. Finding the *Bride* magazine tab, I got a little too excited when I discovered a page labeled *Meet the Team.* Four people down, there was a photo of Sloane Carrick.

The photo was nice, a typical professional headshot, but it didn't capture her personality like the ones from the wedding did. Underneath, I read her bio.

Sloane Carrick is an associate editor. Her career with Bride *magazine began with an internship in her junior year of college, and she has been an integral part of the team ever since. She pens the monthly featured wedding column and is the mastermind behind the uber successful Knot so Seriously YouTube channel where she hosts a weekly Q&A focused on bridal bliss and bloopers. She is a graduate of Binghamton University's School of Journalism.*

Sloane has three obsessions: spaghetti carbonara, cupcakes, and weddings. She began dreaming about her own big day at the age of seven and is currently planning her happily ever after with the love of her life on New Year's Eve.

What the fuck? She's *engaged*? My stomach twisted into a knot, and anger heated my cheeks. We'd sucked face in the coat closet, and I'd felt her up. It was through her clothes, but still, it counted. I stared at the photo, at the sweet smile on her face. Apparently that innocent look was the mask of a *cheater.*

Underneath her bio was a link and the YouTube logo.

Join Knot so Seriously weekly on Thursdays at 9 p.m. Eastern.

I looked at my watch. Nine there was three in the morning here. I'd be fast asleep by then. I tapped my pen on the desk as I gritted my teeth.

Engaged. The best kiss of my life is *freaking engaged.*

I'd wasted an entire morning stalking photos of a woman who

was off-limits. A woman who was a *cheat*. The only thing I hated more than a cheater was one who pretended she *wasn't* a cheater.

I sat at my desk, stewing, for a long-ass time. Eventually, I told myself it was just as well. I didn't need to waste my days pining over a woman who worked for my father and lived thirty-five hundred miles away. In fact, what I needed was *convenience* at this point of my life. Convenient like Melanie Harper, who lived two blocks away and wanted nothing more from me than my dick. I'd spent a few fun nights at her place, and never once did I stalk the website of the company she worked for to read her damn bio. In fact, I wasn't even sure where the hell she worked. Or what she did for a living, for that matter. Graphic designer? Or maybe it was guidance counselor. I was pretty sure it started with a *g*. Game developer? It didn't matter. What mattered was *convenience*. So I picked up my phone and shot off a text to Melanie.

Wilder: Chinese food next week?

I felt better after I hit send.

For . . . *about two seconds*.

Then I was pissed off at how pissed off I still felt. But rather than sit here and let shit gnaw at me, I decided to make good use of the anger and get a workout in. I wasn't accomplishing shit this afternoon anyway. Plus, there was a gym in my building, so it was *convenient*—my word of the day. Bonus, it would stop me from clicking around this stupid computer anymore.

That night, I couldn't sleep. Rolling over, I punched my pillow and stared at my cell on the nightstand. It had to be around four.

Maybe I'll just check out her show for a minute.

It was probably almost over anyway.

See how dumb it is.

I'd had a decent amount of liquor Saturday night. I bet the woman wasn't half as interesting as I remembered. And she wouldn't even know I was there.

I chewed my bottom lip for a while, ultimately deciding if I didn't check out the stupid YouTube show, I'd never get any sleep. And I had work to do tomorrow. So I gave in, got up, and clicked.

The screen immediately filled with Sloane's face. She was covering her mouth, laughing. And I couldn't help it, I smiled at the damn screen. But then, my eyes moved to her hand, *her left hand.* No ring. No engagement ring. Just like the night of the wedding.

"Okay, everyone," she said. "We have about fifteen minutes left, so we're going to open up the Q&A. You can ask any question you want about weddings. Nothing is off-limits, and there's no such thing as a dumb question." She pointed down. "Just type 'em in below, and I'll pick a few to answer."

The blank panel on the bottom half of the screen began to fill with questions. Sloane's eyes moved back and forth for a minute before she read one aloud.

"Okay, first question is from Tatiana. 'How do I gracefully tell the best man I don't want him to give a speech? Ours is loud and crude, and I'm afraid he'll offend my guests.'" Sloane looked at the camera. "Well, Tatiana, I'm not sure there is a gracious way, but if you're not having any other speeches, you could simply tell him you've chosen not to include speeches as part of your wedding because you think it puts too much pressure on the speaker. Or, you might say speeches about you make you uncomfortable, so you've chosen to forego them." She paused, and her eyes went back and forth over the laptop screen again before she smiled. "This next one is a great question. Lily asks, 'Is it bad form to hook up with another member of the bridal party?'" Sloane grinned and looked back up at the camera. "Assuming you're not talking about the bride or groom, I think a hookup between two consenting adults is okay, fun even. As long as you're both clear on what it is."

Hooking up at a wedding gave me an idea. I moved my cursor over to the Q&A box and typed.

Why don't you wear your engagement ring when you're hosting a show about weddings?

There must've been a delay, because it took a minute or two for my question to pop up on the screen. When it did, I watched Sloane's face as she read it. She frowned. "NumberSeventeen asked why I don't wear my engagement ring when I'm doing this show. Well, NumberSeventeen, that would be because I'm not engaged. I was, but things didn't work out."

My heart beat faster. *She's not engaged.*

Screw it. I needed to know if I was the only one obsessing over the kiss last Saturday night. So I typed again:

Have you ever gone to a wedding and made out with a stranger? I almost hit enter, but then decided to make the question a two-parter. *If so, how was it?*

I tapped my fingers on the desk as I waited. Other questions scrolled past, so I wasn't sure she would answer mine again. But when it came on the screen, a sly smile crept over her face.

"NumberSeventeen has another question. She wants to know if I've ever made out with a stranger." Sloane looked into the camera. "In fact I have. Recently, too. And I highly recommend it."

My chest puffed with pride. Generally speaking, I didn't love weddings. An invitation in the mail was about as welcome as a speeding ticket. At least with those you could write a check and be done with it. But suddenly, I was back to looking forward to the next nuptials I had to attend—in three weeks.

7

SLOANE

"How were your last two weeks?" Dr. Amherst settled into her usual chair, picked up her notebook from the end table next to her, and opened to a fresh page before placing it on her lap.

"They could have been better." I shrugged. "I saw a picture of Josh and his new girlfriend. Or rather his new-*again* girlfriend."

"How did that happen?"

"On Instagram. Josh and I still follow each other. The photo was a few months old. Lately that's all I see. Old posts. They must've changed the algorithm or something."

Dr. Amherst smiled. "I miss the old days, when everyone didn't know everything about each other's lives. But tell me, how did the photo make you feel?"

"Like an idiot. The same way I feel when I think back to the email that popped up on his phone a few days before the wedding, with her name on it. I believed him when he said she'd seen the announcement and wanted to wish him luck." I shook my head. "I think the fact that I believed him without question bothers me most these days, maybe even more than the fact that I was left standing at the altar humiliated and the man I loved is back with his ex."

"That's understandable. You placed your trust in someone who shattered it. When that happens, we're left with the fragments of a promise that once carried a lot of weight in our hearts."

I sighed. "I should've unfollowed him."

Dr. Amherst tilted her head. "Why didn't you?"

"I don't know. Maybe I'm a glutton for punishment?"

She smiled. "I think it's more likely the same reason we all look over at a car accident. When something bad happens, our amygdala is stimulated—the part of the brain responsible for processing fearful and threatening stimuli. It sends a signal to the region of the brain that analyzes and interprets things. That, in turn, causes us to evaluate what happened and make sure it doesn't happen to us. Or in your case, make sure it doesn't happen a second time."

"So I'm following Josh to figure out why I didn't see it coming? Or am I following him to keep myself miserable so I won't get into another relationship and get hurt again?"

"Only you know the answer to that."

I sighed. "Isn't there a book that can tell me how to figure it out?"

Dr. Amherst smiled. "Let me ask you, when we met two weeks ago, we spoke about you joining a dating app. Have you done that?"

I shook my head. "Seeing that photo put a damper on the excitement I'd felt about doing it."

"Sounds like you might not need a book. You just answered your own question."

I thought about it. I supposed it made sense. I didn't want to go through what I'd experienced with Josh ever again. When I walked down the aisle on my wedding day, I'd thought it was the beginning of the happiest moments of my life—until my dad lifted my veil and I looked over at Josh's face. I *knew* something was wrong. But I was so damn clueless, I thought someone had died. I actually asked him if his grandmother, who couldn't make that day because she was sick, was okay. The fact that my fiancé of a year and a half was about to dump me in front of all of my family and friends didn't even enter my mind as a possibility. And it wasn't because he suddenly got a case of cold feet, because that does happen. No, it turned out my trusted fiancé had been pining for his ex the entire time we were together. A few days before our wedding, Josh had written her a letter, telling her he wouldn't marry me if there was any possibility he could have a second chance with her. Apparently she showed up at his apartment on the morning of our wedding and admitted she still had feelings for him, too. Yet I'd had no clue about any of it.

So maybe my reluctance to move on did have less to do with getting over Josh and more to do with learning to trust myself again. I nodded. "I'll unfollow him today."

"Baby steps are still steps." Dr. Amherst smiled again.

"Okay. And I didn't sign up for the app, but I did meet someone. And we kissed."

"Oh? Tell me about him."

"He's . . . sort of a jerk who says what's on his mind without regard for hurting another person's feelings. And we argued most of the evening."

Dr. Amherst's brows puckered. "Is there more to that description? Because I'm not sure that sounds like someone who would make a great partner."

I smiled. "He's actually pretty funny. He's got a dark sense of humor. And he has these eyes . . ." I drifted off, remembering how captivating they were. Though it wasn't like I had to do it from memory alone, since I'd looked at the photos Elijah took quite a few times the last couple of weeks. "They're a bright blueish green, maybe turquoise might be the right way to describe them. I was originally calling them azure in my head, but then I looked up the definition of azure and realized his have more green in them. And they're lined with the thickest black lashes."

Dr. Amherst looked amused. "You looked up *azure*?"

I bit my lip. "You'd have to see the eyes to understand."

She smiled. "Okay, well, handsome and funny are a good combination. How did you meet?"

"At a wedding. I was working. He was a guest."

"Will you see him again?"

"Yes, but not for a date or anything. The kiss was amazing, but he's not my type."

"What is your type?"

That stopped me in my tracks. I wasn't sure I knew my type at this point. Clearly it wasn't a wholesome-looking, preppy, blond lawyer with nice manners. "I don't know anymore." I shook my head. "This guy just seemed like a player—you know, the cocky type who's so good-looking he doesn't need to put in more effort than finding a woman a cupcake to wind up in the coat closet for a make-out session."

Dr. Amherst raised a brow. "Is that last part from personal experience?"

I chuckled. "Maybe. But in my defense, I'd had a few drinks. I don't get to eat sugar often, and his eyes are *that incredible*."

She smiled. "We all have our kryptonite. You said you're going to be seeing him again. Is that because you run in the same social circle?"

"No, I'm covering a series of weddings—twelve fraternity brothers who are getting married over one year. They're his friends, so I'm guessing he'll be at them all, too."

"Oh my. So you'll be seeing him a lot then?"

I nodded. "But what happened the first time won't happen again."

"How can you be so sure?"

"Because now that I know what my kryptonite is, I can stay away from it."

I had a two o'clock marketing meeting upstairs after my lunchtime shrink appointment. So I grabbed what I needed and answered an email on my phone as I waited for the elevator. The doors slid open while I was typing, so I entered without looking up. When I finally did, I froze.

Wilder's mouth spread into a cocky grin. A kid stood next to him. He had the same turquoise eyes and dark lashes. They *had* to be related.

I squinted. "Why are you here?" It came out snippy, and his grin grew wider.

"Good to see you, too, Cupcake."

The elevator was packed with people—people I was now holding up by not moving the rest of the way into the car. And everyone was staring at me. So I forced myself to take a spot near one wall. My cheeks felt warm. I was grateful elevator etiquette meant I could turn around and stare straight ahead without having to look at him. I jutted my chin, attempting to look bolder than I felt, and stared up at the numbers, pretending he wasn't less than a foot away.

But damn, I couldn't pretend I had no sense of smell. He smelled *really, really* good, definitely the same cologne he'd worn at the wedding two weeks ago. And my body was doing this weird, tingly-all-over thing. We stopped at the next floor, and I had to step out so two people could get off.

As I got back on, the kid watched me as intently as the man standing next to him. "Are you famous or something?" he asked.

I turned to make sure the kid was talking to me. "No, why?"

"I was going to ask for a selfie, if you were."

I smiled. "Sorry to disappoint."

He shrugged and nodded toward Wilder. "I thought you were famous because he was looking at a bunch of pictures of you on his computer."

I raised a brow to Wilder.

"The *wedding* pictures for the magazine."

The kid chimed in again. "I didn't see any pictures of a bride. You were zoomed in on her."

Wilder slapped a hand over the kid's mouth. "It's considered rude in America to talk while in a full lift."

Everyone in the elevator car chuckled. The next stop was the executive floor, and Wilder said *excuse me,* so I stepped out for him and the boy to get off.

He nodded as he passed. "Have a good day. Maybe I'll see you around later."

The kid snort-laughed. "That means you're definitely gonna see him. I think he's in love."

"Hey, Peaty. I need a favor."

I hit the button to put my cell on speakerphone so I could finish sealing a box at my desk. "What's up, Will?"

"One of the guys at the firehouse was on his way in, but his wife called to say her water broke. So I have to stay. Do you think you could cover me at Carrick's again tonight?"

"Yeah, sure. No problem."

"Can you get there by six? The day-shift guy has to leave by six on Wednesday. His wife's a nurse and works nights, and he can't be late because they have a baby at home. Dad's at the bar today, but you know how that goes . . ."

I looked at the time on my computer. That gave me a little over an hour to run home, change, and get downtown. "I'll do my best."

"Thanks, sis. I owe you."

"I'll add it to the pile of other favors you owe me."

After I hung up, I ran the box down to the shipping-and-receiving department and rushed back to my office to pack up for the day. I turned around to unplug my laptop, and when I faced the desk again, Wilder stood in my doorway.

I jumped. "You scared the crap out of me."

"Sorry." He grinned, not looking sorry at all.

"What are you doing in New York? The next wedding isn't until next weekend."

"I had some business to take care of. I'm in town until tomorrow, and then back a few days later."

"Business with *Bride* magazine?"

He smiled. "No, definitely not. I'm in talks to add an expansion team to the USRL."

"The USRL?"

"US Rugby League."

"Really? That's a thing here?"

He chuckled. "It is, indeed."

"I guess you're into rugby then?"

"You could say that. How about you?"

I shrugged. "I've never watched a game before. But I've seen snippets of it because my dad watches. I know it's a tough-guy sport."

"It's a physical game, yes."

"Did you ever play?"

He smiled again. "Once or twice."

I slipped my laptop into my bag. "Where's your sidekick?"

"Lucas? He's having dinner with our mum's sister."

"Ah, you're brothers. I knew you had to be related. You have the exact same eyes."

"They're from our mother. Lucas and I have different fathers."

"He seems like a whip."

"He's a pain in the ass. Thinks he's twenty when he's only just turned fifteen."

I smiled. "I might have a friend for him. My niece is way smarter than her father and me. Just ask her." I tilted my head. "Look at us, having a civil conversation."

Wilder's eyes dropped to my lips. "Maybe we should argue? I like where that got us better."

I laughed. "I think that was more due to the alcohol and my appreciation for cupcakes."

"Have dinner with me tonight? I'll stop by a bakery and ply you with martinis to increase the odds of a good night kiss."

"Can't. I have to work. In fact, I need to get out of here, or I'm never going to make it."

"Moonlighting?"

"I think you technically have to get *paid* for it to be considered moonlighting. I'm covering for my brother at our family's bar."

"Your brother doesn't pay you?"

"He can barely pay rent half the time. But the pub has been in our family for four generations. It's the third-oldest bar in Manhattan."

"What's it called?"

"Carrick's."

"Your last name."

I nodded.

"Would you have said yes to my dinner invitation if you didn't have to work?"

"Probably not." I grinned. "You're handsome, I'll give you that. But you're also kind of a jerk, and overall you seem like a bad idea. Plus, I'm on a man moratorium."

"Didn't seem like it in the coat closet."

I sighed. "That was a mistake."

Wilder clutched his chest. "Ouch."

I laughed and shoved the rest of what I needed into my bag.

"I'm sure you can bat those thick eyelashes and get any woman you want."

His eyes sparkled. "Apparently not. But I don't give up easily."

I hoisted my bag to my shoulder and walked out the door, leaving him standing just outside my office. Halfway down the hall, I felt eyes on my back. "Stop checking out my ass!"

"Only if you stop walking away from me, Cupcake."

Forty minutes later, I flew through the front door of the brownstone. My niece, Olivia, was sitting on the stairs talking on her cell.

"Why are you talking on the phone in the hall? Your dad's not even home yet."

She shrugged. "I like it out here."

"Whatever." I walked halfway up the flight of stairs to where she sat and kissed the top of her head. "Freaking subway got stuck, so I'm late. I have to be at Carrick's in fifteen minutes. Gotta go change."

Olivia went back to talking on the phone while I climbed the rest of the stairs. At the top, I turned the corner for the next flight . . . and then the next. I reached the fourth-floor landing huffing and puffing and very much missing the old, slow-as-shit elevator I'd taken for granted when I lived uptown. Though the climb was forgotten by the time I caught my breath and opened the door to my *walk-in closet*—something I would never be able to afford if I didn't live here.

My brother Will had bought this brownstone with the life-insurance money he got after his wife died. It had been converted into four separate apartments a half century ago. When one of the tenants moved out a few months after he moved in with Olivia, he'd asked me to live in one of the units in exchange for keeping an eye on his daughter. Will worked twenty-four-hour shifts at the FDNY. I would've moved to help out even without this amazing place, but being in the same building did make it easier when he worked overnights. A year after I'd moved in, Dad had been diagnosed with advanced Parkinson's, so when another unit came up for renewal,

Will opted not to keep the tenant. Instead, Dad sold his apartment and moved into the ground-floor unit here. So I lived with my family. But it was the best of both worlds. We all had our privacy, yet we could chip in and help each other.

I changed from my work clothes—a pencil skirt and silk blouse—into a pair of jeans and a Carrick's T-shirt, tied my hair into a messy bun on the top of my head, and ran back out the door. A flight and a half down, I thought I might've forgotten the keys to the bar, so I stopped midstep to dig in my purse. While I did, I accidentally eavesdropped on Olivia's conversation.

"Eww. It was gross," she said. "You know how boxer dogs sometimes have weird, big tongues? That's what it felt like was in his mouth. Except his tongue was dry, like his lips. Seriously, there was *no* spit in there. He might be cute, but I'm never kissing him again."

Oh shit. Liv is kissing boys? Can't that wait until she's at least . . . I don't know . . . thirty?

I located the keys at the bottom of my purse. My niece definitely hadn't heard me coming, or she wouldn't have been talking so loud. So I stomped my feet down the rest of the flight to let her know I was on my way. I didn't have time to address kissing boys with her now, but we would have a discussion about it the next time I watched her.

I passed her the same way I'd entered. In a rush, I stopped at the step she was parked on and kissed the top of her head.

"Have a good night, Liv. Text me the recipe card for what you want for dinner this weekend so I can pick up ingredients for us to cook together."

"Whatever." She shrugged. It was a typical teenage answer, but I knew she looked forward to our cooking on the nights her dad worked. Her mom had been a chef at a Michelin-starred restaurant here in the city, and we'd been making our way through her recipes for the last six months.

Outside, a cab was coming down the block. I hailed it, rather than chance waiting for the subway. It was five after six when I walked into Carrick's—not too bad. I tossed my purse under the bar, grabbed an apron, and tied it around my waist as I walked toward my father.

"Hey, Dad." I kissed his cheek and looked over at the guy sitting on a stool on the other side of the bar. Frank had been Dad's partner at the NYPD for thirty years. He spent more hours in this place than my father did. "Hey, Frank. How's it going?"

"I brought my own cushion to sit on because my hemorrhoids are so bad. You guys should really get these old stools repadded before someone like me files an Americans with Disabilities Act complaint."

I smiled, shaking my head. "I don't think your hemorrhoids are covered. But just in case, I'm going to have to start charging you for all the beer you drink to cover the cost of replacing all the cushions."

He waved me off. "Let's not go crazy, little miss."

The bar was a little fuller than usual for a weeknight—even had a few faces I'd never seen before. I generally knew most of the patrons since I'd grown up in this place. Almost all of them were either NYPD or FDNY. Most of the ones that weren't didn't last too long with the regular crowd.

I helped a few people, keeping my eye on Dad as he walked over to see what two guys I didn't know wanted. They ordered, and Dad walked over to the row of taps and pulled the lever for Guinness. As usual, he filled it three quarters of the way, and his hand shook as he set it on the counter. I saw the guy eye the beer and make a face, so I walked over.

"That's not full," he grumbled.

I pointed to the sign. "We don't serve sixteen ounces here. Our price reflects that you're getting twelve."

About two years ago, when Dad was no longer able to serve beer without sloshing it all over the counter because of his Parkinson's, we lowered the prices of the beers and hung up a sign saying our serving size was now twelve ounces. It was less of an issue with cocktails, because people didn't expect a vodka seven to be filled to the brim like they did a beer.

The guy shook his hands in front of him. "Maybe you should hire someone to work the bar who isn't an alcoholic with the shakes."

I grabbed one of the bats we kept behind the bar and lifted it to my shoulder. "He's got Parkinson's, asshole. You don't like it, get the fuck out."

He held up his hands. "Jesus, lady. I was just joking."

"I don't find making fun of someone's disability very funny." The bar had gone quiet, everyone paying attention, ready to jump in. I looked around the room. "Do any of you officers find making fun of my dad funny?"

The bar echoed with the sound of stools scraping on the tile floor. Every single guy stood from his chair and folded his arms over his chest. "Nope."

This was why new customers didn't last long. At least this time, I'd be glad they didn't come back. I pointed to the fishbowl on the counter. "That's the tip jar that goes to the Parkinson's Foundation. Maybe stick the apology you owe in there."

A few hours later, things had slowed down a bit. Dad was still hanging around, though most of his cronies besides Frank had gone, and it looked like even Frank was getting ready to take off, too. Dad didn't like to leave me alone here, which was silly, because with our patrons, this place might've been safer than the police station. I went to the back to grab glassware out of the dishwasher, and I figured I'd try to convince him to go home while I restocked, once his buddy was gone for the night. I could tell he was tired, because he was sitting on a stool behind the bar, rather than standing.

I used a hip to open the swinging door leading from the back, a plastic bin full of clean glasses in my arms. Frank was gone, his seat now filled by what looked like might be another new patron. The man had his back to me, so I didn't pay him much attention. At least not until I got closer and he turned.

Then I did a double take. "Wilder? What are you doing here?"

8

SLOANE

I was so confused. Wilder and my father were laughing and smiling like old friends.

Wilder lifted his chin to me. "Hey, Sloane."

"What are you doing here?" I repeated.

He shrugged. "I came in for a beer."

Dad pointed to Wilder. "You know this guy?"

"We met a couple of weeks ago at a wedding I covered for work."

"Why didn't you didn't tell me you knew Wilder Hayes?"

My nose wrinkled. "Why would you care that I know him?"

"Because he's a legend."

"Uh . . . a legend at what?"

Dad shook his head. "You really don't know who this is?"

"My boss's boss's boss's son?"

"He's *Wilder Hayes,* Sloane, one of the best players to have ever played pro rugby."

I looked to Wilder. "You played professionally?"

For the first time, he didn't seem cocky. He looked a little modest even as he nodded. "Yeah, for eight years."

Dad thumbed over at Wilder. "Honey, he's the David Beckham of rugby. He's going to do for rugby what Beckham did for soccer in the US. He's starting his own team, and with his fan base, it's gonna get a lot of attention."

"The team isn't a done deal yet," Wilder said. "The commission votes in less than two weeks on the expansion."

"They'd be idiots not to do it," Dad noted.

"Thank you. That's very kind."

"What can I get you to drink?" Dad asked. "It's on the house."

"I'll just take a beer," Wilder said. "A stout on tap, if you have it."

I needed a minute to let everything sink in. "Excuse me. I need to put these glasses away."

I walked to the middle of the bar and worked on hanging the glasses from the overhead gantry. But every few seconds, my gaze wandered back to Wilder. He was famous? A rugby player? David Beckham? Most perplexing of all, my dad had offered him a *free beer*. Whenever anyone who wasn't a member of the NYPD or FDNY wandered in, he charged them double to discourage hanging around. *No* civilian got free drinks from Dad.

I finished hanging the glasses just as Dad finished pouring Wilder's beer. His hand shook a lot more when he was tired, and I watched Wilder hone in on it. Unlike the guy earlier, Wilder's eyes softened, and he smiled. *Damn it. I don't want to find things to like about you.*

Dad walked over. "I need to hit the head. Be back."

"Okay."

I checked in with a few patrons to see if they needed refills, then walked down to Wilder. "So what are you really doing here?" I asked. "You didn't just wander in for a beer. There's probably a thousand places to get something to drink between here and the office, most of them with friendlier people and glasses without dishwasher spots."

"You said this place was a legend in New York—third-oldest bar, was it?"

"Are you sure it's not because I turned you down and you can't handle that? You seem like the type who always gets his way and might not take it so well when he doesn't."

"I do like to get what I want. But I'm willing to work for it."

I shook my head and sighed. "So you're famous, huh? How come you didn't mention that little fact?"

Wilder shrugged. "Was hoping you'd like me for my personality."

"Your personality?" I laughed. "Really?"

He grinned. "I'm not that bad."

Dad ambled back from the restroom. I nodded toward him. "I should go. He's been here all day, and if he thinks I'm busy talking to you, he'll never leave, and he needs his rest."

"Okay."

Before I could walk away, Dad was at my side. "Why don't you go have your dinner break now?"

"I'm fine. I'll eat when I get home."

"Order something and sit and eat. Or I'm not leaving. I don't want your blood sugar going low when I'm gone."

I frowned. "How about we compromise? I promise to order something that I'll eat when it's slow, and you go home now and get off your feet. Also, you take an Uber, not the subway."

"I'm fine."

"Dad . . ."

Wilder butted in. "I didn't eat yet, either. I noticed an Italian place a few doors down. How about I run over and grab something for us both? I'll be quicker than delivery."

I said *no* at the same time my dad said *great*.

Wilder knocked back the rest of his beer and stood. He lifted his chin to my dad. "You want anything, sir?"

"No, thank you. And it's Harry, please. If you have a sweet tooth, they make fantastic cheesecake."

Wilder nodded and started to walk away. "Be back."

I blinked a few times. "Wait. I said no."

He didn't turn around as he responded. "Your father's right. You need to eat."

"But, but you don't even know what I want."

He chucked a smile over his shoulder. "Sure I do."

Fifteen minutes later, Wilder returned with a large takeout bag. He motioned to the small tables across from the bar and spoke to my dad. "Any particular table?"

"Why don't you go toward the back, where it's quieter?"

My head volleyed back and forth between the two men, who acted like I wasn't here. When I looked to Dad, he gestured to Wilder, who was already approaching the back table. "Run along."

I sighed. "You're leaving in an Uber as soon as I'm done."

Wilder had unpacked a bunch of tins when I got to the table. "How many people are eating?" I asked. "Six containers?"

"I figured I'd get a few choices."

I slid into one side of the booth. "You wouldn't have had to do that if you'd *asked* what I wanted."

He pushed a tin over to my side. "Spaghetti carbonara."

My jaw dropped. "How did you know it was my favorite?"

He grinned and sat down. "I have my ways."

I'd gone to therapy at lunch today, so I was actually pretty hungry. I peeled the lid back and salivated at the smell that wafted through the air. "Why don't I go get us some real plates, and we can share?"

"Sounds good."

I disappeared into the back and returned with plates, utensils, and drinks. Wilder was at the bar with one of the tins. Dad took whatever it was with a big smile.

"What did you give him?" I asked when Wilder sat back down.

"The cheesecake he said he liked. They had plain or blueberries on top. I got the blueberry—loaded with antioxidants and easy to chew. Does he have difficulty swallowing, too?" He paused. "My grandfather had Parkinson's. He had trouble chewing."

I shook my head. "Luckily he doesn't. At least not yet. Thank you for doing that."

"I didn't get us any desserts. I wasn't sure if you could have them."

I tilted my head. "Why do you say that?"

"I noticed the insulin pump on the back of your arm when you were walking away today." He pointed his fork at me. "See? I wasn't *just* looking at your ass."

I smiled.

Wilder opened the rest of the tins, and we loaded up our plates. He eyed mine.

I shrugged and forked a mouthful of pasta. "I didn't get to eat lunch."

His lip twitched. "Wasn't judging. I like a woman who eats. Just taking note of what you picked."

"Why would you do that?"

"For when you come over. I like to cook. And eat pasta in bed after sex."

I covered my full mouth, laughing. "There's so many things wrong with that statement, I don't know where to start."

"You'd prefer I take you out somewhere nice?"

"Don't you live in England?"

"I do. But you can't expect me to always come here. I think it would be nice if you visited me once in a while. Have you ever been to London?"

"No."

"Perfect then. I'll get to show you around."

"Did you bump your head when you walked to the restaurant?"

Wilder grinned. "Just looking ahead."

"Or you're looking at fantasyland."

"We'll see." He shrugged. "Talk to me about this man moratorium. Is it because you're not engaged anymore?"

I had my fork midway to my mouth and paused. "How do you know I was engaged?"

"Same way I know your favorite food is spaghetti carbonara. Your bio on the magazine's website."

I'd forgotten my bio said I was getting married. I needed to change that. Although that didn't explain everything he knew. "I'm pretty sure my bio only says I'm engaged. How did you know I'm not anymore?"

Wilder looked away. "I guess I assumed you weren't because of what happened in the coat closet."

Something told me there was more to it than that. "What was your number when you played rugby?"

"Seventeen. Why?"

Gotcha, NumberSeventeen. I leaned forward, across the table. "Come here."

"You want me to kiss you?"

"No, just lean close for a minute."

The table wasn't that big, so with both of us leaning in, we could've kissed. But I made sure there was a little distance between us. I looked straight into his eyes. "You watched my YouTube show the other night, didn't you?"

Wilder's eyes widened. "I really want to smash my lips against yours right now, but I think I got an in with your father and don't want to ruin it."

I leaned back in my seat. "I freaking knew it!"

Some men might've been embarrassed to admit they'd stalked your company website, memorized your favorite food, and watched you do a wedding-related talk show on YouTube. But not Wilder. His eyes sparkled. "I wasn't happy when I found out you were engaged."

"You thought I was still engaged and made out with you anyway?"

"That's what it looked like, but I hoped I was wrong."

I laughed. "You're a stalker."

"It's a first, trust me."

"I bet it is. Apparently you're a famous rugby player, so I wouldn't imagine it's too hard for you to meet women."

He skirted my comment and redirected to the question that had led us here. "So this man moratorium you're on . . . that start after your engagement ended?"

I nodded. "That definitely contributed. But I'm twenty-six, and I feel like I've had a boyfriend since I was sixteen."

"The same boyfriend?"

"No. I've had a few long-term relationships."

"How long were you with your fiancé?"

"Two and a half years."

"Can I ask why you broke up?"

"He was still in love with his ex." This might've been the first time it didn't sting too badly to admit that. "I had no idea until I was standing at the altar."

"Jesus. What a dick."

I smiled sadly. "Yeah."

He wiped the corner of his mouth. "Well, his loss. My gain."

I laughed. "You haven't gained anything, Mr. Hayes."

He wiggled his eyebrows. "I like the way that sounds rolling off your tongue."

"Rejection?"

"No. You calling me Mr. Hayes."

I had to give him one thing, I'd been smiling since we sat down. Maybe I'd give him two things. He was even better looking than I remembered.

I twirled more spaghetti carbonara onto my fork and stuffed my face. "I feel like you know my life story—from favorite food to my relationship history. What's your deal? Why are you single?"

"Busy. I've jumped through a lot of hurdles over the last year to get this close to adding an expansion team in the US. I should get my name painted on the side of a British Airways jet with all the miles I've flown. Plus, my little brother spends more time at my place than his dad's. He's a handful."

"Is there a reason for that?"

"His dad was always flaky, and then a few years back he got remarried. Brenda is a little too free-spirited to enforce rules for a teenager. Lucas tells her he doesn't feel like going to school, and she tells him to stay home and immerse himself in a book of poetry instead. He also started getting into her pot stash, so I stepped up my time with him."

"Oh boy."

"He's a pain in my ass, but I think we were all pains in the asses at his age."

I smiled. "I take care of my niece a few nights a week for my brother who works overnights. So I very much understand. But I have the opposite problem. Today I heard her talking about kissing a boy. If my brother knew, he'd ground her until she was thirty. So I try to manage what I share with him and give her guidance as best I can. Her mom died eight years ago."

Wilder leaned back, spreading an arm across the top of the booth. "Look how much we have in common already? Family with Parkinson's, helping raise teenagers, we both think I'm handsome."

"Modesty, too." I laughed. "Are you also obsessed with self-help books?"

"I've always thought those were dumb. But I might need a book for my recent obsession."

"What about before last year? How long was your longest relationship?"

Wilder's smile fell. "I haven't dated anyone for more than a few months since college."

"Why is that?"

"You won't like the answer."

"It's okay. I prefer honest answers. I don't love lies that pacify me."

"I enjoyed my single life. I traveled all the time when I was playing. Rugby is big in Europe, and I was the team captain, so . . ."

"So . . ." I said. "We're sort of the polar opposite in that area. I'm a relationship girl, and you're a love-'em-and-leave-'em type."

"Was. I'm not like that anymore."

I tilted my head. "No? How can you be sure if you've never had a serious relationship?"

He grinned. "Because I met you."

I chuckled. "Smooth, Hayes, smooth. I can see why you don't have a hard time getting women. The bullshit flows easily." I wiped my mouth. "But I should get back behind the bar. Dad needs to get off his feet."

"You stay here all night by yourself?"

"It's a cop bar. Nobody gives me any trouble."

"Cop bar?"

"Well, cops and firemen." I pointed to each of the ten guys sitting at the bar. "Cop. Cop. Cop. Fireman. Cop. Fireman. Fireman. Cop. Cop. Cop. My dad worked the first precinct for thirty years. It's a few blocks away. He retired a captain. But he's fourth-generation NYPD, and one of my older brothers is NYPD. The other is FDNY."

"Damn. That sounds like a lot of guns pointed my way if I do something wrong."

I slid out of the booth and stood. "Thank you for dinner."

Wilder followed. He reached for my hand and laced our fingers together. "Let me take you out."

As tempting as it was—as tempting as *he* was—my gut told me it wasn't a good idea. "I don't think so. I'm going to stick to my moratorium."

"How long does it last?"

"A year. I have six months left."

He smiled. "So Ryan's wedding then?"

"Is that who's getting married next?"

He stood and kissed my cheek. "Nope. That's whose wedding is in six months when your moratorium is up. I'll wait."

"You're going to wait six months for me to potentially go out with you?"

Wilder rocked back on his heels. "Yep."

"The man who has never committed to a woman for more than two months is going to wait six months for a woman who *isn't* sleeping with him?"

He shrugged. "If that's what it takes."

I rolled my eyes. "Okay, yeah. Sure."

"You have your man moratorium, and I'll have my miss moratorium."

"Mmm-hmm."

"We'll see."

I cleared the table, separating the garbage from the leftovers. There were a few trays we hadn't even opened. "Do you want to take these?"

"I have an early flight in the morning. You take 'em."

"Thank you. They won't go to waste. One of my brothers or my dad will eat them if I don't."

"I guess I'll see you in a week. At the wedding?"

"I guess so."

Wilder walked over and shook hands with my dad. "Thank you for the beer, Harry."

"Anytime. Come back again, son."

He thumbed over his shoulder, gesturing to the door. "You want a ride home?"

Dad waved him off. "I'm good. I'll jump on the subway."

"You sure? I'm driving one of my dad's cars. He collects old classics. This one is something else—a '64 Pontiac GTO."

Dad's mouth dropped open. "No shit? My dad had a '64 back in '64. Loved that damn car."

Wilder gestured to the door. "Come on then."

"You sure? I don't want you to go out of your way . . ."

My father might've asked the question, but he was already untying his apron.

"Positive."

Wilder waited for Dad to come around the bar. He turned back to me as he pushed open the door for my father and winked. "See you soon, Cupcake."

9

WILDER

"Shit." I looked down at my vibrating phone and groaned, rubbing my forehead. *Melanie Harper.* I'd completely forgotten I'd texted her last week, asking her to hang out when I got back to London. I'd been traveling back and forth so much, I didn't even realize it was Tuesday. Maybe she was canceling? Maybe I didn't even have to waste time thinking this through?

But when I swiped to read the message, a picture popped up. I blew out two cheeks full of air. Melanie was lying in a bathtub, sudsy bubbles covering mostly everything—except two stiff nipples sticking out of the water.

Melanie: Getting ready for our date tonight. My place or yours?

I'd asked her to go out for Chinese food. But she'd gone right to how things were going to end. That was exactly the reason we got along so well. No games. Just straight to it. Neither of us had the time or desire for more. At least I hadn't a few damn weeks ago. Now, though, I had no idea what the hell I was doing. A certain little redhead had me turned upside down.

Six months! I'd told her I was going to wait *six months* for her? Actually, it wouldn't even be waiting for something to happen. It would be waiting for *the chance* of something happening after her dumb moratorium was over. The last time I'd gone six months without sex was—well, it had never happened. Not since I was fifteen and got laid on my birthday the first time. But I also had an early flight back to the US in the morning, so rather than stopping to analyze whether I was really going to do what I'd told Sloane I would, I mentally allowed myself to blame canceling on my travel schedule.

Wilder: Sorry, Mel. Can I get a raincheck? Expansion decision is coming down to the wire and I have to fly out again.

A minute later, my phone lit up with a response.

Melanie: Of course. Best of luck with the team. We can celebrate next week when it's a done deal.

I exhaled a little relief, at least for now. But then my phone vibrated again.

"Fuck my life." I scrubbed my hands over my face.

Melanie had sent another photo. She was standing now, just outside the bathtub—completely naked, except for a few beads of glistening water sliding down her perfect body, and she held a small vibrator in one hand.

Melanie: I'm around the entire month, if you find an hour or two of free time. Until then, I'll take care of myself ;)

I was still staring down at the screen, questioning my sanity, when my assistant, Margot, buzzed in through our intercom system. "Andrew needs to meet with you this morning. He said it's important."

Andrew Emerson was in-house legal counsel for all of my holdings, but lately his time had been almost exclusively dedicated to the expansion team, as was the case with most of the people who worked here. He was also my childhood best friend, more like a brother to me than an employee.

I pressed the button. "Tell him to come by whenever he's ready."

Lord knows I wasn't getting shit accomplished bouncing back and forth between the temptation on my phone and thinking about Sloane. But I forced my nose back to the grindstone, opening my electronic calendar to see what had to be done before I left again tomorrow morning. Less than three minutes later, there was a knock at my door, and Andrew opened it without waiting.

"Guess it's important . . ." I said.

"Yeah, it is." He closed the door. As he came in, I got a good look at him, and my stomach dropped. *Oh fuck.* Whatever it was was *bad.* Andrew was the professional-looking one in our twosome— always clean-shaven, suit pressed razor-sharp, shoes buffed . . . But now he had a face full of scruff, his clothes were wrinkled like he'd slept in them, and I couldn't see myself in his shoe shine.

"What happened? Did we lose one of the committee members we needed for the vote?"

He slumped into my chair and ran a hand through his chaotic hair. "Worse."

"What the hell could be worse than that?"

Andrew looked me in the eyes. "I cheated on Camille."

I froze. This was the last thing I'd expected him to say. "What the hell happened?"

His head fell into his hands, and he yanked at his hair from the roots. "I was out with some of the guys from the advertising department and went to a bar. Had a little too much to drink and started talking to this woman. I've been here for a few weeks, so I guess I was just lonely. None of that is an excuse. I freaking love Camille."

I sat back in my chair, speechless. "Have you ever cheated before?"

He looked offended that I'd even asked. "No, of course not."

"How do you feel about the woman you slept with now? After?"

He frowned. "Well, I feel like shit because I didn't even tell her, at least not that I can remember. But I don't have any feelings for her, if that's what you're asking. It was just a drunken mistake."

"What are you going to do?"

"I picked up the ring a few days ago. I'm supposed to be proposing on our anniversary in two weeks."

I leaned back into my chair. "Oh, man."

"What would you do? Would you tell her or try to pretend it never happened? The woman lives in England, so it's not like Camille's likely to find out."

"I think you're asking the wrong person. You know how I feel about that shit."

Andrew closed his eyes. "Jesus Christ, I'm not even thinking straight. I'm sorry. Of course you'd feel like I should come clean."

"How do you think Camille would take the news if you told her?"

"She'd chop my balls off."

Andrew's girlfriend of four years was an assistant district attorney. I'd seen her in action in court once. She was pretty scary for a five-foot-nothing lady.

I shook my head. "I'm sorry, man."

"I made a mistake, a giant one. She's going to leave me if I tell her."

He wanted me to tell him to forget it ever happened, but that wasn't easy for me. "Did you use protection at least?"

"She had to give me a condom because I didn't even have one. Camille and I haven't used them in years." His eyes grew wide. "What if it was expired? They expire, right? What if I got her pregnant? What if she gave me a fucking disease?"

"Take a deep breath. You don't look so good."

His eyes darted around the room, seemingly as fast as his thoughts. "I don't even have a place to live in New York if she kicks me out."

"That's the least of your worries."

"I'm supposed to fly back in two days. How am I going to face her?"

"Take more time, if you need it. Tell Camille I need you here to work on something. You need to get your head screwed on straight before you get on a plane."

"She won't believe me. She'll know something is off."

Two years ago, I'd plucked Andrew from the blue-chip law firm he'd worked at for ninety hours a week since graduating law school. I'd promised him a better salary and half the hours, though lately he'd been putting in a lot of time because of the expansion team. Camille wouldn't think twice if he said something came up. And my levelheaded best friend knew that. He was just having a meltdown.

Andrew rubbed his temples. "I majorly fucked up. I don't know what to do. I wish I could turn back time."

"Well, I think the first thing you should do is get some freaking sleep. You can't think straight when you're exhausted. Did you sleep at all last night?"

He shook his head. "How could I?"

"That's what I thought. So first things first, go home and sleep. Everything will feel a little clearer once you're not so wired. If you do decide to tell her, this is a conversation you two should have in person, not over the phone or on a Zoom. I'm flying to New York tomorrow morning. If you want, join me. We'll sit together after you've had a decent night of rest and talk it out. Then you'll go see Camille in person."

Andrew blew out a deep breath. "Okay."

I lifted my chin, gesturing to my office door. "Now, go home. Knock back two fingers of that shitty-tasting scotch you drink and pass out. If you decide to fly back with me, tell Margot to change your flight arrangements. I'd say I would stay to be here for you, but I have meetings in New York I can't miss and then another wedding. But I'm only a phone call away twenty-four/seven if you decide to stay in London for a few more days and want to talk."

Andrew nodded and stood. "Thanks, man."

A few hours later, my admin came in with her notepad. "Andrew is all set. I told him to meet you at the British Airways lounge in the morning. It shouldn't be too far from your gate."

"He called already?"

"About a half hour ago."

So much for getting some sleep before making a decision . . . "Okay, great. Thanks."

"Also, Arnot Goncalo will meet you at the game on Thursday during halftime. I told him he was welcome to watch from the box, but he said he likes to watch his son play from the stands, since it's closest to the field."

"Great. Thanks."

Margot checked something off her notepad and kept going. "Your tux has been cleaned for the wedding. I had the St. Regis concierge team pick it up, so they'll deliver it to your room once you check in. There's an email in your inbox that has all of your meeting times and the telephone number for the car service that will be picking you up. Dinner reservations are all made. I wasn't sure if Andrew was going to be joining you at any of the meetings now that he's going to New York as well, so just let me know if you need the number of people adjusted for anything."

I shook my head. "I should be good. Andrew has other stuff to deal with while he's there."

Margot nodded. "I think that's it then. Good luck. We'll all have our fingers crossed, waiting to hear about the vote."

"Thanks, Margot. I don't know what I would've done without you keeping my ass organized this last year."

She smiled. "I am pretty fabulous."

"You are. So take your family out to a nice dinner this weekend and put the bill through as an expense."

"Your version of nice or my version of nice?"

"Whichever is more expensive. Now go home."

"Do you want me to print out your calendar?"

"I'll do it. It's probably the one thing I'm capable of doing without you."

She laughed. "Safe flight, boss."

A few minutes later, I faced the credenza, packing up for the day, when there was a soft knock at the door. I spoke without turning, assuming it was Margot. "You didn't even believe I was capable of doing one thing, did you?"

"Oh, I know you're capable of doing *lots* of things . . ."

I turned to find Anna Destin standing in my doorway. She flashed her signature man-eater smile, and I couldn't help but notice the clingy dress she had on. I diverted my eyes back to my leather bag and cleared my throat. "Hey, Anna. How are you?"

"I'm well." She took a few steps into my office. "Long time, no see. I left you a message earlier today, but didn't hear back. Thought I'd take a chance and see if you were in before I left."

"Sorry about that. It's been a hectic day."

Anna I had met years ago at the company holiday party, when my mom was still alive and running the London magazines. She was older, though I was never quite sure how much. I'd venture to guess she had twelve to fifteen years on me. She was also the VP of sales for all of the mags. At the time, I'd still been playing for England, and I'd never been with a woman in her forties, so when she offered to share a car home at the end of the evening, I said yes. She gave me one hell of a ride that night. It wasn't the smartest thing I'd ever done, but hey, I was single and not her boss. Though it definitely shouldn't have happened again after Mom passed and I took over the ownership of her businesses. There was no excuse for that, especially since it had happened more than once. Except that she was fucking hot and had a mouth so dirty, she could make a trucker blush.

Her eyes dropped to my bag. "Getting ready to leave?"

I nodded. "Yeah."

She tilted her head coyly. "Want a ride?"

First Melanie and her naked selfies, and now Anna. I was being tested today. But even if Sloane weren't in the picture, and even if I didn't own the company Anna worked for, my buddy's news had put a damper on any hookups today. I'd made a lot of mistakes in my life, but I'd be damned if I was going to repeat them.

I lifted my bag to my shoulder. "I have my car here, but thanks."

10

WILDER

TEN YEARS AGO

"What comes easy won't last."

That was the last thing my father had said to me after dropping me off for my first semester at Harvard. At the time, I'd thought he was referring to school.

The blonde currently twirling her hair and smiling from the other side of the bar? She wasn't exactly giving off hard-to-get vibes. I'd noticed her an hour ago. She was impossible to miss—mile-long legs, tiny waist, and red lipstick that I couldn't stop imagining leaving ring marks around certain parts of my body. And I wasn't the only guy who'd noticed, that was for damn sure. I'd watched a half-dozen guys amble up to her, only to be turned away with their tails between their legs. Our eyes had met a few times, so I thought I might have better luck. But that side of the bar wasn't our territory. Final clubs—or what other schools usually called fraternities—split this place in half.

There was no line on the floor or written rules, but I stayed on our side with my buddies all the same. It was something we all knew and accepted—just like the fact that this seat was mine this year. As far as I knew, it had belonged to the captain of the rugby team since the place opened. The one next to me was for the captain of the football team, though he wasn't around tonight. When we weren't here, our seats remained empty—except when people who didn't know the rules wandered in. And they were quickly educated.

I should've been home studying for a test tomorrow, but my teammates had dragged me out to celebrate after our 24–17 win this afternoon. I finished my beer and held it up to the bartender, signaling for another, then made my way to the men's room to get rid of the four I'd already downed. Upon my return, I stopped short, finding my seat filled. Then I saw the legs attached to the offender. I reached around her and scooped my fresh beer from the bar. Legs turned to face me.

"I hope you don't mind me keeping your seat warm." She tilted her head with a smile.

"Not at all. But I'm a little chilly, if you're warming things up."

She plucked my beer from my hand and drank some. "You going to buy me my own, or do I need to drink yours?"

"I've watched half a dozen guys try to buy you a drink tonight. You didn't seem to be thirsty."

She licked beer foam from her top lip. "I don't let guys in bars buy me drinks. It gives them a false expectation that I'm going to do something for them in return."

I raised a brow. "Yet you just told me to buy you one?"

She smiled. "Your expectation might not be false."

I wasn't complaining, but I was curious. "Why is that?"

"You're gorgeous." She squeezed my bicep. "And I saw you play at the game earlier. I was dying to feel your arm."

I already had a big ego, but a good stroking never hurt anyone. Especially from a woman who looked like her.

"I haven't seen you around," I said. "You go to school here?"

"I did. But I had to take the semester off. My parents had problems with the loans, and my dad's sick. I'm waitressing to save up and go back. But it might take a while."

"I'm sorry."

She shrugged. "Not your fault."

"What's your name?"

"Whitney. What's yours?"

"You went to the game today, but you don't know my name?"

She smiled. "Wilder Hayes."

"Why'd you ask if you already knew?"

Her hand was still on my bicep. She rubbed up and down my arm. "Are you going to buy me that drink or what?"

"What are you having?" I lifted a hand to call the bartender.

She shrugged. "I don't know. Maybe a hard seltzer? Something portable, not in a glass."

"You going somewhere?"

She bit her bottom lip. "I hope so."

I ordered her a hard seltzer and added another beer for me. While we waited, I stared at her lips. "I like your lipstick."

"Thank you. I like your eyes."

I looked down. "I like your legs."

She squeezed my arm again. "I like your muscles."

I was standing, so I could see right down her shirt. A healthy amount of cleavage popped out of her top. I lifted my eyes and met hers with a smile. "Fuck the drinks. You want to get out of here?"

Her sexy-as-shit lips curved to a grin. "It's about time."

My dorm room was five minutes away, but it took us twenty because of all the times we stopped to make out. We had half our clothes off in the hall before I even got the door open. It might've been the easiest encounter I'd ever had with a woman.

So my father's words should've set off an alarm.

"What comes easy won't last."

But all the thoughts I had went out the window with the sound of my pants coming undone.

11

WILDER

"Well, it sucks," I said. "But I think you're making the right decision."

Andrew sighed. "I wouldn't be able to look her in the eyes if I didn't come clean. And she deserves honesty."

The following morning, our plane had finally leveled off to cruising altitude, so the crew got up to move about the cabin again. One of the flight attendants, Mia, cast a flirty smile in my direction as she passed.

Andrew noticed, too. "I take it you know her?"

"I take this flight a lot."

My buddy side-eyed me. He knew the answer without me having to spell it out, but just in case he didn't, Mia walked over. I was seated in the window seat. She leaned in, giving me and my buddy a clear view down her blouse as she set the drink I hadn't asked for in front of me.

She smiled. "Staying at the St. Regis this trip?"

I shook my head. "Nah. I have business in a different area."

"Oh. Okay." She stood, her smile morphing from flirty to forced, and rested a hand on Andrew's shoulder. "Can I get you anything else, hun?"

He lifted his still-half-full Bloody Mary. "I'm good. Thanks."

We both watched her walk to the galley area a few rows up. Andrew shook his head. "I thought you said you were staying at the St. Regis?"

I met his eyes. "I am."

"Gotcha." He sipped his drink. "Everything okay with you? It's not like you to turn down a nice offer like that."

I sighed. "Was I that bad?"

"What are you talking about?"

"In the last twenty-four hours, I've gotten invitations from three women I've slept with before."

Andrew stuck his bottom lip out in a pout. "Aww, you poor baby. You're single and got offered sex from three hot women. Meanwhile, I fucked up the rest of my life. Your life really sucks."

I chuckled. "I'm serious. Have I been that big of a whore?"

"You once slept with a woman you met at a bar on a Friday night, and the next day she called and asked if you would sleep with her friend who needed cheering up. And you did."

"What was I supposed to do? Let the woman be miserable?"

Andrew smiled. "You're a whore, my friend. But no judgment here. Especially not now. Besides, it's not like you to pretend to be something you're not."

I frowned.

My buddy's forehead creased. "Seriously? What's going on with you?"

Of all my friends, Andrew knew me the best. He was also brutally honest. I shifted in my seat to see his expression. "Do you think I have relationship potential? I mean, one that lasts more than two months and involves more than just fucking each other's brains out?"

Andrew shrugged. "We've been in one for, what, twenty-five years?"

"I don't mean a friendship."

"I know what you're asking. But I don't think the criteria are that different. A relationship of any kind is built on honesty, trust, and open communication. We have that. So you clearly have the ability to share those things with someone."

"That's being a friend, not a boyfriend."

"The only thing that's really different is the sex, being monogamous."

I pointed to my buddy. "That's the part I'm worried about."

"That's only because you haven't met a woman who holds your interest. Once you do, it won't be hard." He closed his eyes. "And I realize that sounds ridiculously hypocritical considering the reason I'm flying home, but it's the truth. I might be the relationship guy of the two of us, and you're the whore, but I know you'd never cheat after . . ."

I took a deep breath. "I think I met someone. She's got a stranglehold on my interest. I can't fucking think of much else these days."

Andrew's eyebrows shot to his hairline. "Never thought I'd see the day. What's her name?"

"Sloane."

"What's she like?"

"She's smart. Beautiful, with auburn hair and a great figure. And she calls me out on my crap."

He grinned. "I like her already."

"We have great chemistry, and not just the sexual kind. There's an emotional and intellectual chemistry, too. Like, I want to listen to her talk, and when she tells me shit, I feel it in my gut. I don't even really understand it."

"That all sounds great. But why do I feel like there's more coming, like I'm waiting for the big red flags to start waving around in the wind?"

"Oh, there are definitely red flags."

"She married?"

I shook my head. "Of course not. But she was recently engaged. The dickhead left her at the altar. She's like you, has only ever had serious relationships. And she works for one of my dad's holdings—a bridal magazine—and she's got an obsession with weddings. Her family is fourth-generation NYPD, and they also own a cop bar that has so many people carrying they could fight a small war."

"Jesus Christ, Wilder. Why is everything with you go big or go home? You're gonna get your ass shot if you fuck with this woman."

"Tell me about it."

"Does she know who you are? That you don't have the most stable track record when it comes to dating?"

"I haven't hidden anything from her."

"And she wants to give it a shot anyway?"

"Well, I guess that's also a problem."

Andrew's brows pulled tight. "What do you mean?"

"She hasn't agreed to give anything a shot with me. She's on what she calls a 'man moratorium.' Decided not to date anyone for a year after her engagement ended."

"How long ago was that?"

"Six months."

"So you're going to do what for the next six months?"

I frowned. "I sort of told her I'd wait for her."

"Wait for her where? You can't mean you told her you'd be celibate for that long."

My shoulders slumped. "I did, yeah."

Andrew's head fell back in a fit of laughter. He cracked himself up so hard, the jerk snorted a few times.

"Alright, alright. It's not that funny, jackass."

He wiped tears from his eyes. "What's the longest you've ever gone without sex?"

I shrugged. "Maybe a few weeks."

As if on cue, Mia approached a passenger in the row in front of us, seated across the aisle. She bent, practically shoving her heart-shaped ass in our faces. We both took a long look before Andrew's eyes slanted to meet mine again.

"Gonna be a long six months. Good luck, buddy."

The following morning, I pulled up outside the brownstone a half hour early. When I'd invited Harry to come to the Rutgers game on our drive home last week, I hadn't thought to get his number, and now I needed to be at the arena a half hour early. I could've gotten Sloane's number from my dad's office and called her to get it, but I'd only gotten the message about the change in meeting time an hour ago, at 6 a.m. Rather than waking Sloane to reach her dad, I figured I'd take my chances and just show up early. Harry seemed like the kind of guy who would be ready to go.

At the top of the brownstone steps, there were four bell choices. The bottom one read H. CARRICK. I went to press it, but the names above it caught my attention. Three of the four had the last name

Carrick, including the top one, which read S. CARRICK. Did Sloane live here, too? Her whole family, maybe?

As cheesy as it sounded, I felt my pulse pick up. I grumbled to myself, trying to shake off feeling like I was in some sort of lovesick teen movie. When it didn't work, I said *fuck it* and pressed the button for s. CARRICK. Like my buddy Andrew said, *go big or go home*.

But after two minutes, there still was no answer. That turned the excitement I'd felt into something different—*jealousy. Did she sleep somewhere else last night?* When I didn't answer the door in the morning, it was usually because I'd been busy the night before and hadn't made it home. *But*—I talked myself down—that was me, not Sloane. She was probably out for a damn run, or the bell was broken. Or maybe she didn't even live here. *Yeah, that's it.*

I needed to get a move on, so I sucked it up and pressed H. CARRICK. A loud buzzer sounded back, unlocking the outer door. I opened it and walked in through a double set of doors. Harry stepped into the hallway . . . in his bathrobe. *Shit.*

"Hey," I said. "Sorry I'm so early. I didn't have your number. I was supposed to meet someone at the arena during the game to talk about a player, but he texted this morning and pushed the time up."

"Let me get my ass dressed then." Harry waved me into his apartment. "Come on in."

He disappeared into another room before I could shut the door behind me, and yelled from wherever he must've been getting dressed. "There's coffee in the pot, if you want some. Help yourself."

"I'm good. Thanks. I had a cup at the hotel and have a to-go cup in the car waiting. Got one for you, too, in case you want it."

He popped his head out from a doorway down the hall. "This is already the best date I've had in years."

I laughed. "Hey, uh, does Sloane live here, too?"

"Yep. Fourth floor. My son bought this place a few years back. He lives on two, and I'm down here. Got one real tenant on the third."

I nodded. "I think I *accidentally* pressed her bell at first. Hope I didn't wake her . . ."

"Takes more than a little bell to wake that girl on the weekends. She likes to sleep in. She has a lot of energy when she's awake, but she can knock out until two in the afternoon." Harry paused. "Damn it, that reminds me. I gotta return her key to the bar before we go. I borrowed it because my son borrowed mine, and I never gave hers back. She goes into the bar before it opens on Saturdays to do the books."

I noticed a key sitting on the kitchen counter, one with a CARRICK'S PUB key chain. "You want me to return it while you get dressed?"

"If you don't mind, that would be great. But I gotta warn you, it's a four-story walk-up, and she's cranky in the morning."

I smiled. "No problem."

"Key should be on the counter. You might need to pound on the door to get her to wake up."

"Got it. I'll be back in a few."

"I'll be ready by the time you're done."

I took the stairs two at a time, blood back to pumping excitedly though my veins. I told myself my heart was racing because I was running, *not* because I was a giant wuss-bag excited to see a girl. But when I reached the top floor, I might've fixed my hair a little. *Whatever*. Fuck it.

I brought my knuckles to the door and gave it a good, strong knock. There was only her apartment up here, so any sound I heard would mean she was awake. But there wasn't a peep. *Damn, Harry wasn't joking.* She was a solid sleeper.

I knocked again, this time putting some muscle behind it. The door shook, and after a couple of seconds, I heard grumbling. "Alright! Alright! I'm coming."

The door swung open with the same anger I'd heard in her voice. She probably had a scowl to match, too, but I was too busy looking *other places* to notice—like at her creamy thighs and the piercing nipples saluting the morning. Sloane had on a threadbare Back-street Boys T-shirt, sans pants, with a hem that barely brushed the top of her thighs. Also, definitely no bra.

Her eyes widened. "Wilder? What are you doing here?"

I smiled and looked her up and down. "Improving my morning, apparently."

"But, but . . . how do you know where I live?"

"I didn't until a few minutes ago. I came to pick up your dad and saw all the names on the buzzers."

Her nose scrunched up. "Why are you picking up my dad?"

"He didn't mention that he was going to the game today?"

"He did. Well, he said you had given him a ticket to a rugby scrimmage or something. But I guess he failed to mention you were his *date*."

I couldn't take my eyes off the hem of her shirt. I just wanted to glimpse what kind of underwear she had on. *Fuck*. Maybe she's got *nothing* on under there. I should toss the key in the air and make her lift her arms to catch it.

Sloane looked down. "Oh God. I'm not dressed."

"I think you look *fucking great*."

She rolled her eyes, but the corner of her lip twitched upward. "So you're dating my dad because I won't go out with you?"

I leaned in. "*Yet*. You won't go out with me *yet*."

She might've been saying one thing, but I didn't miss the goose bumps that prickled up her arms when I got close. Her body wasn't in denial like the rest of her. I would've loved to see how far I could push, but I didn't want her dad to think I was doing anything shady up here. Plus, I did need to hit the road.

I held out the bar key. "I came to give you this for your dad."

She took it, but I didn't let go.

"Have dinner with me tonight?" I asked.

"Wilder . . ."

"Lunch?"

She smiled. "I'm working at the bar."

"If you weren't?"

She chuckled and swiped the key from my hand. "Then I probably would be sleeping through lunch, if you weren't up here waking me."

I winked. "That's not a no."

"Take good care of my dad, Wilder."

"You got it. And I'll see you soon."

"I can't wait to see when that is, since you seem to show up when I least expect it."

"So, which one are you interested in?" Harry gestured to the field.

I pointed. "Number twenty-two, Leo Goncalo. He's a walk-on, didn't even play in high school or in an organized league. Only experience was playing with his friends on weekends. But he hit the genetic lottery for size and speed, and he has the balls of a cat in a room full of rocking chairs."

Harry lifted his hand to his forehead, shielding his eyes from the sun to watch the action on the field. "Other people interested in him?"

I nodded. "That's why I asked his dad to meet me today. Dad's a tax lawyer, but he's acting as his agent, too. Not smart, if you ask me, but trust is an issue when too many people are suddenly knocking at your door, so I get it. When agents and scouts started lining up two deep at my high school games, all talking shit about the other teams, I had no idea who to trust, either."

"I bet."

"Leo already has offers, and I don't even have a team yet to extend an offer to join. So my chances aren't great, but I wanted to let them know I'm interested and what my plans are if the vote comes through next week."

Rutgers scored, and the crowd went crazy. It reminded me of my college days. After that, we were both glued to the field, cheering Leo on. At halftime, we went up to the club lounge and had a beer.

"So tell me," Harry said. "Are you interested in my daughter, or you just like taking bored old men out?"

I smiled. "I like Sloane, yes. But I would've invited you even if she wasn't your daughter."

"Why is that?"

I shrugged. "My dad taught me to always do right by the people who put their life on the line to protect us. Buy a cop a beer at the bar, pick up the restaurant check for an army private home on leave."

Harry nodded. "I like your dad."

"We had a tough go for a while after he and my mom divorced, but he's always given me good advice, especially on what's important in life."

Harry sipped his beer, which seemed like a difficult task with the way his hand shook. He noticed me looking. "My daughter's always trying to get me to use a straw. But it's hard to look tough sipping beer out of a straw, don't you think?"

I laughed. "Probably."

"She's bought me a dozen special cups—ones with discreet lids inside, handles that rotate to support the tremors—but I prefer the fill-three-quarters method."

I shrugged. "Whatever works."

Harry set his beer on the bar. "I never liked that Josh."

"Who?"

"Sloane's ex."

"Oh."

"Didn't like him from the beginning. A few months after they started dating, Sloane told me she wanted me to get to know him better. So I took him to the gun range for some target practice one afternoon, a place where a lot of cops go. Dumbass thought it was a good place to talk about gun control." Harry shook his head. "He's lucky I didn't bring my gun to the church with the shit he pulled."

"It's gotta be tough for Sloane to work for a bridal magazine after that."

Harry nodded. "That day meant a lot to her. My wife got sick when Sloane was only five. Ovarian cancer. She fought it for two years like a trooper, but in the end it was everywhere. Lily stopped treatment so she could enjoy the last few months she had left. I took leave from work and thought we'd travel and do things before it was her time. But Lily just wanted to be home with her family. Her kids and me were everything to her. I asked her to at least come up with one special thing she wanted to do. She took a week and thought about it and then told me she wanted to marry me all over again."

I felt an ache in my chest. "Wow."

Harry looked away as he continued. "So I threw her the biggest, best second wedding I could plan in two weeks. Even got Sloane a matching white dress to wear on the big day. She stood up at the altar as the maid of honor, and my boys were my best men. It was the happiest day of our lives, even more special than the first time we did it because we were older and wiser, and it meant something that we'd still choose each other after all our ups and downs. It was magical. Sloane smiled from ear to ear all night, and she couldn't stop talking about it when it was over. But pretty soon after, things went downhill. Fast. My Lily died three weeks later. We all took it hard, but Sloane was real bad. The boys had each other and me— but it wasn't the same with her being the only girl." Harry took a deep breath. "Anyway, after that, whenever Sloane was feeling down, she'd throw herself a pretend wedding—even married the dog a few times, which her brothers still tease her about."

I shook my head. "I don't know what to say, except that I'd better not ever cross paths with that Josh for taking something that meant so much away from her."

Harry smiled. "The bottom line is, you seem like a decent-enough guy. But when my Sloane loves, she loves hard. She's had a lot of loss and letdown in her life, and some of that is still healing. I'm not telling you to keep away, because my daughter is a grown-ass woman and has a good head on her shoulders. But I'm asking you to think twice about what you want before you chase her too hard, because I don't want her hurt again."

12

SLOANE

"Holy crap. If you have sexy lingerie under there, I might consider switching teams," Elijah teased.

I smiled and did a twirl. "You like it?"

"You look smokin', Sloane."

I loved the color of this dress, and even I had to admit it hugged me in all the right places. It was a simple slip silhouette with spaghetti straps, but the cowl-neck front showed the right amount of cleavage and made my body into an hourglass. "I figured this beautiful, old mansion on the beach deserved more than the boring little black dress I usually go to these things in."

"*Riiight.* That dress is for the *venue.*"

"What's that supposed to mean?"

"Are you seriously going to tell me you didn't think of a certain blue-eyed Adonis when you were picking out that dress?"

"Absolutely not," I answered *waaay* too quickly.

He chuckled. "Whatever. What's going on with him? Anything new happen since he showed up at your house and took your dad on a date?"

I found lipstick in my purse and stood in front of the mirror lining my lips as I spoke. "I haven't heard from him. It's for the best." I wouldn't admit it, but I was a little disappointed. Wilder hadn't popped in after dropping Dad off after the game, and I knew he'd been in New York the last couple of days. I kept expecting him to show up at the office or the bar. But I'm sure he was busy.

Elijah made a face. "Why? You have to be attracted to him. The man is a work of art. If they hung his mug at the Louvre, I might consider going to a boring-ass museum."

"He's handsome, yes. And I'm actually surprised how much we have in common. But he's a playboy."

Elijah shrugged. "Who cares? You don't want a relationship right now, anyway. What's wrong with having a little fun with the guy?"

I opened my mouth to respond, but then shut it. Twice.

Elijah lifted a perfectly groomed brow. "Got nothing, huh?"

I squinted at him. "Shut up."

"Sloane, the best way to get over someone is to get under someone else. And he's the perfect candidate for a fling. He's a busy guy who lives on another continent. Can't get too attached when you're not seeing each other all the time."

"I work for his dad."

"Big deal. You don't work for Wilder, and he doesn't work for his father, it seems."

"We have completely different lifestyles. The incredible mansion next door where the wedding is being held is owned by the father of the groom. It's their summer place. And this hotel we're in right now? They own that, too. *This* is Wilder's social circle."

"Who gives a shit? None of that matters, especially not if you're keeping it casual and having a good time."

"I don't know." I sighed. "But we should get going. They're using the library as a bridal suite. We should shoot some pictures of it."

Elijah stood. "Okay, but if the bride asks you to fill in for a missing bridesmaid again, you're saying no. I'll put the dress on rather than have you take that one off."

―――

"Why aren't the emergency spray-tan police here?" Elijah whispered.

I giggled. "I think they ran out of solution after using it all on Bridezilla. I can't believe she showed up like that."

The Bridezilla we were referring to wasn't today's bride, fortunately. It was Piper, the horrendous one from last time. Today's bride was sweet as could be. She hadn't even flinched when Piper walked in looking like the Great Pumpkin. I still couldn't believe the woman had showed up looking exactly like what had made her throw a hissy fit at her own wedding. *Unbelievable*. So far Piper's was the only face I recognized from last time, though I suspected many of the groomsmen would be familiar since the series was based on fraternity brothers.

"Is everyone ready to let the guys in?" the mother of the bride asked the room. "I thought it would be nice to make the introductions in here, rather than as you're about to walk down the aisle, since many of you haven't met your partners yet."

A murmur of *sures* went around the room before she opened the door to the library. The first man to walk in was none other than Wilder. He flashed a Hollywood-worthy smile that came with a shy, *aw-shucks* wave.

God, he really is adorable. It struck me as an odd thing to think about a six-foot-two, broad-shouldered professional rugby player, yet he somehow pulled it off. *Freaking adorable.*

The mother of the bride pointed to the ladies standing closest to us—Bridezilla and a pretty blonde who looked like she might be a model. "Wilder, your partner is Amanda."

I frowned. *Great.*

Amanda leaned over to Piper and whispered, "Oh, wow. Is he single?"

Piper nodded. "He's always single. Wilder is a lot of fun, but don't expect more than that."

Amanda licked her lips. "That's okay. *Fun* is all I'm looking for."

I felt a sinking feeling in my chest, like someone releasing the air from a balloon inside.

Elijah scooted closer as I stared down at the ground. "Apparently I'm not the only one who likes your dress."

I looked up to meet a set of stunning blue eyes, and that stupid balloon under my rib cage filled back up with air—at least halfway. Wilder offered a slight nod before walking over to his smiling partner.

"Let's move to the back," Elijah said, "so I can take some candids of this crew."

"Okay." I tried not to pay much attention to Wilder and his pretty partner, but my eyes had a mind of their own. Amanda was a touchy-feely one. Thankfully, it wasn't long before the ceremony started because I could've given myself a headache with all the teeth grinding I was doing.

At the cocktail hour, I took a glass of wine to a quiet table on the outside deck overlooking the ocean and typed some notes about the wedding into my phone for my article. It was beautiful here. The mansion sat on a bluff, and the smell of salt water drifted through the air. The distant sound of waves crashing relaxed me more than the wine.

Then I felt eyes on me. I turned and found Wilder standing in the doorway. I thought for sure he'd come over, especially because I was sitting all alone, but instead he lifted his hand in the type of wave you'd give a casual acquaintance and walked back inside. It left me confused, like maybe I'd done something to upset him and didn't realize it.

Though when the reception started, he didn't *look* upset. In fact, he was all smiles with his partner in his arms as they swayed to the music.

Elijah noticed me watching. "She's his partner. They have to dance together."

He'd said it to make me feel better, but all I could think was, *I was his partner last time. Is that the only reason he danced with me?*

Over the next hour, my eyes caught with Wilder's a few times, but he always looked away. There was no flirting, no secret grins, no winks—nothing I'd come to expect from him. And that might in and of itself have been the problem—*I'd come to expect something from him.*

In between my sulking, I chatted with some of the other guests at my table. One of them was a nice-looking man probably ten years older than me. He was seated two chairs over, but when the table emptied except for the two of us, he got up and took the seat next to me.

"I hate weddings," he said. "How about you?"

I laughed. "Same."

He motioned between us. "And the only thing worse than being seated at the single-friend table is being seated at the kiddie table."

"I'm actually here working."

"Ouch." He reached for his stomach like he'd been punched in the gut. "I stand corrected. There is a shittier table than the kiddie table. The *employee* table."

I laughed again.

The man extended his hand with a smile. "Joe."

"Sloane." We shook.

"So what kind of work do you do, pretending to be a guest at a wedding? Wait—you're not an undercover bodyguard or something?"

"Definitely not."

He rubbed his chin. "Food critic?"

"Nope. But you're getting warmer."

Joe and I talked for ten minutes. He was funny, with a self-deprecating humor I liked, so when he asked me to dance, I should've said yes easily.

"Umm . . ."

"You look like you're on the fence, so let me get my hard sell in. I'm not a very good dancer. I'll probably step on at least one of your toes. But . . ." He held up a finger. "I did grab the cologne bottle without my contacts in earlier, so I probably smell minty fresh. It turns out I slapped mouthwash all over my neck."

I smiled. "Now how can I pass up such an enticing offer?"

Joe stood and held out his hand to me. I scanned the room as we walked, hating that I was looking for Wilder on my way to dance with another man. It was a slow song, so he wrapped one hand around my back and led with the other. Unlike my dance partner at the last wedding, Joe left room for Jesus. Yet I still felt tense dancing with him.

I took a deep breath, trying to relax a bit, and the minty scent of mouthwash washed over me. I laughed. "You weren't kidding. You smell like Scope."

"I was already running late and didn't have time to shower again."

"It doesn't smell half bad. Clean, at least."

Joe smiled and attempted to turn us, but his footwork did one thing and mine did another, and he wound up stomping on my pinky toe. I lifted my foot and winced.

"So sorry," he said.

"You really didn't exaggerate anything, huh?"

We both laughed. I was still smiling when my gaze moved over his shoulder. And landed on a man who was *not* smiling. *Wilder.* His stare was intense, but his face was expressionless. Like earlier, he soon turned away, this time without even the casual wave.

After that, I just wanted to go home. But that wasn't happening until tomorrow since we were four hours from the city. I found Elijah and told him I was tired and ready to head back to the hotel next door. He hadn't found a cute waiter this time, so he left with me.

Back in my room, I changed out of my dress, tied my hair up, and washed the makeup from my face. I'd just slipped under the covers when there was a light knock at my door.

My heart raced upon seeing Wilder through the peephole. The rest of my body joined in when I opened the door. Unknotted bow tie hanging loose around his neck, mussed hair, and a hint of five-o'clock shadow peppering his angular jaw—the man was a sight for sore eyes. He held up a bottle of wine, and his presumption pissed me off.

"Why aren't you with the blonde?"

He frowned. "Because I couldn't do it—even though I wanted to."

I folded my arms across my chest, feeling anger rise within me. "You probably had too much to drink. It happens to men."

Wilder closed his eyes. "That is *not* what I meant. I meant I wanted to fuck some random woman and not be here right now."

I started to shut the door. "Then why don't you go do that?"

He stuck his foot in, stopping it. "*Fuck,* this is coming out all wrong."

I opened the door halfway back and sighed. "What do you want from me, Wilder?"

He raked a hand through his hair. "Can I come in? So we can talk?"

I wasn't sure what was left to say, but I would never be able to sleep without hearing whatever it was, so I gritted my teeth and stepped aside.

Wilder took two steps into the room and stopped, staring at the bed. He shook his head. "Actually, your first instinct was right. You shouldn't trust me in here with you. How about we go for a walk? Maybe on the beach?" He caught my eyes. "Please?"

"Fine. But I need to get dressed."

At least the shirt I'd answered the door in tonight was longer than the one I'd greeted him with the other morning. But I still needed to put on jeans and shoes. Wilder let the door shut behind him and stood just on the other side of it while I got ready.

Neither of us said a word as we walked through the hotel and took a set of stairs built into the bluff down to the beach. It was a beautiful night with a warm breeze and twinkling stars, and the rhythmic sound of the ocean hitting the shoreline tried its best to lull me into relaxing.

"You looked really beautiful tonight," Wilder finally said.

"Thanks."

"Green is your color."

I smiled, and Wilder made small talk about the wedding as we walked side by side along the water's edge. When it seemed he'd run out of ways to fill the space, he stopped.

"Wanna sit?"

I shrugged. "Whatever."

He took off his tuxedo jacket and laid it on the sand, gesturing for me to sit before bending and taking the spot next to it. He looked out at the ocean for a long time before speaking.

"I'm sorry I acted like an ass tonight," he said.

"You don't have anything to apologize for. You didn't do anything wrong."

"Maybe not, but I was avoiding you."

I shifted to face him. "Why?"

He shrugged. "I was trying to do you a favor."

"I don't understand, Wilder."

"I like you, Sloane. I feel like there's something here, something more than physical. That's not something I'm used to. We're built different. Physical is usually enough for me. It's not for you. And you've been hurt recently. I don't want to do it again. My track record sucks. I know you haven't even agreed to go out with me, but I think you feel what I feel, too." He caught my eyes. "Am I wrong?"

My instinct was to say he was, to keep my guard up and protect myself. But he was being honest and vulnerable with me, so I couldn't. My shoulders slumped. "No, you're not."

A cocky grin slid across his face. I pointed to it. "Don't gloat."

Wilder chuckled and bumped his shoulder with mine. After, he held out his hand. I hesitated, but eventually slipped my hand into his.

We both stared straight ahead for a while in silence. When Wilder finally started speaking, he kept his gaze forward. "As long as we're both being honest, I want to come clean about something."

"What's that?"

"I wasn't totally honest with you last week at the bar. Or at least I was strategic in the way I answered."

On reflex, I started to pull my hand from his. But Wilder tightened his grip. "No. You can't have it back yet. I'm gonna need this for a few more minutes."

I looked over, but Wilder had shut his eyes. "The other night you asked me what my longest relationship had been. My answer wasn't a lie, but I skirted what you were trying to get at. I said I hadn't dated anyone for more than a few months since college. What I didn't say was that I had two long-term relationships before that. In high school, I had a girlfriend for two and a half years. Alyssa and I met in tenth grade. Senior year we started partying a lot, mostly typical eighteen-year-old stuff—drinking, smoking pot. One night, we were at some kid's house party. His parents weren't home. Some of the people hanging out were doing more than drinking beer and spiked seltzers. They were taking pills, Percocet and Xanax, but Alyssa played soccer and was going to college on a full ride, and I played on two rugby teams and had already been recruited to Harvard to play for them, so we didn't screw with that stuff. Plus, I had a game the next morning, so I left the party early. Alyssa wanted me to stay, but I always made rugby my priority." He paused and swallowed. "After I left, Alyssa wound up taking a Percocet since her friends were all doing it, and I wasn't around to tell her to cut the shit. As far as I know, it was the first time she'd ever taken a pill that wasn't prescribed to her. Turned out to be laced with fentanyl. She and two of her friends overdosed and died that night."

My hand flew to my chest. "Oh my God. That's horrible. I'm so sorry."

He shook his head. "She wouldn't have taken them if I'd stayed, if I had made getting her home safe my priority."

"No, Wilder. You can't blame yourself for a decision someone else made."

"After it happened, I went on a tear. I got into a lot of fights and caused trouble—even got suspended for a few games for starting a brawl that involved half our team. I was close with my old varsity rugby coach—still am to this day, though I need to get my ass to visit him more often than I do. He's got dementia now. But after Alyssa died, he gave me some leeway. When things spiraled, he sat me down and set me right, told me I was going to lose everything I'd worked for." Wilder nodded. "He kept on me, made sure I stayed in line. Eventually my anger leveled out, or at least I learned how to channel it onto the field. A few months later, I went to college and didn't look back. I swore off relationships after that, at least for the next three years. Then I met Whitney."

Wilder stopped. He picked up a small rock and skimmed it into the ocean. It bounced a few times before I lost track of it in the darkness. "We were together a year." His jaw tightened as he looked straight ahead again, and I watched the bob of his Adam's apple as he swallowed.

"Oh God," I said. "Did she . . . pass away, too?"

Wilder shook his head. "No. She destroyed *me* instead."

I wasn't sure what to say, so I stayed quiet. Eventually, Wilder cleared his throat. "That was my last relationship. It's been ten years." He paused. "A few months ago, when I went to visit Coach Evans, he asked me if I'd found a nice girl to settle down with yet. I laughed and said what I usually say—that I'm not the settling-down type. He patted my knee and told me I shouldn't be afraid, that I needed to stop letting the things that happened years ago keep me from finding love again. I blew off the comment. I've always told myself I wasn't afraid of shit. I just like my life the way it is. At least until recently." Wilder turned and looked into my eyes. "Until the day I met you. Now I can't stop wondering if maybe there's something to what he said."

I squeezed his hand. "Thank you for sharing all of that with me."

"I've never told anyone that story about Alyssa, and I don't think I've said her or Whitney's name in ten years."

I leaned my head on Wilder's shoulder. "Talking about things is usually the first step toward healing. I don't tell too many people, but I go to therapy."

"I don't have a therapist, but I have Coach, my old rugby coach. He's who I've always talked to. He's forgetful and confused a lot of days now, yet he's still better at seeing what's going on with me than I am."

"He was your coach in college?"

"Middle school and high school. But we've stayed close over the years. We talk on the phone every week. I don't get to see him enough lately because I've been so busy. But I need to rectify that."

We sat for a few more minutes, staring at the ocean. What he'd shared was a lot for me to take in, but I imagined it was tougher for him to let out. Then a few noisy people pulled our attention back to the staircase where we'd come down from the hotel.

Wilder dropped his head. "Shit."

"What?"

"It's the guys. We have this tradition whenever we're anywhere near water—started the first year of college, the night we all got inducted into our fraternity. It's the reason I don't invite any of them to my dad's summer home in the Hamptons anymore."

I was about to ask what the tradition was, but I didn't have to. The crew of guys weren't even at the bottom of the staircase yet and were already stripping out of their clothes as they ran toward us.

"Fuck." Wilder stood and waved his hands in the air. "They

don't see us sitting here." He shouted to his friends, "Hey, jack-asses! I'm sitting here with a lady."

One guy yelled as he struggled to pull his pants off. "She's a lucky freaking girl."

Another guy yanked his shirt over his head. "Get your ass in the water, Hayes! Or you know what happens—we're carrying you in with all your clothes on."

Wilder shook his head. "Sorry. They're wasted and a bunch of idiots sober. I'm not going to be able to stop them."

I smiled and climbed to my feet. "It's okay. I should get some sleep anyway. We're leaving early in the morning."

Wilder nodded toward the stairs. "I'll walk you back."

"You don't have to. You should enjoy your friends."

"Trust me, I'm not going to miss anything. Those jackasses are going to be in there floating on their backs with their shriveled dicks hanging out for a while. I'll come back down after I walk you."

I chuckled. "Okay."

When we got to my hotel room door, Wilder took both my hands. "Is having dinner with a friend who is a man against the rules of your moratorium?"

I nibbled my bottom lip. "Friends, huh?"

"Think about it." Wilder held out his cell phone. "Can we at least exchange numbers in case you decide in my favor?"

I smiled. "Sure."

"'Night, Cupcake." He took his phone back and kissed my fore-head. "I'm here for another week. I'll leave the ball in your court."

"Good night, Wilder."

Inside my room, I leaned my forehead against the door, my chest feeling full again. The balloon in there was getting a workout today. *Damn, that man is so much more than meets the eye.*

13

WILDER

TEN YEARS AGO

"I can't freaking believe it." My buddy Andrew shook his head. "When did you find out?"

"A week ago."

"Didn't you use protection?"

I raked a hand through my hair. "We did at first. But we weren't seeing anyone else, and she's on the pill."

"Isn't that thing supposed to be like ninety-nine percent effective?"

I blew out two cheeks full of air. "I've always been an over-achiever."

"What are you going to do? You're leaving for England in a few months."

"Not anymore."

Andrew's eyes bulged. "*What?* It's all you've talked about since we were kids. Playing for England is your dream."

"I'll postpone. Or I'll play here in the US. It's not too late to qualify for next year's draft in the MLR."

"You know that's not the same thing. Rugby here is shit. You might as well play professional Ping-Pong."

I frowned. "It's growing fast."

He shook his head. "Name one player here who has a seven-figure endorsement."

Of course I couldn't. Not here anyway. England? New Zealand? South Africa? Definitely. But the sport didn't make household names and faces in the US. "You know I don't need the money."

"I know. But don't you want to play against the best? In a stadium full of eighty thousand people?"

That's what hurt the most. I didn't mind not making money. My father had enough to last generations. But I wanted to be the best, and in order to *be* the best, you had to *play* against the best. There wasn't a player from the United States ranked in the top fifty. It sucked. But what the hell was I going to do? My girlfriend was pregnant. I couldn't move to another country right before she was about to give birth.

Andrew sighed. "Do you love her at least?"

"I haven't been with anyone else in four months."

He frowned. "That's not a yes. That could mean she's a great lay."

I pointed. "Watch it."

"Seriously, Wilder. This is a big fucking deal—changing your entire life for someone. Do you love her or not?"

"I'm content."

"I'm content when I sit on my grandmother's couch and she makes me her homemade gnocchi. Doesn't mean I want her to have my baby and uproot my entire life."

I raked a hand through my hair. "Doesn't matter what I want now. Because it's happening. We're having a kid."

14

SLOANE

Friday afternoon, I was sitting at my desk finishing up some work when my phone vibrated with an incoming call. I got excited, thinking maybe it was Wilder, only to get the ultimate letdown when I read the name on the screen. *Josh.* My ex was the absolute last person I felt like talking to—even seeing his name irked me—so I let the call go to voicemail. But I was curious, so when my phone chirped with a new message, I couldn't help myself and pressed play.

"Hey, Sloane. Long time, no talk. I couldn't decide whether I had a better chance of you reading a text from me or answering my call. Or maybe I'm kidding myself and I have no shot at either. At least I got to hear your voice on your message." He paused, and for a few heartbeats I thought that was it, that he'd hung up. But then he spoke again. "Anyway, I miss hearing it. I'd like to talk, if you have some time. So . . . yeah. Call me back. Please?"

I shook my head. *What balls.* Though I realized this might've been the first time I'd thought of Josh and *only* gotten angry, not sad. A few months ago, a call like that would've thrown my whole day off, but now, I didn't find it too difficult to get back to work.

A few hours later, a CNN alert popped up on my phone. Most of the time, I ignored them, but this particular one snagged my attention. *US Rugby League approves expansion team.*

I swiped to open. *Oh wow. How have I not googled this man for old photos yet?* The article had two pictures of Wilder at the top. The first must've been from his playing days—his teammates had him on their shoulders as he held a gold trophy of some kind in the air. He had no shirt on, and his chest was so carved with muscles, it didn't look real. I pinched the screen and zoomed in. *Wow. Just wow.* It took a solid minute of drooling before I panned up and studied his face. He didn't look that much different than he did now—same smile, same sparkling eyes. It said something when those peepers weren't the *first* thing to catch your attention.

The second photo was of him in a suit, looking handsome, but serious. Underneath, the article gave details about his ownership of the new team, along with two billionaire investors, and the stadium they were already in talks to secure. I hadn't heard from Wilder since the night of the wedding, when he'd left the ball in my court to get together. I'd thought about him every day—even picked up my phone and debated texting him on more than one occasion. But in the end I always chickened out. Now, though, I had an excuse. In fact, it would be rude of me not to reach out. At least that's what I told myself as I started to type.

> **Sloane:** Congratulations! I just read the big news on CNN. You did it!

I'd thought he might be busy with press and stuff, but the circles on my phone began bouncing around immediately.

> **Wilder:** Thank you. What are you doing tonight? Maybe my *friend* can help me celebrate . . .

I smiled, wishing I could, but I had Olivia tonight.

> **Sloane:** Sorry, I can't. My brother has a twenty-four-hour shift that started this morning so I'm making dinner for my niece at seven, followed by watching double episodes of *Pretty Little Liars*.
> **Wilder:** I'm a good cook, if you need some help . . .

I smiled.

> **Sloane:** I'm sure that's how you want to celebrate getting your own professional rugby team—with a fourteen-year-old

whose hobbies are rolling her eyes and giving monosyllabic responses.

Wilder: You'll be there, right?

I felt my brows dip.

Sloane: Yes, of course.
Wilder: Then there's nowhere I'd rather celebrate.

My heart went pitter patter. Before I could type back, another text came in.

Wilder: My brother is here, too. I think they might get along. His hobbies are rolling his eyes at me and busting my balls.

I nibbled my bottom lip, which was going to be swollen from all the gnawing the last few days. How could I say no when he'd achieved such a major accomplishment today? It was the *friend*ly thing to do, wasn't it? And what could happen with two teenagers around? Nothing, of course. Not that anything would happen if we were alone, either, but . . .

Maybe I should bake a cake to celebrate? *Cupcakes* . . . yum.

And shoot, I needed to get my eyebrows done on the way home. *Is my apartment clean?*

I looked at the time on my phone. If I left by five, I could stop at the grocery store and pick up ingredients, take the 1 train over to Libby to get my brows shaped, and still have time to clean and freshen up my makeup.

Freshen up my makeup. Yeah, it was the *friend*ly thing to do. I rolled my eyes at myself, but also picked up the pen from my desk and started writing a list of things I'd need. Then I added a few more quick stops I should probably make. *Shoot. I better get out of here a little early.*

A few minutes later, I was busy chewing on my pen, deciding if I needed anything besides under-eye concealer from Sephora—I hadn't slept so well last night—when my phone buzzed.

Wilder: You still there?

Oh my God. I'd gotten so engrossed in planning all the crap I
needed to do that I'd forgotten the most important thing: the invitation. I shook my head.

Sloane: Dinner at 7?

The little dots bounced around.

Wilder: We'll be there. Thanks for the invite, even if I did have to
invite myself, friend.

<hr>

"Why is this guy coming over again?"

I opened the oven door and slipped two cupcake pans inside.
"I told you, he's celebrating that he gets to start a rugby team
here."

"Who plays *rugby*?" Olivia snarled.

"It's a very popular sport in Europe. There's a professional
league here, too. It's just not as popular as football or soccer. But
Grandpa watches it. He actually went to a game with Wilder."

"Wilder." Olivia scoffed. "Stupid name."

"Can you please be civil when they're here?"

"Why? Is this guy your boyfriend or something?"

"No. He's just . . . a friend."

The buzzer rang, and a flurry of butterflies flapped their little
wings in my belly. I frowned down at my stomach. *Did you not just
hear me say he's a* friend? I shook my head and grabbed a bottle of
wine out of the fridge. "Can you press the button to let them in,
Olivia, please?"

She mumbled something, but did it. I opened the wine to let it
breathe and went to the door, pointing my finger at Olivia. "Be nice
to Lucas."

Her response was a typical eye roll.

Wilder came up the stairs first, with his brother behind. They both held bags in their arms. Wilder's mouth curved to a flirtatious grin when he saw me. "Hey."

I smiled. "Congratulations, Mr. Team Owner."

He shifted the bags to one arm and kissed my forehead. "Hello, gorgeous."

Lucas rolled his eyes.

I stepped aside for Wilder to enter and smiled at his mini-me. "Hi, Lucas." *Right this way, to the other half of the I-hate-everything matching set.*

He lifted his chin. "Whassup."

Olivia was busy texting on her phone and didn't bother to look up as they entered. I cleared my throat. "Olivia, this is Wilder and Lucas. Guys, this is my niece, Olivia."

She managed to hold back an eye roll, but the bored look on her face remained as she lifted her nose from her cell. Though it changed when her eyes found Wilder. She blinked a few times with an open jaw.

Yeah, tell me about it, girl.

She looked away, attempting to cover for her face, but she got hit with a second punch when she saw Lucas. Olivia had her mother's nice, year-round-tanned skin, but I could've sworn I saw a pink blush dust up on her cheeks.

"Olivia is in ninth grade," I said.

Wilder nodded to his brother. "Lucas, too."

"Oh, I thought he was a year older."

"He's got an early birthday, so he's one of the oldest in his class."

Lucas straightened his spine. "And I'm the tallest."

Wilder chuckled. "Yes, that you are."

There were a few awkward seconds as the two teens looked anywhere but at each other. Wilder raised the bag in his hand. "I didn't know what you were making, so I got red and white wine." He gestured to his brother. "And that bag has dessert. One is sugar free."

"Thank you." I gave Olivia a nudge. "Why don't you put the desserts away and see if Lucas wants a soda or some water or something?" I took the other bag from Wilder. "Thank you for this. I already opened a bottle of cab. Or would you rather me open what you brought?"

"Whatever you have is fine."

Lucas walked over to the art I had hanging on the wall. "Where'd you get this?"

I smiled and looked at Olivia. "My super-talented niece painted it."

Lucas's eyes widened. "Really? You're into manga?"

She shrugged. "I drew that a few years ago when I was into Shojo, but I'm more into Josei now."

"Josei's cool. I spray-paint Seinen."

"You *used to* spray-paint," Wilder said. "You're not going to destroy public property anymore, *right*?"

Lucas rolled his eyes.

"There's a comic book store around the corner," Olivia said. "They just had a big Seinen mural painted. You want to go see it?"

"Hell yeah."

Olivia looked to me.

"It's fine with me, if it's okay with Wilder."

Wilder shrugged. "Go for it."

I wagged a finger at my niece. "Just be back in twenty minutes. We're going to eat soon."

"Alright."

The two of them rushed out the door, and I shook my head. "Well, that was a quick bonding moment."

"He's super into that Japanese art stuff. A little too into it. He was grounded for a month after he spray-painted the side of an abandoned building in London. He and his buddies used it as their canvas."

"Oh, that's not good."

"I would never let him hear me say it, but the art was pretty kick-ass. It was an improvement to the crumbling old building. Obviously he shouldn't have done it, though."

I nodded. "You want some wine?"

"Definitely."

I took down two glasses and poured while Wilder looked around. "Your place is nice. It fits you."

I passed him a glass. "I'm not sure if that's a good thing or a bad thing."

He looked over at a small crystal chandelier I'd hung in the kitchen. "It's girly, but not over the top. Sophisticated, but curious. Makes me want to look around a little more."

I chuckled and leaned my hip against the counter, sipping my wine. "So is Lucas why you aren't out celebrating the big announcement today?"

Wilder's brows pulled together. "I am celebrating."

"I meant celebrating somewhere good."

"This is exactly where I want to be."

"You just became the owner of a professional team you've worked two years to obtain, and you want to be at a fourth-floor walk-up?"

"I guess I misspoke. If I had my choice, we'd be out celebrating somewhere you didn't have to cook. But I'm *with* exactly who I want to be with."

I tried to ignore the warmth that spread through my chest, which had nothing to do with the wine in my hand. "So what happens next with the team?"

"A lot." Wilder took a deep breath. "And fast. I'm flying to Spain tomorrow morning and Sweden the next day. We've been in negotiations with a few players, and first priority is getting them signed."

"That sounds exciting. I've never left the United States."

"Really?"

I nodded. "The next wedding is in London. I can't wait."

"I'm going to be busy for the next few weeks. But why don't you come in a few days early so I can show you around?"

"That's sweet of you to offer. Can I . . . think about it?"

Wilder's eyes dropped to my lips. "Full disclosure. I'm not being sweet. I want to spend time with you."

I felt my face grow warm, so I cooled myself with a sip of wine. "Did you see the photos from the wedding last weekend?"

He shook his head. "I've been busy."

I smiled. "There's one of you that's hysterical. Let me grab my laptop. It's in my bedroom. Be right back."

"You sure you don't want help carrying it? I could join you?"

I chuckled. "Make yourself comfortable. Actually, not *too* comfortable."

I went down the hall to my bedroom. When I came back, Wilder was seated on one of the stools that was usually tucked under the island counter. He pointed his eyes to a business card sitting on top. "You work on Saturdays, too?"

I peered over to see what he was talking about. It was an appointment card for Fifth Avenue Bridal at 9 a.m. tomorrow. "Oh, that." I shook my head. "No. That's personal, not magazine-related. I made an appointment to sell my wedding dress."

"*Huh*. Guess I never thought about what you do with the stuff if the wedding doesn't happen."

"I should have gotten rid of it by now. I'm never going to wear it. But I'm pretty attached to it. I bought it almost a decade ago."

"I thought you were only dating the guy a few years?"

I smiled. "I was. I bought it before we met. I saw it in a magazine. *Bride* magazine, oddly enough. It was long before I even worked there. I'd had this picture in my head of what my wedding would look like since I was a little kid, dress and all. One day I was flipping through a magazine at the doctor's office, and there it was—my dream dress. So I figured out who had it in stock and went to see it in person. I was only seventeen. I hadn't even planned on trying it on. But I wound up cashing in the savings bonds I'd had since I was born and buying it."

Wilder looked a little scared, which made me laugh. I pointed to his face. "I really wish we'd gone on a date, so I could've told you that story at dinner. You look terrified. I bet you would have bolted before dessert." I shrugged. "Anyway, as long as I'm letting my crazy out, I might as well let it all hang out. The appointment tomorrow is my third one. I've tried to sell it twice before."

"What happened?"

"Well, the first time I made it to the front door, but I couldn't bring myself to go in. The second time, I went in and spoke to one of the women who worked there. She took the dress out of the bag to look at it and a woman who was shopping walked over and asked if it was available for sale—she wanted to try it on. I pretended to get a call and rushed out. I couldn't part with it."

"What's the attachment? The dress, the dream, or the douche-bag?"

That made me smile. "You're asking a really good question. I'm over the douchebag, but I'm not sure if it's giving up the dress or my dreams that upsets me more. Maybe it's a little bit of both?"

"You can dream new dreams. Ones that are bigger and better."

I sighed and nodded. "Or maybe it's time I live in the land of reality. But let's not talk about my issues. I want to hear more about your team."

Wilder's eyes lit up as he spoke about all of his plans and ideas. He rambled for a solid twenty minutes before coming to a lull. "Sorry." He smiled. "I was babbling. You're probably dying to eat just so I'll shut up for a few minutes."

"Not at all. I find you inspiring. It's a reminder that I used to have goals of my own that didn't link my happiness with my love life."

"Like what?"

"I wanted to be an author, write books. I used to love my job, but I went to school for journalism and creative writing."

"What kind of books would you write?"

"Honestly, probably romance. It's all I read. Well, that and . . ." I looked over at a stack of books on the kitchen shelf. "Self-help books."

"You were reading one of those the night I came to your office. Do they work?"

"Sometimes when I'm reading them, I get invigorated by the ideas and outlook they have. It's sort of like getting a pep talk from the coach before a game."

"I can relate to that."

I nodded. "Except after it's over, you probably kept the excitement you felt by playing in the game. An hour or two after I shut the book, I forget everything I just read."

"So play the game after the pep talk," he suggested. "Start writing the book you always wanted to write."

"I guess . . . Maybe."

"I should be your coach, encourage you to follow your dreams. But selfishly, I also want to have a reason to see you every month, so you can't quit your current job anytime soon."

The front door burst open. Lucas and Olivia were laughing and talking like the best of friends. They offered us a chin lift and disappeared into another room.

I pointed. "Who were those happy children?"

Wilder shrugged. "Fuck if I know."

"I won my sixth-grade spelling bee," Lucas said. "Wilder has a tattoo on his ass. And Wilder is so afraid of clowns, he once pissed himself at the circus."

"I did not piss myself. I spilled my drink."

Lucas cracked up. "Because you jumped out of your seat when that clown came near you. That counts as pissing yourself."

Wilder grumbled and shook his head. "I thought the truths and lies we told playing this game were supposed to be about ourselves."

Lucas smirked. God, he really looked like his older brother. I glanced over at Olivia, who was currently gazing at the boy much the way I looked at Wilder. I wasn't the only one with a little crush.

Lucas pointed to me. "You go first. Which is the lie, Sloane?"

"I'm going to say . . . Wilder has a tattoo on his ass is the lie."

Lucas pointed to Olivia. She smirked. "He definitely looks like he could have an ass tattoo. I'm going with Lucas didn't win the spelling bee."

Wilder grumbled and gestured across the table at Olivia. "I'll vote with her."

My eyes widened. "You have an ass tattoo?"

"Show it to 'em." Lucas nudged his brother with his elbow. "Come on, show it to 'em."

"I think I'll pass on taking down my pants in front of a fourteen-year-old girl. Thanks, Lucas. People get arrested for that."

I couldn't stop laughing. This board game had turned out to be more fun than I'd thought, even if I was the only one whose game piece was still stuck at start. It was sort of like two truths and a lie, except when you guessed correctly, you moved your piece forward a few spaces.

"It's your turn, Aunt Sloane."

"Oh gosh. I'm going to sound boring after an ass tattoo." I looked over at Wilder. "You better tell me what it is later."

He winked. "I'll show you."

I wasn't sure how many hours we played, but I couldn't remember the last time I'd laughed so hard for so long. My face actually hurt a little. Eventually Wilder looked at his watch. "It's almost midnight. We should probably get going. We have an early flight in the morning."

I grinned. "Need to get home and put on your mud mask, huh?"

Wilder closed his eyes and dropped his head while the teenagers enjoyed my teasing. Lucas had revealed a lot of dirt on his brother tonight, most of which involved girly habits, like using mud masks, taking baths with candles, and watching the *Real Housewives* shows. "I'm going to kick your ass, kid," he growled. But it was all in good fun.

Lucas and Olivia said goodbye after exchanging phone numbers, and Olivia gave him one of her recent drawings. She stayed behind while I walked the guys downstairs and out front. Lucas waved goodbye and jogged to the car, giving Wilder and me a minute alone.

"He's a good wingman," I noted. "Did you train him to be adorable and then let you end your evening with privacy?"

"Adorable? He told you I listen to Taylor Swift while working out and have an ass tattoo."

I laughed. "Oh my God. What is the ass tattoo?"

"I'm not telling you. Gotta keep the mystery alive."

A light breeze blew, catching a piece of my hair and pushing it across my face. Wilder fixed it. It was such a simple thing, but it took the moment from laughing to more serious.

"I had a really good time tonight," he said.

"So did I."

"I hope you'll come to London early."

I wanted to get on the plane and go, though when he looked at me like he was right now, it scared the crap out of me. It wouldn't be hard to fall for Wilder Hayes, that's for sure. And maybe a little piece of me was already starting to. But I needed to be smart. "I'll try."

He kissed my forehead. "Thank you for having us."

My chest felt hollow as I watched him walk to the car. When he got to the door, he looked back and waved again before I went inside.

Olivia was waiting in the kitchen when I got back. "Oh my God. Did you see his eyes?"

"Wilder's?"

She looked at me like I was nuts. "*No!* Lucas's. When Mom was alive, we went to Turks and Caicos, and I remember looking down from the plane as we landed. His eyes are the same color as the water there. They're not really blue or green, but blue-green."

I smiled. "Yeah, Wilder's are the same."

"And he likes Josei *and* Seinen. I gave him one of my Josei drawings, and he's going to spray-paint me a Seinen version of it and mail it to me. Can you make sure he knows I live on the second floor? I forgot to give him my apartment number."

"I think it'll get to you if he uses mine or even just the house number."

"He lives in London, and his mom died, too."

"Yeah, I know," I told her.

Olivia rarely mentioned her mother, so I found it pretty amazing that she'd apparently already had a conversation about her with a boy she'd just met. But it was good for her to talk about it.

For the next half hour, she rambled on about things Lucas had told her, things they'd talked about. It was clear she had a crush. There was just something irresistible about those brothers. And it was becoming a challenge to fight it already . . . with six months left of my moratorium.

15

SLOANE

I pulled the door closed behind me at eight thirty the next morning, garment bag draped over one shoulder, feeling confident that today was the day. Two steps down the brownstone's front stairs, I looked up and nearly lost my balance. "What . . ."

Wilder leaned against a car, a to-go coffee cup in each hand, smiling. "Morning." He nodded. "I thought you could use a wingman, someone to help you get the job done on the third try."

"But I thought you had a flight out early this morning."

"I did. Made it a little later."

There were very few times I'd been rendered speechless. Hell, even when Josh broke my heart at the altar, I'd found words—most of them were curses, but I'd had *words*. Now, though, I could only stand and stare.

Wilder pushed off the car, set one coffee on the roof, and walked over to me. He extended the cup in his hand and reached for the garment bag. "Trade?"

I nodded, my jaw still slack, and didn't move.

Wilder took the weight of the bag and tucked the coffee cup into my hand. Somehow I put one foot in front of the other and followed him to the car. After he'd opened the passenger door for me, he laid the dress out in the backseat and jogged around to the driver's side.

I blinked at him. "I cannot believe you changed your flight to come with me to sell my wedding dress."

He shrugged. "I figured Lucas could use some sleep. He was up chewing my ear off about Olivia for an hour once we got back to the hotel."

I smiled. "Oh God. Olivia did the same. I think we might have a problem."

Wilder turned the key to start the car. "Yeah, if my ball-busting little brother gets a Carrick for a girlfriend before I do, I'm never gonna hear the end of it."

A loud chirp sounded from inside my purse.

"Is that your phone?" Wilder asked.

"No." I rummaged through my purse for my cell. "It's an alarm for my insulin pump."

"You okay?"

"I'm sure it's nothing. It usually is." I opened the pump app. My supposed blood-sugar reading flashed on the screen. If it was right, it would be a problem. But sometimes the reader just needed a reset. To be on the safe side, though, I needed to go back upstairs. "Can you just give me two minutes? I'm going to run back inside and double-check that this is a bad reading with an old-school finger prick."

"Should I come?"

"No. I'm fine. I'll just be two minutes, really."

I huffed it up to my apartment, did a quick stick of my finger, and inserted the slip into the glucose monitor. Sure enough, my blood sugar was fine. I needed to talk to the doctor about the increase in alarms at my next appointment.

Back downstairs, I climbed into the passenger seat.

"Everything okay?" Wilder asked.

"Perfect. The machine just does that once in a while."

"Okay." He smiled. "You ready to get rid of that dress?"

I took a deep breath. "I am. And this was really so sweet of you, Wilder."

He put the car in drive, but kept his foot on the brake, looking over at me. "Told you, Cupcake. Not sweet, just want to spend time with you." He winked. "Plus, the sooner you put old dreams to bed, the better my chances of getting you to go out with me."

I didn't buy for a minute that he didn't have a sweet side, but I also didn't call him out on it. The bridal shop was only a half mile away, so ten minutes later, we parked. I took a deep breath as he opened the door for me to walk through first.

"Hi," I said to the woman at the counter. "I have an appointment to sell a wedding dress."

"It is used?"

I frowned. "Yes, but I only wore it for an hour because . . . Well, I only wore it for an hour."

She pointed to a hook on the top of a tall silver pole next to the register. "You can hang it there. It'll take me a while to inspect the dress and research the value. If you want, take a look around a bit. There's a section of cocktail dresses in the back. Most people check that out, since we only give store credit."

"You only give store credit?"

The woman nodded.

"Is that a new policy?"

"Been that way as long as I've worked here. So at least two years."

I sighed. How the heck did I not know that? "Maybe I should . . ."

Wilder looked at me. "Are there other places that give cash?"

I shrugged. "I think so?" I chewed on my fingernail, debating.

Wilder put his hand on my shoulder and gently guided me to turn. Once we were facing each other, he put his other hand on my other shoulder, sort of like a coach talking to his player.

"You have ten more weddings you can buy dresses for."

He was right, but . . .

Wilder must have read the hesitation on my face. He leaned in and spoke more softly. "Do you want to keep that chapter of your life open?"

I shook my head.

"Then sell the dress, Sloane."

I took a deep breath and nodded, looking over at the sales clerk. "I'll take the store credit." It felt good to say. I smiled at Wilder. "Thank you."

"Anytime. Now come on . . ." He slung an arm around my shoulder and walked us toward the back of the store. "You're going to try on sexy shit for me as a reward for being such a good friend."

My smile grew. I could handle that.

Ten minutes later, I exited the dressing room wearing a dress so low-cut, I'd checked twice to see if it was on backward before coming out.

Wilder's face slid into a dirty grin as he stared at my very on-display cleavage. "Now that's a keeper."

I chuckled. "I'm practically naked."

"I know. It's freaking *great*."

I'd turned to go back into the dressing room when a display caught my eye—a wedding dress that reminded me of the one JFK Jr.'s wife, Carolyn, wore on her wedding day.

Wilder followed my line of sight. "You see something you like?"

"That dress is amazing."

He pointed. "The gown? Does it look like the one you're selling?"

I shook my head. "It's nothing like mine. But I think it might be the first dress since mine to give me goose bumps." I lifted my arm to show him.

Wilder shrugged. "Why don't you try it on?"

I snort-laughed. "We came here to get rid of a wedding dress. I'm not doing that again, buying a dress for a fantasy that doesn't exist."

The salesclerk made her way back to the fitting room. She held out a piece of paper. "This is the best I can do on the gown. It's a beautiful dress, but it's pretty old."

I swallowed hard looking at the number written on the sheet. It was maybe 10 percent of what I'd paid years ago.

Wilder caught my eye. "It's not about the money, right?"

I sighed. "Yeah. You're right." I looked to the salesclerk. "It's a deal. Thank you."

A little while later, we pulled up to the brownstone. I had two new cocktail dresses and still a small store credit left.

"What time is your flight?" I asked.

Wilder glanced at his watch. "Three and a half hours from now. I have to pick up Lucas and get this car back to my dad's garage before we head to the airport. So I do have to get going, though I wish I didn't."

"I don't know how to thank you for today. I feel lighter already. Freer."

Wilder winked. "That might've been my hope all along. See you in London—maybe a few days early?"

I smiled. "Yeah, I think you might."

16

SLOANE

"So today is going to be a fun one," I said into the camera. "We're making a dos-and-don'ts list for brides leading up to their wedding. And to help us, I have a special guest—Anna Wren from Park Avenue Wedding Planners. Anna has planned some of the biggest and most luxurious weddings in New York, including those of celebrities and Wall Street tycoons. She's one of the most sought-after planners, and her fifteen years of experience have taught her a thing or two about good etiquette." I took a breath. "And then toward the end of the show, I have a *giant* announcement I can't wait to share." I pressed a button to split the screen, and Anna went live with me. "Hi, Anna. Are you ready to get started?"

She pretended to crack her knuckles. "I am."

We jumped right into the list, starting with simple stuff like:

Do take into account all of your bridesmaids' body types when selecting dresses.

Don't ask people to be backup bridesmaids. (I didn't even know that was a thing.)

Do make sure dress fittings and rehearsals are at a convenient time for everyone involved.

Don't fire your bridesmaid because she gets pregnant.

Most of the list was pretty comical, consisting of things I hoped most people wouldn't need to be told, but brides got caught up when it came to their weddings. Anna and I laughed our way through the entire segment, and pretty soon it was time to ask the viewers for their input.

"Alright, ladies, you have our list. But we want to hear from you! So, we're going to open the chat for you to give us your thoughts on what else we should add to our list."

The suggestions rapid-fired in one after another, most of them *don'ts,* which clearly showed how many people have had bad bridal-party experiences.

Don't ask your bridal party to chip in for your honeymoon. (Huh?)

Don't tell your bridesmaids they must hold off on getting engaged until after your wedding so they won't steal your limelight.

Don't forbid your bridal party from eating the day of the wedding so they won't look bloated in pictures.

One in particular caught my attention as it rolled in.

Don't make your bridal party spray-tan themselves orange so they all have an equal amount of melanin.

The viewer's handle? NumberSeventeen.

A tingle ran up my spine at the thought of Wilder watching. The man was traveling nonstop and pulling together a brand-new professional sports team, but he'd remembered my weekly show? It was almost nine o'clock here, so nearly two in the morning his time—assuming he was back in England tonight. He was like Waldo lately, popping up in my Instagram feed all over the place in different countries.

I smiled at the camera, feeling slightly flushed. "Alright, I think we'll add NumberSeventeen's *don't* to our list—not requiring your bridal party to get matching spray tans so no one in particular stands out—and call it a day." I rubbed my hands together. "But we still have the big announcement, which I'm going to share with you by reading a letter I received from a viewer. But first, I want to thank Anna for all of her help today."

Anna waved. "Thank you for having me! And if we've made one person into less of a Bridezilla, I think we've done our job."

"Definitely."

"Bye, Sloane!"

"Bye, Anna!"

I pressed the button to go from split screen to just me and lifted a paper from my desk. "Alright, everyone, here we go. This is the letter I received from a wonderful viewer named Larisa . . . 'Dear Sloane, I've been a fan of your show since I got engaged two years ago. A friend told me about one of your segments on unique venues, and I watched it and wound up booking a small farm you featured up in the Hudson Valley for my wedding. Unfortunately, things haven't worked out, and my fiancé and I called off the wedding a few days ago. The entire thing is already paid for—in excess of fifty thousand dollars spent on the venue, catering, photographer, floral arrangements, hair and makeup, even a honeymoon suite. All of it is nonrefundable and going to go to waste, so I thought maybe I could turn something negative into something positive and pay forward the blessing I was able to afford. Would you be interested in running some sort of a contest with your followers to give away a pretty amazing wedding package? Best, Larisa Maven.'"

I leaned forward, unable to contain my excitement. "Of course I would! In fact, I've already spoken to Larisa several times and verified with all of the service providers that the services are transferrable. *This is happening, everyone!* The only thing you need to get is your dress. Larisa was going to wear her grandmother's, which she obviously wants to keep."

The comments section had been busier than usual all day, but now the messages were coming in so rapidly, I couldn't even read them.

"So here's the deal. One lucky person is going to win this *ahmazing* wedding. To enter, all you have to do is tell us why it should be you, in three hundred words or less." I pointed down to where a link had started flashing on the screen. "Just click below to submit your entry. We'll keep the contest open for five days and announce the winner live on our next show! Good luck, and happy wedding planning."

My laptop wasn't even shut when my phone buzzed with an incoming text. I smiled and swiped.

Wilder: Great show. That's some contest.
Sloane: I know. I was tempted to go buy back my wedding dress and donate it to the package. But I thought better of it. LOL.
Wilder: I'm glad you didn't.
Sloane: What country are you in now?
Wilder: I'm back home in England finally. I can't believe it's

only been twelve days since I left New York. It feels like twelve months.

Sloane: Were your travels productive?

Wilder: For the most part. Your haircut looks nice, BTW.

I was shocked he'd noticed. It was only a trim.

Sloane: Thank you. You're very observant.

Wilder: I once dated a girl who dyed her hair from blond to jet black. She wasn't happy when I didn't notice the change. So I think I have selective observation skills.

I smiled.

Sloane: My niece has her nose in her phone even more than usual. I'm pretty sure she and Lucas are texting nonstop.

Wilder: I took him to dinner when I got home earlier since I haven't been around. He barely said two words he was so busy on his cell. That explains it.

Before I could type back, a second text came in.

Wilder: Will they be related when we get married? It's been too long of a day for me to do the math on that.

I chuckled.

Sloane: Married, huh? We haven't even had a date yet.

Wilder: Maybe it's time we changed that . . .

I chewed on my fingernail, debating whether I should ask about his current dating life. A few of the photos I'd seen of him in the last week had included women—attractive ones. They could have been employees or business partners or . . . I wasn't sure I wanted to know the answer. But maybe if I did, I'd stop stalking the man's Instagram.

Sloane: Speaking of dating, are you still on your miss moratorium?
Wilder: It's the longest I've been celibate since I was fifteen.

I chewed on my lip.

Sloane: How long has it been?
Wilder: 29 days, 9 hours, and 11 minutes.

I laughed.

Sloane: You don't really know the minutes and hours, do you?
Wilder: Nah. Made that part up.

I swiped over to my calendar and did a little math before re-sponding.

Sloane: I have you beat. 251 days.

The little circles started to bounce around, then stopped before starting again.

Wilder: Wasn't your wedding date six months ago—a hundred and eighty days from when we met last month? That would be 220.
Sloane: Yes. But we didn't have sex for a month before the wedding. I was trying to make our wedding night special.

Those dots started moving again, then stopped. Thirty seconds later, my phone rang.

Wilder spoke before I could even say hello. "We are *not* doing that shit before our wedding."

The gravelly sound of his voice woke up the butterflies in my belly, but the thought of having sex with Wilder at all sent them fluttering still lower.

I laughed. "And here I thought I was the only one who made wedding plans before there was even a proposal."

"I don't give two shits about the when and where, but I care about being cut off from having you beneath me."

"Beneath you? What if I'm more of an on-top girl?"

Wilder groaned. "You're killing me, Cupcake."

I couldn't stop smiling. "Why are you up so late? It's after two there, isn't it?"

"I wanted to see you."

My heart melted. "You stayed up to watch my show? That's so sweet."

Wilder went silent for a minute. I thought we might've gotten disconnected. "Hello?"

"Yeah," he said. "I'm here. Was just debating sharing something. But I think it might be better if I didn't."

"Well, now you *have* to share."

"I don't know if you're going to like it."

"Tell me anyway."

"I wanted to watch your show, but it's not because I'm sweet, Sloane."

"Okay . . ."

"I've been feeling sort of frustrated the last few weeks. You know, not dating and all. So I thought I might . . . take care of business while watching."

My eyes bulged. "You masturbated to my show?"

"I didn't. I felt like too much of a piece of shit. But that had been my plan. I figured phone sex was out of the question since you hadn't agreed to a date with me yet."

A vision of Wilder sitting in his bed, carved eight-pack on display, hand wrapped around his thick . . . "Oh my God." I covered my mouth. "That's hot."

His voice lowered a few octaves. "Oh yeah?"

A nervous giggle escaped. "You don't happen to have a show of your own I can watch?"

He chuckled. "No, but I'm sure you can find plenty of clips from my playing days."

I could do that . . . This time it was me who went silent. But I hadn't realized until Wilder spoke again.

"You're thinking about it, aren't you?"

"Oh my God." I swallowed. "We need to change the subject."

"It won't be half as fun, but if that's what you want . . ." He paused. "How about we talk about your trip to London? The wedding is in a week and a half. You haven't given me an answer about coming in a few days early."

I'd thought about his offer enough, but hadn't decided. I wasn't so sure I could trust myself alone around Wilder for a few days. Especially now that I was planning my Google search for after we got off the phone. I wanted to take the next step with him, but I was afraid. "I have a few work things I'm not sure about the timing of," I lied. "Can I let you know in a day or two?"

"Sure." Wilder's voice was throaty, sexy as hell, but he sounded exhausted.

"You sound tired."

"I am. It's been nonstop for almost two weeks."

"I'll let you go then."

"Alright, but before we hang up, I wanted to ask a favor. A business one."

"What's up?"

"I'm working on getting office space in the city for the management and support staff of the team. But until then, a few people are going to use some space in my father's building. A floor down from you, starting tomorrow."

"Oh, wow. Okay."

"One of the people who's going to be parked there is my friend Andrew. He's my in-house counsel. We have a bunch of press releases that have to go out—new player announcements, contracts signed, management hires. They all go through Andrew, but then they usually pass through Millie in my office, who cleans up the wording and fixes the grammar. Andrew graduated top of his class at Yale Law, but he must've slept though English in undergrad. Millie went out on early maternity leave today, so I'm hoping maybe you could hook Andrew up with a proofreader or a copy editor he could work with."

"Oh, I can do it for you."

"Really?"

"Sure. With one condition."

"Name it?"

"You have to tell me what the tattoo is on your ass."

"I'm trying to make a good impression. Don't make me tell you about a stupid mistake I made."

"How about if I promise not to hold it against you? I'm dying to know."

"Does that mean you've been thinking about my ass, love?"

"Just tell me."

He chuckled. "The numbers one, two, and seven. I made a stupid bet against my biggest rival the last year in the league. We lost, and that was the final score of the game. Twelve–seven."

I covered my mouth. "Oh my God. So you have a losing score tattooed on your ass for the rest of your life?"

"It wasn't my finest moment. But in my defense, we'd beaten them every single game for nine straight years. It seemed like a no-brainer, and I fancied the idea of leaving that mark on my rival my last year in the league."

"Seems you got a little ahead of yourself."

He sighed. "Apparently that's a habit of mine."

I laughed. "I'll stop down when I get in tomorrow to introduce myself to Andrew and pick up the stuff you need proofread."

"Thank you. I appreciate it. One more thing and then I'll let you go."

"What's that?"

"Are the replays of your shows online right away after your live?"

"Yeah, why?"

He let out a sinister chuckle. "'Night, Cupcake."

"Hi. Andrew?"

The tall, lanky, clean-cut guy flashed a boyish smile. "I'm guessing you're Sloane?"

"I am. How did you know?"

"Wilder described you, right before he threatened my life about keeping my eyes to myself." He covered his face playfully and extended his other hand to the guest chairs. "Please, have a seat. I don't want to get my ass kicked like in sixth grade when I told a girl Wilder liked that he sits down when he pees."

I laughed. "Does he?"

"He did for a few weeks." He took his hand from his face. "He broke his ankle playing rugby and was in a hard cast up to his knee. Fucker could still catch me when I ran away from him."

"You two have been friends a long time then?"

"Since we were in the carriage. Our moms were best friends." Andrew leaned back in his seat and rubbed his bottom lip with his thumb. "So you're the one, huh?"

"The one?"

"The one who has my boy all knotted up into a pretzel. I've never seen him this way. Usually he doesn't remember the name of the woman he's talking to."

My face fell. Andrew noticed and put his hands up. "That wasn't supposed to come out like that. He's not a jerk or anything. Well, he is a jerk, but not because he treats women badly and can't remember their names. He's a jerk because he held me down and shaved half of my moustache during my *Top Gun* phase."

I smiled. "It's fine. I get it. Wilder hasn't tried to hide who he is."

"That means he likes you. Most guys who like a woman try to put their best foot forward, show them their good side. But not Wilder. If he cares about you, he's protective—even wants to protect you from him. He gave me a hundred reasons why I shouldn't take the job before we started working together."

A woman knocked on the open office doorway. "Mr. Emerson?"

"Andrew, please."

"Your first appointment is here. I put him in the conference room and gave him some coffee."

"Thank you, Laura."

Andrew shook his head. "One thing's for sure, life with Wilder is never boring."

"I bet." I smiled. "I'll let you get to your appointment. Wilder said he had some press releases he needed a copyedit on?"

Andrew searched around the piles of papers on his desk and pulled out a pack of stapled ones. "Thank you for doing this."

"No problem. I have two meetings this morning, but I'll get them back to you as soon as I'm done."

"Thanks a lot. It was really nice to meet you, Sloane."

"You, too."

I went back up for my meetings, and then it was almost one by the time I got back downstairs with the edits. Wilder hadn't been kidding—his friend wasn't great at grammar. I'd made a lot of corrections.

Andrew was on the phone when I walked in, but he smiled and held up one finger. "Sorry about that," he said when he hung up.

"No problem. Here are your press releases. I made some changes."

He looked down and smiled. "The mighty red pen. Thank you for this."

"Anytime."

"Did you eat lunch yet?"

"Not yet. I wanted to get that done first."

He nodded toward the door. "Me neither. Can I buy you lunch to say thank you?"

"That's not necessary."

"Come on. I'll tell you about the fall of seventh grade when Wilder started wearing his dad's shit—cologne, sweaters—to come off more mature when he hit on our thirty-year-old math teacher. He was thirteen at the time."

I laughed. "How can I refuse that invitation?"

Andrew grabbed his suit jacket from the back of the chair. "You can't. Let's go."

I snort-laughed and covered my mouth. "I'm definitely going to sip his drink the next time I see him drinking out of a can. If he likes cosmos so much, why didn't he just make a batch and drink it out of a red plastic cup?"

"We were fifteen. He thought he had to act like a tough guy, and tough guys drank beer on TV, not red drinks in martini glasses.

So he'd dump out the beer and pour in girly drinks—cosmos, Malibu and pineapple—I wouldn't be surprised if he had hard Shirley Temples in there sometimes."

"I guess it's a good thing he grew up to be so brawny, since he has a penchant for things that might get him teased. Lucas already spilled that he likes mud masks and watches reality TV."

Andrew held up a finger. "He's also a closet Swiftie. He'll deny it, but the dude knows every word to 'Shake it Off.'"

My phone buzzed, giving me a fifteen-minute reminder about my afternoon meeting with the boss. I wiped my mouth with a napkin. "Gosh, I didn't realize how long we've been siting here."

"I've got enough material about Wilder to amuse us for days," Andrew said.

"I bet you do. So we might need another lunch sometime."

He grinned. "It would be my pleasure."

I'd started to slide out of the booth when Andrew reached across and touched my arm. "Hey, I feel like we've had a lot of laughs at my friend's expense. So give me one minute more to tell you a few things about him."

"Okay . . ." I settled back into my seat.

"I couldn't afford to go to Yale for undergrad. My family is comfortable, but not eighty-thousand-dollars-a-year comfortable, and I also have four siblings. Ivies are competitive. All the kids have better than a four-point-oh, so there aren't many academic scholarships. Then at the last minute, a scholarship came through—a full ride. I thought it was strange, but I wasn't looking a gift horse in the mouth. Two years ago, when I started working for Wilder, I was looking through some files for paperwork I needed, and I found a file with the name of the organization that had given me the scholarship. Wilder had taken some of the money his mother left him and set up a charitable foundation just to pay my tuition without me knowing. He knew I'd never take the money from him if he tried to give it to me directly."

"Wow."

Andrew nodded. "To this day, he doesn't know I know. So please don't share that with him. But that's the kind of guy he is. And it's not just money. When we were in high school, he played for one of the national junior rugby leagues, but he played for the worst team. He could've played for the one that won the championship every year. All the teams were clamoring for him. But his coach from middle school coached the shitty team. Guy has some health problems, and Wilder still visits him to this day."

I nodded. "He's actually mentioned his coach."

"Recently I screwed up royally with my girlfriend. I was going to hide it from her, but Wilder talked me into coming clean. He might have a history with the ladies, but he's always been honest." He paused. "My point is, Wilder's only going to tell you the bad shit. But it's not hard to find the good stuff, if you take the chance to get to know him. He keeps most people at a distance, but the ones he lets in are there forever." Andrew pointed to me. "And if you tell him I gave him any compliments, I'll deny it."

I smiled. "Your secret is safe with me."

I went back to work, and later that afternoon, I was sitting at my desk still thinking about what Andrew had said. Hadn't I already seen glimpses of the man he'd described? The loyalty to his brother. Small things like bringing me sugar-free desserts after finding out I'm diabetic, changing his flight to come with me to sell my old wedding dress, and inviting my dad to a rugby game. There was a soft heart under that hard exterior. And I couldn't deny that I was ridiculously attracted to him. My heart began to race before my brain caught up.

Screw it. I'm doing it.

I was tired of staying in and reading self-help books to figure out who I was. It was time I figured it out by living. So I picked up my phone and texted.

Sloane: If the offer is still open, I'd love to come to London a few days early.

17

SLOANE

"Your seat is this way . . ." The flight attendant pointed to her left, so I headed down the aisle.

But she had to have made a mistake. The seats were all too spacious in this section. I double-checked the seat number on my ticket as I walked to 9B. Another flight attendant walked over, greeting me with champagne.

"Umm . . . I'm not sure I'm in the right area."

He took the boarding pass from my hand and gestured to a roomy chair that converted to a lay-flat bed. "This is it."

"But this doesn't look like economy."

He smiled. "It's definitely not."

"I bought an economy ticket, though."

"You probably got upgraded based on your status with the airline."

I shook my head. "I don't even have a frequent flier account."

"Well, then someone likes you. Maybe the gate agent gave you a little present." He shrugged. "However it happened, this is your seat. So relax and enjoy it." He held up the flute again. "Would you like some champagne, or I can add a little orange juice and make a mimosa?"

"*Ooh,* I love mimosas."

"Get settled in. I'll be back in a jiffy."

My seating area was almost as spacious as my office, so I wasn't going to complain about the upgrade for a long flight. Though I did wonder if the secret admirer responsible for this was Wilder and not the gate agent. Either way, I had work to do during the flight, so it would be nice to spread out and not have someone reading my laptop over my shoulder.

I settled in and took out my phone to switch to airplane mode. As I did, I noticed a missed text.

Josh: Hey. I know you probably hate me, but do you think we could talk? It won't take long.

Ugh. That was not happening—definitely not on this trip. There was nothing left to say. He'd said it all at the altar. I slid the button to airplane mode and tucked my phone away for takeoff just in time to receive my mimosa.

A little while after we hit cruising altitude, the flight attendant served a delicious breakfast—complete with fresh fruit, entrée, warm croissant, and dessert. They even had sugar-free dessert options, not to mention another complimentary mimosa. This was definitely better than the cardboard-box meal I'd paid twelve bucks for on my last flight to Florida. While I spooned rich yet diabetic-friendly cheesecake into my mouth, I opened my laptop and called up the first submission to the wedding contest.

We'd received more than two thousand entries, so I'd enlisted a few of the other staff writers to help sort through them all. Now it was up to me to narrow down the finalists. When I'd decided to read through the essays on the plane, I hadn't considered how emotional many of them would be. Some of the reasons people wanted a free wedding really tugged at the heartstrings—from being poor to suffering from depression and finally finding her soulmate. There was even a sixty-seven-year-old woman who had been married to a man who abused her for forty years. She'd finally left him and found true love.

I cried reading more than one of them, but it was the last essay that hit me the hardest. The woman's wedding was all planned—for a year from now. She wanted to win the giveaway because her father had been diagnosed with stage-four pancreatic cancer and likely had only a few months to live. I reread the last paragraph of the letter for a third time, tears streaming down my face.

I had big plans for my wedding next summer—lose thirty pounds, get fit, save for a honeymoon in Fiji, have a bachelorette party in Vegas.

But I now realize the only thing important is having my daddy walk me down the aisle. If I win the wedding next month, I'll happily pay it forward and give away my day next year with everything prepaid.

I wasn't sure if I felt this one so deeply because the woman's story reminded me of my mom's dying wish to marry my dad all over again when she had end-stage cancer, or if it was the mention of a honeymoon in Fiji—where Josh and I were supposed to go. Or maybe it was my lack of sleep on this long flight and my hormones being a little out of whack. But when we landed, I was glad Wilder was still in Italy and wasn't going to be able to pick me up because my face was blotchy, my eyes swollen, and my nose chafed from cheap airline tissues.

After passing through customs and immigration, I followed the herd of people to get my luggage. A bunch of drivers were lined up behind a metal barrier, holding signs. Wilder had arranged a car, so I looked for my name as I passed. The first three signs were typed, with logos of the names of the car service. When I scanned the fourth one, it struck me as odd that it was written on what looked like a brown paper bag with pen. I had to squint to read the name. *Cupcake.*

My eyes jumped to the person holding it, and my heart stuttered.

The guy might've been wearing a baseball hat and dark sunglasses, but that cocky smile only belonged to one man. Wilder's face fell when he got a look at me, and he hustled around the barrier and grabbed my shoulders. "What happened?"

"What do you mean?" I asked. I'd momentarily forgotten what a disaster I looked like. *Shoot.* I would've fixed my face a little if I'd known he was going to be here.

"You've been crying."

"Oh. Yeah." I touched my warm cheek. "It's nothing. I was reading sad stories on the plane and got upset."

He visibly relaxed. "You scared the crap out of me."

I smiled. "I'm fine. But what are you doing here? I thought you were supposed to be in Italy until late tonight."

He leaned down and kissed my forehead. "I was too anxious to see you."

Out of the corner of my eye, I caught two women looking our way. One pointed, and the other lifted her phone like she was about to take a picture. Wilder put his head down and turned us. "Come on, let's get your luggage and get out of here before the paparazzi find out. They're not as bad here as they are in the States, but they've been following me nonstop since the news broke about the team."

Wilder kept a protective arm around my shoulder, hugging me close as we made our way to the luggage carousel. We huddled in a corner where Wilder could keep his back to the crowd, which meant all of his attention was on *me*.

He flashed a crooked smile. "What the heck were you reading on the plane that hit you so hard?"

"Submissions to the wedding-giveaway contest. Entrants had to write a short essay on why they should win. Some of them really hit home."

He rubbed at my cheek with his thumb. "Mascara."

"If you would've warned me that you were coming, I would've cleaned up a little."

"Nah. This is why I like you. You're just you." He stroked my face, and I felt it down to my toes. "Thank you for coming early. I can't wait to show you around."

I wasn't sure I'd ever understand why a ridiculously handsome guy who could have any woman he wanted and was busy getting a new professional sports team off the ground would *want* to show me around, but I could see in his eyes that he was being sincere.

The luggage carousel made a loud chirping noise and jerked to a start. Bags started flowing as Wilder told me about his trip. He'd landed only a few hours earlier. As we chatted, I kept one eye on the conveyor belt, but there was no sign of my luggage, not even after twenty minutes. The people standing around waiting dwindled to just me and a few others, and eventually we watched the same lone purple suitcase and set of golf clubs circle around a dozen times before the belt came to an abrupt halt.

"Uh, what's happening?" I asked.

"Shit. I think your bag must be lost."

"Lost? No. It can't be."

He gestured toward a small office I hadn't noticed. "The baggage-claim office is over there. Sadly, I've been there recently."

"You've had your luggage lost?"

"Twice."

"How long did it take for them to find it?"

"I got it back the next day both times."

"Great. I usually take a change of clothes in my carry-on bag, but I had so much work stuff to carry, I didn't this time. I don't even have underwear."

Wilder wiggled his brows. "I'll make a stop at the lingerie store if you model them for me."

The baggage-claim office had me fill out a bunch of paperwork and took my phone number, promising to contact me as soon as they located my bag. Wilder and I left with only my carry-on filled with work.

"I'll have my assistant follow up with them and send a messenger to grab your bag when it arrives. It'll be quicker than waiting for the airline to drop it off."

"Oh. That would be great. Thank you."

Wilder led me to a small Volkswagen parked in the short-term lot. "This is us," he said.

"Such a normal car. I would've expected something flashier, Hayes."

He opened the back hatch and grinned. "It's my assistant's. My car is slightly more memorable. We swapped to throw off the paparazzi."

"What do you normally drive?"

"A vintage Aston Martin in Caribbean blue."

"I don't know what that is, but it sounds expensive."

He shut the hatch. "My father got me into old cars."

I started to walk around to the passenger side, but Wilder stopped me. "You driving?"

"Definitely not."

He chuckled. "Then why are you getting in on the driver's side?"

I looked at the car. "Oh!" I laughed. "Sorry, I forgot they drive on the other side of the road here."

Wilder opened my door before sliding behind the wheel. Not only was the steering wheel on the wrong side, the car was a stick shift.

"Don't you get confused driving here one week and in New York the other?"

"Sometimes, like after a few weeks of driving in the States and then I come back here and pull into a roundabout. It takes a bit for my brain to work it out. Luckily, there's always traffic in both places, so I can mostly just follow the flow."

We drove out of the airport lot and onto a busy highway. Maybe I was delirious from lack of sleep, but I couldn't take my eyes off the way Wilder's big hand wrapped around the gear shift and took control. Then again, there wasn't much I *didn't* find sexy about the man these days. Usually it was the opposite—I'd think a man was handsome and the more I got to know him, the less handsome he became.

I forced my eyes back to the road.

"Did you sleep on the plane?" Wilder asked.

I shook my head. "I drank too much coffee beforehand. I'd planned to work since I can't sleep sitting up and thought I was stuck in a middle seat in economy. By the way, did you do that? Upgrade me to first class?"

He shrugged. "You're my guest. I wanted to make sure you were comfortable."

"Thank you. It was incredible. I've always peeked at the prices of those tickets and didn't understand what the fuss was about for all that extra money. But I get it now. I had a full bed and could've probably slept the entire flight if I wasn't all caffeinated. Even the food was good."

"Really helps on quick trips. When I do the red-eye, I can usually knock out for five to six hours and be functional for meetings when I land."

"I can see that."

"I also changed your hotel. Hope you don't mind."

"Umm . . . no, I guess you would know better. I just picked a chain I knew."

"You're at the Rosewood now." He looked over with a cheeky smile. "It's closer to my place. How about if I drop you there so you can get some sleep, and tomorrow morning I'll scoop up your suitcase and bring it with me when I come to pick you up? I'll have some coffee in the restaurant while you unpack and get ready."

"That sounds perfect. I don't know how to thank you."

"I can think of a few ways . . ."

I shook my head. And then a few minutes later, my mouth fell open. I figured Wilder had moved me somewhere nicer, but I didn't expect iron gates leading to a grand Edwardian courtyard. The opulent building was rather intimidating as we pulled up.

"Here we go."

"Wilder . . ." I looked over at him. "I can't stay here."

His brows pulled together. "You don't like it?"

"It's gorgeous. But it must cost a small fortune."

"Don't worry about it. You're my guest."

"That's very sweet, but . . ."

He met my eyes. "I just wanted you to stay somewhere nice. I don't expect anything, Sloane."

"Oh, I know. I wasn't thinking you were, but . . ."

"Let me take care of you while you're here, okay?"

I took a deep breath and nodded. "I'm not so good at that—letting people take care of me."

"I noticed. Now come on. Let's get you checked in, and then I'll go home and crash, too."

I smiled. "Okay."

At the front desk, Wilder slipped a black card to the check-in clerk while I looked around in awe. The hotel was sophisticated and contemporary, yet somehow still had a distinctly British feel. After a minute, the clerk gave me keys and pointed us to the elevators.

Wilder walked with me, passing me my work tote after pressing the button at the elevator bank.

"How does eleven sound? Is that too early with the five-hour time change? I heard a rumor you like to sleep."

I smiled. "I do. But I'm too excited to see the city to waste a full day."

"Good." He kissed my forehead. "Get some sleep. I'll be back in the morning to collect you."

The elevator doors slid open, so I stepped inside and turned around.

Wilder smiled. "I'm happy you're here, Cupcake."

My insides grew warm. "I am, too."

This is definitely better than the three-star I had booked.

The lotion I pumped out of one of the pretty glass canisters in the bathroom smelled like fresh lavender as I rubbed it into my arms. This was by far the nicest hotel I'd ever stayed in. My suite was huge—with a separate living room, an airy bedroom, and a marble bathroom with a soaking tub and walk-in shower that could easily hold six people. It was now a few minutes before ten on Wednesday morning, and I still had the plush hotel robe wrapped around me. I didn't want to put my dirty clothes from yesterday back on after getting out of the shower. Maybe I should, though, rather than answering the door for Wilder like this?

I was still nibbling on my lip, debating a quick change, when there was a knock. *Welp, guess that decision is made for me.* I tugged the belt of my robe tight, did a check in the mirror, and reached for the door handle. To my surprise, it wasn't Wilder standing on the other side of the door. It was a woman dressed to the nines, her hands filled with shopping bags.

The woman smiled. "Good morning. You must be Sloane?"

"Yes?"

"I'm Emily Bloom. Mr. Hayes's personal shopper."

"His what?"

She lifted her arms. "I think you're going to love what he picked out."

"He? I'm sorry. I'm not following?"

She leaned back and checked the room number on the side of the door. "This is four ten. You are Sloane Carrick, aren't you?"

"I am."

She had an amused smile on her face. "I guess Wilder didn't tell you I was coming this morning?"

"No, he didn't."

"Then let me back up. I'm a personal shopper and stylist. I pick out clothes for my clients, most of whom are too busy to go shopping or don't want the hassle of putting together their wardrobe. Wilder is one of my clients. He called me early this morning with an SOS. He said someone special was visiting and the airline had lost her luggage. So we were at the stores when they opened this morning and together we picked out a bunch of great outfits."

"We?" I remained mired in confusion. "Wilder went with you?"

She smiled. "He did indeed. Normally I can't even get that man to stop in at the store to have the tailor take a suit in. I have to send the tailor to him. So you must be very special."

My cell phone rang from somewhere inside the room. I looked over my shoulder and back to the woman, still confused about what was going on, even though she'd just explained it to me.

"Is it okay if we come in?" she asked.

"We?" I poked my head out into the hall. Sure enough, another woman stood behind her carrying even more bags—and there was also a full rolling rack of dresses. "Oh my gosh. I think Wilder has lost his mind." *Though . . . I do need something to wear today.* "But yes, come in."

My phone went to voicemail before I could grab it, but Wilder's name was on the screen. I pressed the button to call him back. "Are you insane?"

I heard the smile in his voice when he answered. "I guess Emily got to you before me?"

"Yes, Emily and half the contents of a boutique have arrived."

"I called the airline this morning. They still don't have your luggage."

"Well, that stinks, but you didn't need to go shopping for me."

"I actually had fun. Especially picking out your underwear and bra. What size do you wear anyway? I guessed a thirty-four C."

That was *exactly* my size. Though I was torn between being

impressed and feeling unsettled that he could guess a woman's bra size. The latter, I assumed, was because he'd felt all shapes and sizes.

"Wilder, you can't do all this."

"Sure I can. Already did."

"Wilder—"

He cut me off. "I have to jump on a quick conference call. I'll pick you up at eleven. Be downstairs. And I like the green top best. Later, Cupcake."

I turned around to find Emily and her assistant laying out outfits all over the living room. I shook my head. "I'm sorry. But I can't accept all of this."

"Your boyfriend knows you well." She smiled and kept going. "He said you might say that, so I've been instructed not to take anything back. Sorry."

There was another knock at the door. Still feeling bamboozled, I went to answer it. A man in a suit stood behind a full room-service cart. He smiled. "Good morning. Where would you like your breakfast set up?"

I shook my head. "I didn't order anything."

"The order was called in by a gentleman. He said you might be confused."

I rolled my eyes. "Of course."

The man I needed to argue with wasn't here, and I was starving since I'd slept through dinner last night, so I stepped aside. "Come on in. Join the party."

18

WILDER

She wore the green top. This woman was killing me.

Sloane stepped out of the elevator and looked around the lobby. I stood just as she found me and couldn't help but grin as she approached.

"Alright, alright. Don't gloat," she said. "I'm wearing the green because I like it best, and it's also the most practical—not because you said it was your favorite."

"Right." My smile widened.

Sloane squinted. "You know, I can go back upstairs to change and keep you waiting another half hour, if you want?"

I caught her hand, weaving our fingers together. "Not a chance. You look gorgeous."

She rolled her eyes, but the corner of her mouth tilted upward. She liked my compliments, even if she pretended she didn't.

"Come on . . ." I tugged her along. "I have a whole day planned."

The valet had kept my car waiting nearby. The kid jogged to get it and pulled it to the curb. When he got out, he went to open the passenger door, but I waved him off. "Got it."

"Now *this* is more what I would expect you to drive," Sloane said as she buckled in.

"Because it's hot and sexy?"

She laughed. "Because it's flashy and looks like it could get you in trouble." She glanced to the center console. "It's not a stick shift?"

I shook my head. "Are you asking because you want to drive?"

"Definitely not. I just kinda liked watching you drive the other one."

I slipped the car into gear. "I'll switch with my assistant permanently."

She laughed like I was kidding. "So, what are we going to see first? The London Bridge? Big Ben? Buckingham Palace?"

"Actually, none of those. I thought today I'd show you my favorite places in London rather than the touristy crap. Tomorrow I'll take you to all the sites where you can buy a snow globe and an I heart London T-shirt on the way out."

Sloane rested her hand on my arm, and I felt a jolt. *Damn* . . . what would it feel like if she touched me a little lower, maybe on my third arm?

"Thank you for doing this," she said. "All of it. The flight, the hotel, going shopping early this morning so I would have something to wear. It's so thoughtful."

And I was . . . thinking of her. I was up to my eyeballs in contracts, meetings, paperwork, and negotiations—so much so that I hadn't slept that well last night because I kept remembering more things I needed to do and adding to my list. But right now, right at this moment with Sloane wide-eyed excited to see the city? I didn't give two shits about any of that. I couldn't even remember what was on the damn list now. That scared the shit out of me as much as I welcomed the break.

I winked. "The things I'll do just to touch your underwear."

The first stop on today's sightseeing tour was my absolute favorite place in London. I'd never come here with anyone before, and as we approached, I started to wonder if it was such a good idea to bring Sloane. I couldn't put my finger on why the place was so special to me, but I hoped she wasn't bored with my pick. Though as soon as we walked into the park, Sloane's eyes widened. She looked like a little kid walking into Disney for the first time, and whatever nerves I'd had about bringing her here immediately settled. It helped that the sun was hitting just right, making everything glow like the forest in *Twilight*.

"What is this place?"

"It's an old church called St. Dunstan in the East. It was originally built in 1100 AD. It was damaged in the Great Fire of London in the 1600s and later rebuilt—only to be destroyed again during the Second World War. Now the ruins are a public garden."

Sloane looked up at the remnants of the church's stone walls. Ivy and creeping vines weaved through archways that had once held stained glass, but today sun streaked in from the other side, creating a magical feeling.

"Wow," she said. "It doesn't seem real."

I smiled. "I know."

She pulled out her phone. "This would be an amazing place for a wedding. I need to take some pictures."

I shook my head.

"What?"

"Nothing. Take your pics." I stood off to the side, watching Sloane smile as she angled her phone and snapped photos from all different perspectives. I never thought the day would come when a woman mentioned the word *wedding* and I didn't break out in hives. And I certainly never imagined I'd take out my phone and sneak a few pics myself. But it gave me a warm feeling to see Sloane love the place as much as I did—a different warm feeling than I'd had a couple of hours ago picking out thongs. Which reminded me . . . My eyes dropped to her ass to see if I could make out whether she was wearing one I'd picked out. Sadly, I couldn't.

We wandered around the small park for a long time, finding all the little hidden places and reading the informational signs I'd read a dozen times before. On our way out, Sloane stopped at the stone archway where we'd started. "What do you love about this place?" she asked. "I mean, aside from how beautiful it is?"

I shrugged. "That's a good question. I don't know really. I guess I like it because it's been destroyed so many times, and yet it never falls."

Sloane nodded. "Yeah. It feels . . . hopeful."

Our eyes caught. I wanted so fucking badly to kiss her. I wasn't a romantic guy—my idea of romance was drinking a little wine on the balcony off my bedroom before plowing into a woman on all fours on my bed ten feet away. But Sloane? I wanted to dip her in the middle of the ruins of a medieval church. Which meant it was most definitely time to get the hell out of here.

Stop two wasn't as dreamy-eyed, at least not for most people.

I took her to Wembley Stadium—the place I'd played for more than eight years. It was closed to the public today, but the guys in security all knew me, so they let me give Sloane a private tour.

We walked out onto the field through the tunnel I'd walked out of hundreds of times before, and Sloane looked up at the empty stands. "Wow. How many people does the stadium hold?"

"Ninety thousand."

She shook her head. "I can't imagine what this must feel like with all the seats filled and people cheering your name, wearing your jersey."

I looked up, remembering those days. "It was great when I did well, but it was brutal when I had a bad day. Same fan cheering you on the way in could be throwing his empty beer bottle at you on the way out."

"That didn't really happen, did it?"

I pointed to the scar on my hairline. "Playoff game. Six stitches. It was the worst game of my career."

"I can't believe someone threw a bottle at you."

"I deserved it. My head was up my ass that day." I smiled at the stands, picturing them full. "There were more good days than bad though."

"I bet you were the most popular player with the women."

I wasn't touching that comment with a ten-foot pole. "The fans were interesting. That's for sure."

"Do you miss it?"

"Yes and no. I took advantage of the celebrity that came with it—walking into any club I wanted, never getting in trouble for stupid shit I did—but after a while you start to realize none of it is real. People want to be friends with you for the wrong reasons, women want to be with you because of your name, not who you are. After you fall for it a few times, you start to retreat. I guess on the plus side, it taught me to value the people in my inner circle."

"Like Andrew?"

I nodded. "He might technically work for me, but I need him much more than he needs me. I'd be screwed without him."

Sloane smiled. "He speaks highly of you, too—in between the stories of what a jerk you are."

I grinned. "Wouldn't have it any other way."

Sloane pointed up to the rafters, to the six oversized jerseys hanging there. "Your jersey is still up there?"

I nodded. "They retired it the year after I stopped playing."

"Wow. That's a big honor, right?"

For a change, I downplayed the accomplishment. "I guess."

We both stared up for a while. I didn't realize I was smiling until Sloane interrupted. "What's going on in that head of yours?"

"What do you mean?"

"You look like your thoughts are up to no good."

I smiled. "I was just thinking, I'd love to see you wearing my jersey."

She laughed. "I may have to, if they don't find my luggage soon."

I lowered my voice. "Well, if that's the case, I was thinking just the jersey—no underwear, no bra."

"Hey, Hayes! Can I get your autograph?"

I had my hand on the restaurant door, about to open it for Sloane, when a kid who was probably about thirteen or fourteen yelled over. "Do you mind?"

"Of course not."

I walked over to the kid and his friends. The one who'd yelled took off his sneaker and held it out to me.

"You have something for me to sign it with?"

"Shit. No."

"Watch your mouth." I thumbed to Sloane, who stood next to me. "There's a lady here."

The kid looked her up and down and grinned. "She's hot. Is she your girlfriend?"

I chuckled. "I'm working on it. Maybe you can help me out? Tell her how good a player I was."

The kid looked at Sloane. "He was great. The best. Except for that playoff game where you sucked."

I frowned. "Thanks, buddy."

The kid looked over his shoulder at his friends. "Don't one of you have a pen?"

They all shrugged.

I shook my head. "Hang on a second."

I went into the restaurant and asked the maître d' to borrow something to write with.

Back outside, I uncapped the felt-tip marker as I spoke to the kid. "What's your name?"

"Rinaldo."

"You play rugby?" I scribbled my name along the side of his sneaker.

"Twenty-eight points so far this season."

"Nice. How are your grades?"

The kid's face fell. "School sucks."

"If you're lucky enough to make it to the pros, you get maybe eight, maybe ten years. School is what teaches you to make good decisions and not get ripped off. You can do well in more than one thing." I handed him back his sneaker.

The kid looked back at Sloane. "School wouldn't score you her. Rugby will."

"Dude." I shook my head. "She didn't even know who I was when I met her."

"Really?"

I mussed his hair. "Keep yourself out of trouble, huh?"

I noticed a few people starting to point and break out their phones, so I put my hand on Sloane's back and guided her into the restaurant. We were quickly seated at a quiet table in the corner, and I ordered a bottle of wine and some appetizers.

Sloane smiled. "You're really good with kids. Not just the boys outside, but your brother, my niece . . ."

"I get a lot of practice with kids, since I'm a big one."

"You know, for a guy who came off as a cocky bastard when we first met, you're pretty shy about taking compliments."

"I'm not shy about taking them for the things I deserve to be complimented on—rugby, good looks, my talent in the sack . . ."

She chuckled. "Don't ruin the moment, Hayes."

I smiled.

Sloane sipped her wine and ran her finger along the top of the glass. "Do you want kids someday?"

I expected to hear sirens, the flashing of warning lights in my head. But it didn't happen. That question should've scared the crap out of me more than the fact that I hadn't checked my phone or thought about my new team since we sat down, but for some crazy reason, it didn't. "I want a slew of them. All boys. Enough to build my own rugby squad."

"You better watch it. God has a funny sense of humor when you say things like that. You'll wind up with eight girls."

I drank my wine. "What about you? You want kids?"

Sloane nodded. "I don't know about a team of them, but yeah, I do. I loved growing up with my brothers."

"Speaking of brothers, Lucas tried to talk me into flying Olivia out with you."

"Oh gosh. She would've loved that. But she has school."

I reached across the table and took her hand. "Plus, I wanted you all to myself."

Her cheeks pinked, and I couldn't stop my mind from wandering. Her skin was so responsive, coloring when she was embarrassed or shy—what would it look like when I was inside her? Pouty mouth parted, skin flushed as I looked down at her, big, green eyes rolling back in her head as I sank deep. I wasn't a missionary fan usually. I preferred a woman up on all fours, taking her from behind, or maybe a little reverse cowgirl so I could watch my dick slide in and out. But with Sloane, I knew I would want to watch her face.

Fuck. I shifted in my seat, feeling my pants grow snug at the thought of it. Sloane said something, but I had no idea what the hell it was because I was too busy trying to ward off embarrassing myself.

Grandma . . .

Missing the shot with one second left on the clock in the big playoff game . . .

7832 + 9408 . . .

The time I walked in on my father getting a blow job from his sixty-year-old girlfriend . . .

That did the trick. Except now I had no damn idea where we were in the conversation. I was relieved when the waiter showed up with the food we'd ordered, interrupting things. We both dug in, and it made me happy to see Sloane wasn't a salad girl.

"So what made you finally decide to come early?" I asked. "Other than my charm and begging?"

Sloane laughed. "Actually, it was your friend Andrew."

"Andrew?"

She shrugged. "Just the way he talked about you."

"Ah . . ." I nodded. "He's seen me naked in the locker room."

"That wasn't exactly what we spoke about, but close. Though I can tell you I'm already really glad I came."

"It was the sexy shoes I picked out, wasn't it?"

She smiled. "Those were beautiful. But the company has been better than any of the things you've treated me to."

I tipped the bottle of wine into her glass, emptying what was left. "Are you up for another stop?"

"What did you have in mind?"

"One touristy thing. The London Eye is not too far. If we get out of here in the next half hour, we can catch the sunset over the city."

Her eyes lit up. "I'd love that."

And I couldn't freaking wait to show it to her. Plenty of my friends had come to visit and wanted to do all the touristy things, including the Ferris wheel. Normally, I'd bow out, tell them I had work to do and let them have at it alone. Yet right now, I was more excited to wait in line for an hour at a tourist trap, knowing I'd get to watch her face light up when she saw the city, than I would be finding naked triplets in my hotel suite—which did happen once.

I wanted to show Sloane Carrick everything—and not just London. The goddamned world.

Her eyes sparkled in the moonlight.

Suddenly, I'd turned into damn Shakespeare. At least in my

head. Which I was glad for, because saying what I was thinking out loud would sound corny as hell. Even if it was true.

Sloane leaned forward in the car, absorbing the view from the top of the London Eye. It was a gorgeous, clear night with the majestic River Thames winding its way beneath us, creating a path to all the touristy spots—the bridge, the tower, Houses of Parliament—everything lit up and glowing. But none of that held a candle to the woman sitting next to me. I could've stayed up here all night, watching her take it all in.

"This is amazing, Wilder. This whole day has been like a fairy tale, like a dream come true."

I smiled. "I'm glad you enjoyed it."

A brisk wind picked up a lock of her hair, pushing it across her face. I reached out and brushed it from her cheek. Sloane's eyes dropped to my lips, and I would've bet my new team that if I'd leaned in and pressed my lips to hers, she wouldn't have stopped me. And I wanted to taste her more than anything. But something kept me from doing it.

I could see in her face that she was waiting for it, too. I didn't want to leave her hanging, so I felt the need to explain myself. I looked down at her lips again before meeting her eyes. "I want to kiss you more than anything. But I don't think that's a good idea."

She blinked a few times, then looked away, almost embarrassed. "Yeah, of course."

I reached out and tilted her head back to me. "I feel like you'd kiss me back right now. Am I wrong?"

She diverted her eyes again. "Probably not."

"This might sound stupid, but this day has been amazing—magical even. And right now, it feels like one of those big moments in a movie, the kind that's easy to get swept up in. Do you know what I mean?"

"I guess."

"And I don't want you to kiss me because we're caught up in some romantic moment. I want it to be about us, and only us."

Sloane took a deep breath and sighed, but nodded. "I actually do get it. I've gotten myself caught up in more than one fairy tale."

My eyes dropped to her lips once more. "But fuck, I want to bite your pouty mouth."

She chuckled and shook her head. I had effectively ruined the most romantic moment of my life, and I was torn between being proud of myself for wanting her to want me for the right reasons and wanting to kick my own ass for not pouncing and taking advantage. Either way, the moment had passed, thanks to me, so instead of an epic romantic kiss, I put my arm around her shoulder and snuggled her to my chest, dropping a kiss on the top of her head. "I'm really glad you're here."

She looked up at me. "I am, too."

An hour later, Sloane yawned as we pulled up to her hotel.

"Tired?"

"Yeah. And it's weird because you would think I'd be wide awake since it's only four o'clock at home."

"Traveling takes a lot out of you. Plus, you probably adjusted last night after not sleeping on the plane."

I opened the door to the lobby just as my cell buzzed. It was my assistant. I'd texted her earlier for an update on Sloane's lost luggage.

"Not great news on your bag." I put my hand out for Sloane to enter first.

"They didn't find it?"

I shook my head. "They put a tracer on it, but they don't even know what country it's in."

She sighed. "It could be worse. I could *not* have a fairy godmother who bought me a brand-new wardrobe."

We walked to the elevator. "Do you mind if I walk you up?"

"Not at all."

The doors slid closed, and a sudden wave of nerves hit me. I felt like thirteen-year-old Wilder. *Should I try to kiss her? What if she invites me in? Are my palms freaking sweaty?*

I didn't get a chance to finish debating things before the doors glided open once again. Sloane's room was a few doors down. She found her key in her purse and looked up at me, chewing on her bottom lip. "Would you . . . want to come in for a little while? Have a drink or something?"

I wanted to *or something* more than anything, but the nerves I saw in her eyes answered all the questions I'd been kicking around in my head. "I'd love to. But I'm gonna pass and head home."

"Oh." She looked down. "Okay."

I slipped two fingers under her chin and nudged until our eyes met. "I'm saying no because you looked nervous that I might say yes. Not because I don't want to."

She smiled and shook her head. "Okay. Thank you."

I kissed her forehead.

"You know," she said. "I never would've taken you for such a gentleman."

I leaned close. "Fair warning, Cupcake. When I come into your room—not if, but *when*—the gentleman in me will be staying at the door."

19

SLOANE

"So, tell me everything." The car door was barely closed before Elijah started the interrogation. He looked around the back of the stretch limousine. "And does this thing have champagne or what?"

The uniformed driver looked in the rearview mirror. "There are two bottles in the cooler on the left side. Glasses are on the right. Would you like me to wait so you can pour before I start driving?"

"Pour?" Elijah waved him off. "What's there to pour? You said two bottles and there's *two* of us. Do you have straws?"

The very British driver looked appalled. Elijah couldn't have cared less. He waved goodbye to the man as he pushed the button to raise the privacy screen.

I shook my head. "You are so rude."

"Me? He's the one butting into our conversation." He pulled the chilled champagne out of the cooler box and turned the bottle to face me. "*Ooh* . . . Dom Pérignon. The company really went all out for this trip."

"I doubt it was the company."

"What do you mean?"

"Wilder's been intervening on all the plans the company made and upgrading them—my flight here, my hotel. I'm sure the car service that was supposed to pick us up for the wedding tonight was a Volkswagen Rabbit before he quietly stepped in."

Elijah pulled the cork from the champagne with a loud pop, then put his mouth over the top to catch the foam bubbling out.

"Classy." I laughed.

"No judging." He swallowed a mouthful of champagne and used the back of his hand to wipe his cheek. "Or I'll stick my tongue in the hole before I give you your bottle, and you do *not* want to know where this tongue was last weekend."

My nose scrunched up as I plucked the other bottle from his hand. "No, I definitely do not."

The wedding tonight was at Hedsor House, a country estate forty-five minutes outside of London. So I slipped off my gorgeous but extremely high-heeled sparkly new shoes.

"Wow. Jimmy Choos." Elijah gestured to the floor with his champagne bottle. "Someone didn't get the same shitty three percent raise as me at Christmas."

"They were a gift from Wilder. As was this dress. I don't even want to know what they cost."

"So you're like Cinderella going to the ball? Except your fairy godmother is a hot rugby player." He wiggled his brows. "Tell me, is he big and brawny all over? God couldn't be so cruel as to give a man with those shoulders and that face a tiny dick."

I sighed. "I wouldn't know."

"You didn't go all the way yet?"

"We haven't gone *any* of the way yet. Wilder hasn't even kissed me since I landed in London."

Elijah's jaw dropped as he covered his heart. "Oh my God. Is he gay? *Please, please* tell me he's gay?"

I laughed. "He's not gay, but he has been a gentleman."

My friend wrinkled his nose like he'd smelled something sour. "Yuck. Why?"

"It's my fault. The guy scares the crap out of me."

"You've seen the outline and it's that big?"

I chuckled. "No! I meant he makes me feel things."

"Well, clearly not the good kind of things if he hasn't touched you."

"I'm serious."

Elijah lifted his knee onto the seat and turned to face me. "You fell off the horse—or in Josh's case, the jackass—and now you're afraid to get back on. I understand that. I really do. But, honey, this isn't another donkey. This is a fucking unicorn we're talking about. They don't come around very often."

"I know. But the fact that he *is* a unicorn makes it even scarier. I mean, if I couldn't hold on to the donkey, how the hell can I expect to saddle the unicorn?"

Elijah frowned. "What Josh did is not about you. It's about him. You can't be afraid to take chances because you got hurt. Life is all about taking chances. Sometimes we jump off the cliff and splatter to the ground. But sometimes we jump off and fly."

"Wilder and I are just so different. I'm a serial-relationship person; he's a serial dater. He's first class to Europe. I sit in the middle seat on my flight to Florida because I'm too cheap to pay for seat assignment. I live in New York in a house with most of my family, and he lives in London and has been on his own since he was eighteen. This month, he got approval to start his own professional rugby expansion team. He's been traveling around the world signing players for weeks. I read three self-help books and went to therapy."

"You know what that sounds like to me?"

"What?"

"A bunch of excuses because you're a chicken shit."

My shoulders slumped. "I hate you."

"Let me try a different approach. What about having fun? No expectations, just get back on the horse and *ride, girl, ride.*"

I smiled. "Now that is tempting . . ."

"So do it. Listen to Nike and *just fucking do it.*"

"I don't think Nike said it exactly like that."

"They should have."

Hedsor House was breathtaking. A private Georgian estate set on a hundred acres of manicured gardens, it made me wonder how I'd ever thought my wedding venue was special. Even the ceremony was beautiful. The bride and groom cried as they exchanged vows, making my own eyes well up with tears. Wilder and I had shared secret smiles a few times, but he'd been on groomsman duty, and I'd been busy talking to the bridal party to get material for my article. After getting off to a rough start with Piper's wedding, this group had proved themselves to be sophisticated and tasteful, and the series had turned out to be a smart addition for the magazine. All because of a nip slip . . .

At the cocktail hour, I noticed a willowy brunette walk over and greet Wilder with a big hug and kiss. She was difficult to miss, being drop-dead gorgeous and probably close to six feet tall. When he spoke, she leaned in, gave good eye contact, and rested her hand on his arm or his chest. A woman could spot another interested woman a mile away, and it made me wonder if the ease with which she touched him was because they'd previously spent time touching each other. I looked the other way and went to the bar for a glass of wine, rather than let it bother me. Though the simple exchange dented my confidence.

But once the reception was in full swing, Wilder made his way over to my table.

"Can I have this dance?" He held out a hand.

"Sure." I smiled.

Wilder led me to the dance floor, pulling me close as we slipped into the crowd of people. His hand rested at the small of my back, making my skin tingle.

"Not leaving room for Jesus again, huh, Hayes?"

His lip twitched. "Have I mentioned you look gorgeous tonight?"

"You have. But thank you. A girl can never hear it too many times. And thank you again for this beautiful dress."

He nodded. "I intentionally picked one with an open back, for this very moment." His fingers stroked my bare skin. "The things I'll do just to get to touch you."

I giggled, trying to lighten the moment, but the sexual tension was so thick, my breaths felt more like pants already.

Wilder spun me around the dance floor. "Is it weird that I really like shopping for you?"

"No, but I've noticed you seem to like shopping in some departments more than others. I think I have two outfits left, yet I have twenty thongs and lacy panties."

"I never knew dressing a woman could be so titillating."

"Titillating, huh?"

"Every time I pick something out, I imagine myself peeling it off of you."

His hand at my back tugged me closer, and I suddenly felt every hard inch of his body. *Every* hard inch. I gasped.

Wilder moved his mouth to my ear. "I've been this way since the damn day I met you. It never fully goes down."

"Maybe you should see a doctor?"

He groaned. "A psychiatrist. Because my mind seems to have only one track lately. *You.*"

There was something so sexy about the way Wilder wasn't afraid to tell me what he thought. Our attraction wasn't a one-way street, but I hadn't had the courage to admit that—at least not yet. I took a deep breath. "You know, I . . ."

My words trailed off when a woman appeared beside us—the tall brunette from earlier. She was even more stunning up close. She flashed a megawatt smile and looked only at Wilder. "I hope you won't find me too much of a daft cow if I cut in?"

Great, that face comes with an equally sexy British accent.

Wilder's grip on me tightened. "Maybe the next song."

As if on cue, the band played the last note of the song and rolled into a new one.

She smiled. "It seems the band agrees we should dance."

But Wilder still hadn't loosened his hold, so I helped him along, wiggling from his grasp. "It's okay. You two enjoy."

"Sloane—"

But I kept going, not stopping until I was back at my table. Unfortunately, Elijah wasn't around to distract me, so I sat there alone, watching the two of them glide around the dance floor while I micro-analyzed everything—the way her hand rested on his chest, how his held her hip. They definitely had history, and that didn't make me feel good.

When the dance was over, Wilder came right over. "Sorry about that."

"It's fine." I forced a smile that probably made me look like the Joker. "No big deal."

"Natasha and I went to college together."

Great, Harvard. Beauty, British, and brains. I continued to pretend it didn't bother me. "That's nice."

Wilder's brows pulled tight. "Are you angry with me?"

"Of course not. Why would I be angry? Dance with her all night, for all I care."

His jaw hardened. "Really? You wouldn't mind if I danced with her all night?"

"Why would I? We're just friends."

The muscle in his cheek ticked. "Don't do that."

"Do what?"

"Pretend that's all we are. You know that's bullshit."

I looked away, shaking my head. "I'm sorry, Wilder. I shouldn't have come to London early. I'm giving you the wrong impression."

"The wrong impression?"

"Yes, the wrong impression."

He stared at me in silence, but I refused to meet his gaze. After the longest time, he frowned. "Whatever. Have a great time tonight."

I felt tears threatening as he stalked off. One of the ladies sitting a few seats away looked at me with concern in her eyes. She leaned forward like she was going to ask if I was okay, so I abruptly stood to avoid her and went in search of the ladies' room.

When I found it, there were a few women chatting near the sinks, so I locked myself in a stall to collect my feelings. I blotted my eye makeup and took a mint from my purse before flushing, even though I hadn't used the toilet. The bathroom chatter had quieted, so I opened the door, expecting to be alone. But I wasn't.

The tall brunette, *Natasha,* leaned over a sink, lining her lips in blood red, but her eyes moved immediately me. She flashed a vicious smile. She'd definitely been waiting for me to come out. "Hello."

I nodded and stepped to the sink. "Hi."

She grinned. "You must be American?"

I knew I had a New York accent, but I didn't think one syllable showcased it.

Her smile widened at my confusion. "Brits don't say *hi.*"

"Oh." I turned on the water and tried to pay attention to getting my hands wet, but it was impossible to ignore her studying my face in the mirror. I looked up and met her gaze. "Can I help you with something?"

"Actually, I thought I'd help you."

"And how would you do that?"

"By giving you some advice on Wilder Hayes."

My jaw clenched. I wanted to tell her I didn't need her advice, but I also couldn't bring myself to stop her from talking, because I was equally curious.

She turned to face me directly. "I saw the way you look at him."

"And how is that?"

"Like he's the catch that he is. Let's face it, the man is the full package." A dirty grin crossed her face. "And bonus—he has a *very full package*."

I wanted to come across as cool and collected, but my skin betrayed me. I felt heat rise from my neck to the top of my head.

The woman's eyes gleamed when she saw my face. "Oh my. You've got it bad, and you haven't even fucked him yet."

I turned off the water and reached for a paper towel. "Does this conversation have a point?"

"I'm only trying to save you some heartache. Wilder is an easy man to fall for. He's handsome, rich, intelligent, and the best lay I've ever had. But he's also emotionally unavailable."

It felt like steam might billow from my nose and ears, I was so angry. "Did you ever think that maybe the reason he wasn't emotionally available is because *you* were just an easy lay?"

"And you think he wants something more from you?"

I dried my hands and tossed the paper into the garbage. "I don't know. But where did he go as soon as he could get away from you?"

The woman's eyes narrowed. At least I'd landed one punch. I straightened my spine, pretended to fluff my hair in the mirror, and walked out without giving her the satisfaction of looking back. Though underneath all the strut and confidence, I felt myself crumbling. I just wanted to go home—not even back to my beautiful hotel, but home to New York.

Elijah was at our table when I returned.

"Do you think we can get out of here early?" I asked.

"Are you okay?"

I didn't want to get into it now, so I lied. "I feel a headache coming on."

"I'm supposed to get photos of the giant cake, remember? It's like six feet tall or something."

Shoot. I'd forgotten about that. Some famous cake decorator in London had spent days making it, and we'd planned to include it with our spread.

Elijah stood. "You go. Take the car home. I'll get an Uber or something."

I wasn't sure if Ubers were even a thing this far out in the countryside. Plus, this was part of my job, and Elijah and I were a team. I wasn't going to leave him high and dry.

I shook my head. "It's fine. I'll just take a few aspirin and get some fresh air."

"You sure?"

I forced a smile. "Positive."

I disappeared outside for a while, taking a walk along the beautiful tree-lined grounds while I went over the mess tonight had become. I'd been jealous. That's how it had started. I wasn't unattractive. In fact, I could confidently say I was pretty. But there was a mile between me and that bitch from the ladies' room, at least on the outside. She'd made me feel small, and in turn I'd lashed out at Wilder, who hadn't done anything wrong other than dance with a woman he clearly—by the way he'd held on to me—hadn't wanted to dance with. I hadn't wanted him to see that I was insecure, so I'd pretended it hadn't bothered me, that we were nothing to each other. Which, deep down, I knew was crap.

I walked for the better part of an hour, until my feet started hurting in my heels. While the time alone had brought me clarity, and I could see that I'd acted immaturely, it was also a stark reminder that I wouldn't do well in Wilder's world. Imagine if we took things further and the newspapers ran pictures of him with a pretty fan while I was a continent away? I couldn't imagine how many opportunities the man had thrown at him each week. I'd be sitting home, questioning what he was doing, while he traveled the world, and that wouldn't be fair to either of us.

I didn't want to miss the cake cutting, so it was time to go back inside. Elijah was waiting out front when I walked back to the door.

"There you are. I've been looking all over for you. Are you okay?"

I smiled. "Yeah, I feel better. Sorry to make you worry."

He slung his arm around my shoulder. "They're going to do the cake soon. Then we can get out of here."

"Okay, great."

"I should warn you before we go back in, though, your guy is pretty liquored up tonight."

"Wilder?"

He nodded. "Caused a bit of a scene a few minutes ago. He fell into the dais, and his buddies had to help him up off the floor."

I sighed. "Thanks for letting me know."

Back at our table, I kept an eye on Wilder. He was sitting with his friends, drinking some sort of amber liquid from a glass. I'd never seen him have more than a few glasses of wine or beer, and it looked like he didn't hold more too well. His hair was mussed, his tie was missing, and he slouched to one side.

Luckily we were nearing the end of the evening, so we didn't have to wait long for the cake. The giant, seven-tiered confection stood taller than the bride. It was over the top, yet also stunningly beautiful with hundreds of flowers and details like I'd never seen before. I was glad I hadn't made us rush out and miss it for our feature.

After, I wasn't sure how to end the evening with Wilder, but I thought it might be best to avoid confrontation in his condition. I looked over at Elijah. "You ready to go?"

He nodded. "I'll go outside to text the driver and let him know we're ready. I don't get service in here, but he said he was parking ten minutes away, so it shouldn't be long." He lifted his chin toward Wilder. "You going to say goodbye?"

I shrugged. "I'm still debating."

"Okay. Be right back."

The more I watched Wilder, the drunker he seemed to get. He was standing now, the front of his shirt partially untucked, leaning on his buddy Louis, who was practically holding him up. I didn't want to make a scene, so I decided to slip out unnoticed. But as I took one last look, I saw the brunette from the bathroom strut over. My jaw clenched as I watched. Her claws were all over him. Elijah returned from calling the car just in time to catch the show on the other side of the room.

"Who's that?" he asked.

"Some bitch. She cut in while I was dancing with Wilder and tried to scare me off in the ladies' room."

Elijah and I looked on as Natasha slipped under Wilder's arm—the one that wasn't around his buddy. He wasn't paying any attention to her, really, but that didn't stop her from curling into him and laying a hand on his chest.

"Does that piss you off?" Elijah asked.

"What do you think?" I deadpanned, feeling like I might crack a tooth with how hard my jaw was clenched.

He grinned. "Well, go do something about it. Stake your claim, girl."

Adrenaline pumped through my veins. "You know what? I think I will. If nothing else, I'm not going to let her take advantage of the state he's in."

I started walking before I could talk myself into realizing this was a bad idea. Natasha saw me coming first. She smirked as I approached, and she held Wilder tighter.

"Hello, again," she practically cooed.

"Let go of him."

Wilder turned, noticing me for the first time. Though he had to lean forward and squint before he could determine who I was. "Sloane!" he said. "Where you been, baby?"

I gestured behind me. "Elijah and I are leaving now. Would you like a ride back to London?"

He looked over at Natasha and slurred his words. "Sloane doesn't want me. Isn't that the kicker? Everyone *always* wanted me, and I never wanted them back. Now, I finally want a woman, and she doesn't want me." Wilder wobbled on his feet, and his buddy grabbed him. Louis and I had met at the previous weddings. I smiled at him.

"Hey, Louis? Would you mind helping Wilder to the car? It should be out front by now."

"No problem, Sloane."

None of us acknowledged Natasha before walking away, which gave me a sense of satisfaction. Once we were in the limo, Wilder spread out across the backseat with his head on my lap. I was pretty sure he hadn't noticed Elijah. Five minutes later, he was snoring.

Elijah grinned. "He's even hot when he's sleeping."

I looked down and brushed Wilder's hair from his face. "I kinda wish he wasn't."

"Wasn't what? Hot?"

"Sort of. Hot, a celebrity athlete, wealthy, this body . . . ."

"Umm, are you drunk, too?"

I smiled. "He'd be just as much of a catch without all that."

"If you say so. Where are we taking him, anyway? Back to our hotel?"

I hadn't thought about the logistics. But I should probably take him home. Though . . . I had no idea where that was. "I'd rather take him to his place, but I don't know his address. Do you think he has a wallet on him?"

Elijah wiggled his brows. "I volunteer to check his pants pockets."

I chuckled. "I'll try his jacket first."

His wallet was the first place I checked, on the inside of his tux jacket, which had his name embroidered on the inner pocket. I'd assumed by the way his tux fit that it wasn't a rental, but this was yet another reminder how different our lives were. None of my friends owned a tuxedo.

If that didn't point out the difference enough, pulling up to the address on Wilder's license was a flashing neon sign. *Wow*. The building looked like it belonged on the cover of *Wealth* magazine. Modern and sleek, with curved glass and an entrance that had to be two stories high—it was pretty damn intimidating.

"How are we going to do this?" Elijah asked. "You think they have a luggage cart or a dolly?"

I laughed. "I'm sure that would raise a few eyebrows, if we wheeled him in. Let's start by trying to wake him." I placed my hand on Wilder's chest and gently shook him. "Wilder? You're home."

He gripped my hand and grinned. "I smooth-talked you into coming home with me after all?"

"Something like that . . . Do you think you can walk?"

"I can do more than walk . . ."

I smiled at Elijah. "At least it seems like he's back to himself a little more than when we left."

Slipping my hand under Wilder's head, I lifted and helped him sit up. Once his feet were on the floor, he blinked over at Elijah. "Oh, hey, man. When did you get here?"

"Just now." Elijah chuckled and looked to me. "Want me to help you get him up?"

"I don't need any help getting it up," Wilder said. "Trust me."

"Should I wait here?"

I shook my head. "He said our hotel was near here. I'll just grab an Uber so you don't have to wait."

"Are you sure?"

"Yeah. I'm going to help him up and make sure he's okay."

Elijah winked. "Right. Got ya."

"No, really."

He opened the back of the limo, still grinning. "Let me at least get the doors."

Once we were inside, I waved goodbye to Elijah and turned to the task at hand. Wilder's forty-five-minute power nap had made him a bit more steady on his feet, but he was still pretty drunk. "What floor do you live on?" I asked as we stepped into the elevator.

"Top."

There were thirty-eight buttons and one marked PH. "Thirty-eight?"

He yawned. "Penthouse. The code is zero-zero-one-seven."

NumberSeventeen. I smiled to myself thinking back to how he'd stalked my YouTube channel when we first met and found the keypad underneath the buttons and entered the numbers. Before I could push the PH button, it illuminated. *I guess it knows where we're going.*

The car sped up to the top floor, and the doors opened right into an apartment. I stepped off tentatively. "Is this you?"

Wilder peeled off his jacket and let it fall to the floor as we walked in. "You want a drink?"

"No, thank you."

"Don't mind if I do . . ."

I thought he'd had enough, but at least he was home and safe. Wilder headed to a bar off the living room and poured something from a decanter while I looked around. The apartment was even more fabulous than I would've guessed from the fancy outside, and that was saying something. Floor-to-ceiling windows lined the living room, showcasing a lit-up London beneath. I lived in what I considered to be a decent-sized space due to my brother's generosity, but my entire apartment could fit in this room, and there were hallways going in two different directions, too.

"Your apartment is beautiful."

He swallowed the contents of his glass in a second gulp. "But that doesn't get me points with you, does it?"

I sighed. "You don't need points, Wilder."

"Tell me, what I do need?"

I wished it were that easy. But it wasn't about him. It was about me.

When I took too long to answer, Wilder frowned. "I'm going to bed."

"Alright."

"You're welcome to stay. There's three bedrooms. Or go." He smiled sadly. "But I know which you'll be choosing."

Wilder bumped into the kitchen counter on his way down the hall and disappeared into the last room on the left. I waited, listening to make sure he got to bed okay. The apartment went quiet, so I waited a few more minutes, then tiptoed down the hall to check in. Wilder was passed out, on his back, with his shoes still on. I figured the least I could do was make him comfy. So I went in, slipped off his shoes, and covered him with a blanket. I looked down at his beautiful face, feeling so torn. I was crazy about him. But . . . what if he was just in it for the chase? He'd said himself that everyone had always wanted him, except me. Maybe it was the challenge that was enticing. After all, he was a competitive athlete.

Eventually, I took a play from his book, leaning down and kissing his forehead before turning off the light. On my way out, I looked around to see if everything was in order. The cap was still off the decanter, so I closed that up and rinsed the glass he'd used in the sink. A laptop sat on the island, a screen saver of some sort flashing photos, one after another. Catching something familiar in the millisecond it was on-screen, I walked over for a closer look. And I gasped when I realized what it was.

Me.

It was me.

One flashing photo after another. All *me.*

I stood there dumbfounded, watching it over and over to get a good look at each of them. Most of them had been taken at St. Dunstan in the East, the church ruins he'd taken me to on my first day here. I knew he'd taken a few pictures, because we'd posed for selfies. But these were of only me. Me smiling up at the sun with my eyes closed. Me smelling one of the sweet-scented flowering trees. Me trying to balance in one of the archways and almost falling. Me laughing.

I felt a physical ache in my chest. As much as he denied it, Wilder *was* sweet. He was thoughtful and caring. Everything he'd done for me since I arrived—no, since I'd met him—had shown me that. But I'd wanted to believe it was all a ploy to get me into bed. Because anything more scared the crap out of me. If I didn't take a chance, I couldn't get hurt. And there was no getting *a little hurt* by Wilder Hayes. Because Wilder was *big love.* The kind that doesn't just take a piece of your heart when he leaves, but punches a gaping hole right through it.

I looked toward the elevator, then back to the hall that led to the bedroom. Then back at the elevator. One choice was simple— walk out that door, get on the flight tomorrow night, and never look back. The other choice was complicated—messy and scary as hell. But . . . I looked over at the screen saver once more and realized there was no choice.

In the end, it wasn't even a conscious decision to stay, my feet just started moving on their own. I strode down the hall, took a deep breath, and opened the bedroom door. Wilder was conked out, but I wanted to be here to tell him how I felt when he woke up. So I slipped into bed beside him, rested my head on his warm chest, and shut my eyes, feeling at peace for the first time in a long time.

Though when my eyes fluttered open the next morning, *peace* wasn't what I felt. At least not pushing up against my ass . . .

20

WILDER

What the . . .

Sloane? In my bed? I lifted the covers and looked down at myself. Still dressed.

So was she. I wasn't sure if I should be disappointed or grateful that I didn't remember what the hell had happened last night. But I really liked the way it felt waking up wrapped around her. Though I had to pee pretty bad. And I had no idea how the heck I was going to extract myself from the tangle of limbs without waking her. Also, *damn* . . . my dick was right up against her ass. I was a guy, so I often woke with an erection. But right now, I was hard as a rock. It was probably a good thing she was still sleeping, or I might get my ass kicked.

I inched back, trying to slip my arm from beneath her when Sloane's head suddenly turned.

"You're awake?" she said.

"Sorry. I was trying to get up to go to the bathroom without waking you."

"I've been awake for a while."

She pushed up to her elbow, releasing my arm, and I slipped from the bed and headed to the bathroom. But as soon as I was upright, my head started pounding. *Fuck.* What the hell did I drink last night?

Standing in front of the toilet bowl, I unzipped and attempted to pull my rigid cock down enough to hit the water, but that wasn't happening. Not even close. I was too damn hard. So I had to lean forward, palms against the wall behind the toilet and angle in. I cursed under my breath as the stream started, trying to remember something about last night—any little bits and pieces.

I remembered the moment Sloane had walked into the mansion. She'd looked so freaking gorgeous in that green dress. I'd been standing at the top of the stairs, watching the people down below. She'd entered looking straight ahead, so it gave me the chance to take a long look without getting caught.

I remembered snapping a picture of her talking to Elijah and laughing, when she wasn't looking.

I remembered us dancing.

I remembered how good she smelled, how goose bumps had prickled along her arms when I touched her, but she tried to act like she wasn't affected.

I remembered telling her that every time I picked something out for her to wear, I imagined myself peeling it off of her.

I remembered her gasping when she felt my hard-on up against her belly on the dance floor.

But then . . . it got fuzzy.

Until it didn't.

I shut my eyes.

Natasha.

Fucking Natasha cut in.

Great. Just great.

I finished peeing, washed my hands, splashed some water on my face, and looked in the mirror. I looked like shit. About the way I felt at the moment, I supposed. A shower was in order. But I needed to get clothes from the bedroom and let Sloane know first. So I took a deep breath and attempted to *look* like I didn't *feel* like I'd been run over by a Mack truck. I opened the bathroom door.

Sloane was sitting up in bed now, wearing one of my T-shirts and a pair of my sweats rolled at the waist. Her eyes dropped to my crotch and widened.

"Sorry," I said. "It has a mind of its own."

She smiled. "I know. I thought your leg was poking me in the ass when I woke up. Yet you were still snoring like a baby."

I frowned. "Sorry."

She waved me off. "It's fine. I could've slept somewhere else if it bothered me. I didn't help myself to a tour of the place, but I noticed a lot of doors, so I assume there are other alternatives somewhere."

I took a seat on the edge of the bed next to her and ran a hand through my hair. "What happened last night? Some of the evening is . . . foggy."

"What do you remember?"

"Not enough . . ."

"Well, let me summarize for you. I acted like a jealous asshole, and you got upset and drank too much."

My brows lifted. "*You* acted like the asshole, not me? Are you just trying to make me feel better?"

Sloane shook her head. "No. I was definitely the asshole."

"Did it have something to do with a woman who cut in while we were dancing?"

She nodded. "The lovely Natasha also cornered me in the bathroom to make sure I knew you'd slept together and that I shouldn't expect anything more than a good lay."

I dropped my head and closed my eyes. "I'm sorry."

"Don't be. You didn't do anything wrong."

"Maybe not last night. But the life I've been leading has come back to bite me in the ass, and that's my fault." I shook my head. "Not just last night, but in general. You have doubts about my intentions, and I really can't blame you. You do the same thing over and over enough times, people start to be able to predict the future. Even I question if I'm capable of being the man you deserve. I don't want to hurt you, Sloane."

She bumped her shoulder with mine. "I think both of our pasts are getting in the way of our future. I won't lie and say your dating history doesn't give me some concern, but it's not the biggest reason I've been keeping you at a distance."

"It's not?"

She shook her head. "My own past has left me with a lot of insecurities and self-esteem issues, if I'm being honest. I was afraid to believe you actually liked me, and this wasn't just about the chase."

"Was? Does that mean you believe me now?"

She smiled. "Well, it's either that or you're a serial killer."

I laughed. "I'm not sure I'm following."

"I saw the screen saver on your laptop, with all the pictures of me. It made me understand how *you* see me, instead of how *I've* been seeing me."

I brushed a piece of hair from Sloane's cheek and looked into her eyes. "I see you as beautiful, inside and out."

Her face went soft. "I believe you do. I'm not sure you're right, but I finally understand that's really what you see."

"Good." I kissed her forehead. "Because this is one thick skull to get things through."

She smiled. "That's not the first time I've heard that."

I took her hands. "Will you let me take you out now? On a date?"

"When?"

"Tonight."

"I can't. I'm leaving. My flight is at nine. I have to be at work on Tuesday."

"But you would go out with me if your flight wasn't today?"

She nodded. "Maybe we can do it next time you're in New York?"

No way in hell was I waiting another day, much less until I got back to New York, now that she'd said she'd give me a chance. I looked around and found my phone on the end table. The little battery symbol at the top was red, but at least it was working. I called up my contacts and scrolled down to D. Finding the name I wanted, I hit the call button and brought the phone to my ear.

Sloane's cute little nose wrinkled. "Who are you calling?"

I held up a finger and waited. One ring. Two rings. Three. I started to think he wasn't going to answer, but then a deep voice came on.

"Hello?"

"Hey, Dad."

Sloane's eyes bulged.

"What's up, kiddo?" my father said.

"Do you remember that park I had you take Mom to years ago, when you came to stay with her at the end?"

"The church ruins she loved so much?"

"That's the one."

"Beautiful place. What about it?"

"They sometimes do weddings. I was thinking . . . since your team is here anyway, maybe they could stay an extra day or two and cover it for the magazine for a future spread."

"It's funny you should say that. Because when I was there with your mom, I asked her to marry me again."

"Weren't you still married to wife number three?"

Dad sighed. "That's why she said no."

I laughed. "And probably why you're on marriage number four."

"You make a good point." Dad chuckled. "But sure, if the team doesn't mind staying, I think it would make a great story."

I grinned and met Sloane's eyes. "I don't think they'll mind an extra night or two."

"You run it past them and tell them to let Bill Winkler know what they decide. He runs the magazine division."

I wiggled my eyebrows. "I'll definitely run it past them. Thanks, Dad. Talk to you soon." I hung up and tossed my phone over my shoulder with a shit-eating grin.

Sloane shook her head. "I'm terrified by how quickly you came up with that story."

I weaved my fingers with hers. "Will you stay and have dinner with me? We can go back to the park tomorrow or the next day and do a shoot."

She bit her lip. "What about Elijah?"

"Obviously he'll have to stay, too. But I'm not taking him to dinner. I want you all to myself."

Sloane rolled her eyes, but I saw a smile. "I'll talk to him."

"Thank you."

"But first, you need to make me some coffee. I've been up for hours and I'm dying."

"Yes, ma'am." I stood, tugging her up with me. "Come on. I'll start it brewing and then take a quick shower, if you don't mind."

"Okay."

I led Sloane out to the kitchen and lifted her onto the counter next to the coffee maker. "I'm going to make it. But I'm also going to show you how." I winked. "So you can make it if you're up before me on our next sleepover."

A little while later, I was in the shower. I wasn't sure if it was the hot water pelting my shoulders or the fact that Sloane was most likely going to be staying that cured my hangover. But I came out feeling like a new man. I started to get dressed, but then thought better of it and kept just the towel wrapped around my waist. (And I might've done a few dozen push-ups in the bathroom, because you can never look too good.)

Sloane was sitting in the living room with her coffee when I walked out. Her eyes followed the drops of water still running down my chest. She swallowed, and my dick twitched in response—it really did have a mind of its own. Sloane noticed.

I didn't have to look down to know there was an outline now—a nice, thick one. I fucking loved seeing her eyes all over me, seeing how I affected her. But there was a fine line between showing off and being a giant asshole, so I poured a coffee and excused myself to get dressed. When I came back, Sloane was standing at the windows, looking out at London. I walked up behind her.

"This view is incredible," she said.

"I can't complain."

"How long have you lived here?"

"About five years. My first place was a one-bedroom. I needed somewhere bigger since Lucas stays over a lot. And this is closer to his school. I'm going to guess I didn't offer you a tour last night?"

She smiled. "You passed out on the drive home. You're lucky you made it to the bedroom."

I nodded. "Come on. I'll show you around."

Down the hall, I opened the door to my office first. It was filled with team pictures, a shitload of trophies and plaques, and the usual equipment—laptop, printer, scanner. Next, I showed her Lucas's room. It was a mess, but at least the bed was sort of made.

"He's not the cleanest or the most organized kid."

She looked around at the walls. "My niece would love the artwork in here."

"You'll have to come back and bring her."

The tour continued on to two bathrooms, a small room filled with weights and exercise equipment, and then we headed to the last door at the end of the hall, the spare bedroom. I opened the door, but quickly pulled it shut.

"What?" she asked. "Is someone in there?"

"No . . . I, uh . . ."

"What's in there that you don't want me to see?"

"Nothing."

She frowned. "You're not a very good liar, Wilder."

I didn't want her to think the worst, like I was hiding a bed with chains and a torn pair of panties my sex slave had forgotten the other night. So I decided to come clean. I rubbed the back of my neck. "It just arrived yesterday morning."

"What arrived?"

I pushed the door open and held my hand out for her to enter first.

Sloane hesitated before walking in. "Oh my God. You have my suitcase! Why didn't you tell me it came?"

"I was going to. Just not until today. I was afraid if I told you yesterday, you'd wear the dress you brought and make me return the one I got you."

"So?"

"I really wanted you to have it. Plus, I couldn't wait to see you wear that green dress."

She laughed, covering her mouth. "Oh my God. You are insane."

I slung my arm around her shoulder. "I blame you. You won't let me see you naked, so I have to get off on shopping for you."

"You better be careful. You have really good taste, and you buy things I could never afford. I might not let you see me naked just to keep you shopping."

"What if I promise the shopping will get *better* after I see you naked? I could end the tour with another visit to my bedroom?"

She smiled and shook her head. "I should get back to my hotel and talk to Elijah."

"Can I make you breakfast first?"

"Shopping for me, cooking for me . . . a girl could get used to this."

I winked. "That's what I'm counting on, Cupcake."

21

WILDER

"You look like you're thinking something very inappropriate right now."

"That happens a lot when you're around." I stood as Sloane returned from the ladies' room and took her hand. "Dance with me anyway."

She smiled. "Okay."

The evening had been perfect. I'd taken her to my favorite restaurant, we'd shared a delicious meal, and now I pulled her into my arms and rested my cheek against hers as we swayed to live music. "Did I tell you how beautiful you look?"

"I think three times."

I spun us around. "Must be true then."

"Thank you for the dress. But I have my suitcase and could've worn the one I was going to wear to the wedding."

I'd gone shopping after dropping her off this morning. This time, I didn't even call Emily, my personal shopper. I went to the department store all by myself, though I did get some help from a saleswoman when it came to matching shoes. I wasn't sure what the hell had come over me lately. Maybe I was losing my mind, but I wanted to do everything for Sloane—buy her things, drive her places, cook for her. Hell, when I'd shown up at her hotel room earlier this afternoon and she was still getting ready, I'd wanted to brush her hair for her. Normally I didn't even want to make my own coffee, so it was completely out of character for me.

"I like doing things for you."

She looked up into my eyes. "You really do, don't you?"

I shrugged. "No fucking idea why. But I do. I can't remember the last time I picked out my own underwear, yet I want to dress you from head to toe. Is that weird?"

She smiled. "Yes. But it's also very sweet."

"What did I tell you about thinking I'm sweet?"

"You know what I think?"

"What?"

"I think you *are* sweet, but you don't want people to know it."

"Oh yeah? Would you like me to tell you what I was thinking about when you were walking back from the ladies' room?"

"What?"

I slid my hand to her delicate neck and stroked my thumb up and down the front. "The gurgling sound you'll make when I stick my dick down your throat and don't let you breathe."

Sloane gasped. "Oh my God."

I grinned. "Not so sweet then, eh?"

She moved her mouth to my ear. "I don't know. I haven't tasted it yet."

I groaned. "Every single time I've danced with you, from that very first wedding, I've had a hard-on."

"I know. Because you don't leave room for Jesus."

"I don't know what it is about you, but there isn't room for air between us."

We danced from one song into the next, enjoying a moment of comfortable silence. I didn't think I'd ever felt so content. But the lady in my arms must have been doing more than enjoying the moment. Sloane shifted to look at me. "Thank you for being persistent."

"I don't think I had a choice, sweetheart. I couldn't get you out of my head."

Her face turned serious. "You make me nervous, Wilder."

"Right back at ya, sweetheart. There's never been a time in my life when I wasn't trying to get somewhere. When I started playing rugby, I wanted to play in college. When I got to college, I wanted to play in the pros. When I went pro, I wanted to be the best in the league. When I retired, I wanted to own a team. I've always been on the run, trying to get somewhere. But since I met you, the only place I want to be is where you are. It scares the crap out of me, and some days I'm not sure if I've lost my mind for feeling this way or if I've finally figured out the meaning of life."

Sloane's eyes welled up. "How are you even real?"

When the song ended, we sat. I wasn't hungry, yet I ordered dessert because I didn't want the night to end. But when the waiter brought the check, I couldn't drag things out anymore. Panic washed over me as we walked to the valet.

"Will you stay with me tonight?" I asked. "You can stay in the guest room, if you want. I promise I won't push you to do anything you don't want to. I just don't want tonight to end, and I want you there when I wake up in the morning."

Sloane smiled. "I'd like that a lot."

I hadn't been nervous around girls since I was a teen. But when it was just me and Sloane in my apartment, I had no idea what to do with myself. I opened a bottle of wine and poured us each a glass while Sloane looked out the window at the nighttime view of London. I passed her a glass and stood just behind her, keeping a bit of distance.

"You're awfully quiet." Sloane sipped, looking over her shoulder at me.

"I don't want to fuck anything up."

Her brows pulled. "What would you fuck up?"

"I don't know. It feels unnatural to not have my hands on you. But I'm afraid if I touch you, I won't be able to stop."

"Why would you have to stop?"

"I don't want to scare you away with too much, too fast."

She smiled and turned to face me. "You told me at dinner that you wanted to hear the sound of me choking while you filled my throat, and I'm still here."

My eyes dropped to her neck. I swallowed. "There's so much I want to do to you."

Sloane tilted her head and spoke softly. "Like what?"

I lifted my eyes and met hers. "You really want to know?"

She nodded.

I sucked back a big gulp of wine and allowed my eyes to rake up and down her body. "For starters, I want to tear that dress from your body."

"I saw the tag on this dress. Maybe we can unzip it?"

I shook my head. "I'll buy you another one. I want the pieces on the floor, scattered around your feet while I spend a few minutes looking at you in nothing but your bra and underwear and those sexy-as-fuck heels."

Sloane sipped her wine. "Sorry, can't do that."

"No?"

"I don't have anything on underneath this dress."

I hissed out a breath. "Did you do that for me?"

She nodded. "Will just the heels work?"

"I might have to add a picture to my screen saver collection."

Sloane smiled. "Then what?"

I lifted my chin, gesturing to the window. "Then you press your hands to the glass and bend over, and I'll drop to my knees and lick you while you look out at London."

"Is the window privacy glass?"

A slow smile curved across my face as I shook my head. "Is that a problem?"

Sloane shivered. "No."

I stepped forward and ran a single finger along the bare skin of her back, starting at the top of her spine. "*Lick you* might not be the right words. I'm going to devour you, bury my face in your pussy, and eat you until you come all over my tongue. I want you dripping."

Sloane's voice was breathy. "Oh God."

I stepped fully behind her, pulled her hair to one side, and sucked along her pulse line. Her head lolled back, giving me full access. When she let out a little mewl, I pushed up against her, letting her know she wasn't the only one affected.

"I've dreamed of tying you up, making you writhe in my bed until you beg."

"Is that payback for making you wait?"

"Fifty-one days."

Sloane blinked, as if from a haze. "What's fifty-one days?"

"How long I've been waiting. Since the day I met you."

Her features slackened. "You know how many days it's been?"

"I know everything about the time I've spent with you."

She swallowed, seeming to let my comment sink in. "I think we need to get back to the dirty talk or I'm going to ruin the moment with a sappy cry. I can feel the Hallmark tears marching toward my eyes now."

My lip quirked. "Not a problem."

"Tell me what else you've dreamed about."

I nipped at her shoulder blade. "I want to watch your face while you come."

"That's still sweet. What else you got?"

"I have a typed-up list of shit I want to do to you. I was going to alphabetize it, but I wasn't sure if numbers came before letters, or do I spell out sixty-nine?"

She smiled. "I can't tell if you're serious or not."

I lifted my chin to her glass. "No more talking. Finish your wine."

I might've been teasing about the typed-up list, but I wasn't exaggerating when I said I'd spent hours imagining things I wanted to do to her. Yet her lifting the wineglass to her mouth and doing what I asked might have turned me on more than anything. I watched as she swallowed the last drop before I took the stem from her hand and set it on the counter next to my half-full glass.

Tonight's dress had spaghetti straps and an open back with a short zipper that started at the waist. It would have taken two seconds to unzip and take it off. But tearing the straps was so much more fun. I grabbed the flimsy material from her shoulders and yanked. The silky fabric slid down her body in a way that would forever stay seared into my brain. It puddled to a pool of green around her feet.

I stepped back, though my body vibrated with the need to touch her. "Turn around. I want to look at you."

I'd imagined this moment more than once, what she would look like standing before me naked. But whatever I'd conjured in my head didn't hold a candle to the real thing. Her gorgeous, real tits were full with the most perfect lilt to them. Purply-pink nipples stood at full attention, hard peaks begging to be sucked. I salivated staring at them, and I hadn't even made my way down to the rest of her yet. My heart pumped so fast that it felt like I might die if I didn't get started. Then my eyes dropped lower.

Oh fuck. Can you have a heart attack from need? Because that clean-shaven pussy was about to test the theory. I licked my lips, feeling like a little kid in a candy store, not sure what sweet treat to start with. So much for all the mental planning I'd done . . .

I took a step toward her, ready to dive in, and was met with a hand.

No.

No. No. No. She can't be putting the brakes on now.

I froze, holding my breath. "What?"

Sloane's lips curved to a wicked grin. "You told me what *you* wanted. But you didn't ask what *I* wanted."

Fuck. I shook my head. "I'm sorry. I didn't think . . ."

But before I could finish groveling, Sloane dropped to her knees.

Naked.

Except for the stilettos.

I was caught completely off guard, so much so that I stood with my jaw hanging open while she unbuckled my pants and unzipped me. Sloane tugged my pants down, wrapped her little hand around my painfully hard cock, and looked up at me.

"I want you to make me choke."

I thought I might come right then and there. My cock throbbed. "Fuck," I hissed. "You are . . . perfect."

I'd said it before she touched me, and I meant every damn word. But when she licked her lips, lowered her jaw, and took me into her hot, wet mouth, I thought I might be the one to sappy cry. Usually when a woman got on her knees, she gave you a show—licking the head seductively, sucking along the shaft like it was a lollipop, wrapping her hand around and pumping to get things started—but none of it was necessary. Not when a woman takes you down her throat in one swallow.

Jesus.

Fucking.

Christ.

She can deep throat. My head fell back with a groan.

Sloane pulled back, keeping suction tight as she slid me almost fully out of her mouth, then lunged forward, taking me into her throat once again. I looked down, watching her head bob, and tears prickled at the corners of my eyes. It was that freaking good.

Was it too soon to propose?

Would her father be pissed if I didn't ask him first?

Shit, I hadn't even met her brothers yet.

Not even thoughts of marriage could slow down the orgasm already barreling down on me. She needed to ease up or this was going to be embarrassing. "Sloane. Jesus, baby. You have to slow down."

Her answer was to look up at me, reach for my hand, and put it on the back of her head, urging me to guide her rhythm. *Fuck.* She wasn't just giving me her blessing to fuck her face, she was telling me to do it. My fingers curled into her hair, and my hips began to thrust.

I couldn't breathe. The sensation of her warm, snug throat constricting around me was the only thing that mattered. I could've gone deeper, but she already had so much of me, so I stopped an inch or two shy of my hips pressed to her face.

"Fuuuuck," I groaned. "Just like that. So, so good."

My fingers loosened in her hair as I pulled back out, almost to the tip. Then tightened as I eagerly pushed back in.

Sloane moaned, and I felt it in my balls. I pushed in a little farther, still not all the way, but enough that I was riding that edge. But this time, when I stopped the last inch from going in, she looked up at me, reached for the hand already at the back of her head, and urged me to push more.

Fuck.

That did it. I pushed past the point of no return and fed her my full length. Her throat constricted around me as she made a gurgling, choking sound. My eyes rolled into the back of my head. It was nirvana, the best thing I've ever heard and felt in my life. But I was seconds away from pumping down her throat, which undoubtedly was going to be an explosion. Choking her once was a gift, a second time was greedy. So I reached down, gripped under her arms, and guided her to her feet. Then I kissed that magical mouth.

Change of plans—I scooped her into my arms and stalked through the apartment.

"What about the window?" she asked in a daze.

"Fuck that. No one is seeing you look like this except for me."

I set her down in the center of my bed, undressing the rest of the way in record speed. She looked like some sort of goddess, hair fanned out all over my pillow, a real-life wet dream. I made a mental note to tell my housekeeper not to wash the sheets, so I could smell her while I jacked off to the memory of tonight after she was gone. The thought was laughable, really. I was already making plans to watch the rerun, and the show hadn't even started yet. But I knew it was going to be that good. I'd known it since the first day we met. And that was before I had any inkling she could deep throat better than a porn star.

I pushed her thighs open, spreading her wide. She was pink and perfect, glistening and so fucking lickable. I hovered over her, rubbing my nose against the top of her slit, and inhaled deeply. I was going to bury my face in that sexy smell, and it was highly possible I wouldn't wash that for a long time, either.

Just like she'd done to me in the living room, I didn't start small. No. I dipped down as far as I could go, almost to the crack of her ass, and licked one long stroke from back to clit. *Fucking delicious.* She moaned, and the sound shot straight to my cock. I'd thought nothing could be better than her swallowing me, making choking sounds to take every last inch. But this—hearing her pleasure— this was pure heaven. I'd never quite understood the bible verse that said it was *better to give than receive,* at least when it came to head. *Getting* was always better, at least until today. I wanted to eat her all night long, make her moan my name until the words formed a damn song.

Sloane's back arched off the bed. I lifted a hand to her stomach and nudged her down, using a firm grip to keep her in place. Then

I went in for another lick. But it wasn't enough. Not even close. I spread her legs wider and tunneled in, fucking her with my tongue. Her head thrashed from side to side while she moaned my name. Back in my playing days, the roar of the crowd chanting my name could make me feel invincible. But this—hearing Sloane scream— charged me up more than a packed stadium. My entire face got in on the action—lips, tongue, teeth. Hell, I used the scruff on my cheeks to work her with friction. I couldn't get enough. And from the sounds she was making, neither could she. I couldn't be sure which of us was enjoying it more.

"Wilder! Oh God." She yanked my hair.

I wanted her to pull harder. So I sucked on her firm little bud and slipped a finger inside. I was so fucking turned on that I started fucking the bed, hips thrusting against the mattress, while my tongue lapped at her juices and my fingers pumped in and out. I was totally obsessed and consumed, and I never wanted to come up for air.

Then it happened. I felt the clench around me, her words trailed to an incoherent babble, and Sloane came all over my tongue. It was . . . glorious. Holy. Other freaking worldly.

And the best part? It was only the beginning . . .

22

SLOANE

I panted as I stared at the man hovering over me.

"I . . . I, oh God."

Wilder smiled. "I'll take that as a pet name."

I tried to roll my eyes but apparently that took too much energy. Even my eyeballs were sated. "I can't feel my arms and legs," I said.

"That's okay. The only thing I want you to feel is my cock."

I managed to lift my head and look down. "That thing is scary."

Wilder leaned in and kissed me. "You didn't seem too afraid of it when you were on your knees."

"Ignorance is bliss. That was before I knew the true size of it. It actually choked me—that wasn't for your benefit."

He smiled and trailed a finger over my neck. "You are incredible."

I flashed what was probably a goofy smile. "You're pretty good at what you just did, too."

"I'm glad you think so, because I plan to spend lots of time doing it."

My arms and legs felt like jelly, but when Wilder kissed his way to my ear and started to tell me all the other things he planned to do to me tonight, I suddenly got a second wind. The dirtier his words became, the more desperate I grew to have him inside me. Though Wilder still seemed firmly in control. So I decided to rattle him with a taste of his own dirty-talk medicine.

"I've never done that—had someone go down on me while I sucked their dick."

Wilder's eyes darkened. "But you want to?"

I nodded. "I can't wait to try it with you."

"What else haven't you done?"

"I don't know. Lots of things. My ex wasn't the adventurous type."

"Thank fuck. I already knew he was a moron."

I smiled and scraped my fingernail over Wilder's broad shoulder. "I want to try new things with you."

Wilder reached between us and fisted his cock. He slid his thick head through my wetness but kept going until he reached my ass, then circled my tight hole. "How about here? Would this be new?"

I nodded.

Wilder grumbled a few curses before looking up and thanking God. But I didn't want to talk anymore, so I took the flesh of his bottom lip between my teeth and tugged.

He hissed. "I may never let you go back to New York."

"Stop talking and kiss me."

He grinned. "Yes, ma'am."

Wilder pressed his lips to mine. It didn't take long for things to grow heated, and soon we were both panting again. He pulled back and kept our gazes locked as he pushed inside me.

"Jesus Christ." He swallowed. "You're so tight and wet."

His body shook as he moved in and out slowly, each time pushing a little deeper. It had been a long time since I'd been with a man, and I'd never been with one his size, so my body needed to go slow, though the tension in Wilder's jaw told me it wasn't easy. Once I was fully ready, he took my hands and weaved our fingers together, pulling them up and over my head.

His eyes jumped back and forth between mine. "You are so damn beautiful. And I am crazy about you, sweetheart."

I felt my eyes fill with tears. Wilder never took his gaze from mine as he moved faster, in and out rhythmically. Soft thrusts grew hard, and gliding grew to rooting deep into my body. The only thing that stayed the same was the way he looked at me. It made me feel so vulnerable, yet somehow safe.

Everything else disappeared, except for our connection—mind, body, and soul. The moment was so powerful, I gave in to it, letting myself be lost in this man. When I began to come undone, Wilder smashed his lips to mine, taking my breath away. "Oh God . . ." My body started to throb on its own, and my eyes closed. "I'm gonna . . ."

He pulled back. "Open, sweetheart. I want to watch you give it to me."

It hit like a storm, a fury tearing up everything in its path, and it took all I had to not surrender and allow my eyes to close. My muscles pulsed, and Wilder read my body, speeding up his pace, chasing his own release. He pumped in and out, the sound of our wet bodies slapping against each other echoing around the room, before burying himself deep and releasing with a growl.

I'd expected Wilder to roll off and collapse after what he'd just done. Lord knows that's what Josh always did. But this man was nothing like my ex. Wilder kissed me softly, gliding in and out with a smile on his face as we caught our breath.

"If that's just the beginning," I said, "I can't imagine what it will be like by the end."

Wilder shook his head. "Maybe there won't be an end, and things will just keep getting better."

The next morning I woke to my cell phone ringing. I felt around the nightstand, not ready to lift my head or wanting to open my eyes. Grabbing it, I squinted one eye open and considered ignoring the call. But Elijah would only call back, so I swiped. "Hello?"

"Where are you?"

My other eye opened, and I pushed up to my elbows. "What time is it?"

"Umm . . . Fifteen minutes after we were supposed to meet at the park."

I was so confused. "But we aren't meeting until one."

"I know. It's one fifteen, girly."

I jolted upright. "Are you joking?"

Elijah chuckled. "I really hope you were busy balling all night and it's not that you were watching a *Law and Order* marathon."

I looked over at the man next to me, the one who had kept me up until all hours. "Umm . . ."

"Fuck yeah!"

Elijah screamed so loud that Wilder's eyes opened. He looked about as happy as I felt to be awake. I covered the phone. "It's the middle of the day. I was supposed to meet Elijah for the photoshoot at the park."

"Is that him?"

I nodded.

Wilder held out his hand. "Let me talk to him."

"What? Why?"

"Give me the phone, Cupcake."

I pulled the cell from my ear, but hesitated to hand it over. Wilder plucked it from my hand.

"We're going to need an hour," he barked into the phone. "There's a café at the corner of Cross and Baker, on the southeast side of the park entrance. Go have lunch. It's on me."

I could hear Elijah speak, even from where I sat. "Okay, but an hour is a long time. I'm going to need a bottle of champagne with lunch."

"Have at it."

"The good stuff. Not the cheap shit that gives you a hangover."

"You have no budget. Buy the best bottle they have. But you don't get to give Sloane shit for being late when we get there. Deal?"

"Umm . . ." I shook my head. "The words *no budget* are very dangerous to say to Elijah."

Wilder's eyes dropped to my bare chest. "Buy two bottles. We might be longer than an hour."

I wasn't sure if Elijah responded or not, but Wilder swiped to end the call and tossed the phone over his shoulder. He scooped under me and rolled until I was on top of him. I yelped, but the smile on my face was impossible to hide.

"Now say good morning to me properly." His voice was deep with morning grog, but it was *so* damn sexy.

I figured he meant a kiss, but I was in a playful mood. "Good morning."

"I said properly."

"How exactly do I say good morning properly?"

"With my cock inside of you."

"Inside of me where?"

He clasped his hands behind his head. "Any hole will do."

I slapped his chest, laughing. "You're so crass."

He cupped his ear. "Did you say in your *ass*? Okay, but we're going to be a lot later than an hour then."

I shook my head, laughing. "How are you even thinking about sex after last night? I lost track of the number of times we did it."

Wilder reached around me, pressing his dick to the crack of my ass—his *very hard* dick. "You're in bed with me naked. The better question is why are we even going to the park?"

I bit my lip. "We have to be fast because I need to shower."

"I'll do you one better." He climbed to his feet, standing on the bed, and took me with him. "Shower sex. Two birds, one stone."

Wilder carried me to the bathroom, cradled in his arms, and set me down to turn the water on. Once it was warm, he stepped in and tugged me along. Water rained down over us, and Wilder said good morning properly—with my hands splayed wide on the tile, while he fucked me from behind.

23

SLOANE

The sound of the apartment door creaking open made me lose my place midsentence. Unfortunately, I was filming Knot so Seriously live, so I couldn't run to see the man I assumed had just walked in, though my heart wanted to. It had been a week since I'd seen Wilder, and it felt more like a month.

He strolled into the bedroom and flashed a cocky smile as I spoke to the camera. I'd warned him that I might still be live when he arrived, but would leave my door open. My show normally ran about an hour, give or take. But today it would definitely be on the short side.

Wilder looked so sexy in his well-fitted business suit. Then again, I thought he looked sexy in jeans and a T-shirt. Or a tuxedo. Gosh, and the photos I'd seen of him in rugby shorts—those thick thighs. And don't even get me started on how he looked naked. I *really, really* liked him that way best.

He'd watched my show before, though never right in front of me. So it was a little nerve-racking. Wilder quietly set his bag down and took off his suit jacket, being careful to stay behind the camera while I cleared my throat and spoke into it.

"Alright, everyone. I think it's time I opened up the discussion so you can tell me what you think about the list of rules the team at *Bride* magazine and I came up with for bachelor and bachelorette parties. But first, let's do a quick rundown of what we have, so you're ready to comment.

"Number one—The party shouldn't be held the night before the wedding. We don't want any hungover brides or grooms.

"Number two—No strippers. If you need to see another woman

or man naked one last time, maybe you aren't as ready to get married as you think.

"Number three—No destination parties, like Vegas or the Caribbean, that cost a small fortune. Weddings are already expensive enough for your bridal party."

I held up a finger. "Of course, if you live in Vegas or the Caribbean, or if you and your friends are all loaded and have private jets, then ignore this rule and have a great time.

"Number four—Do not, under any circumstances, leave the tab for the bride or groom to pay. This is a party where everyone attending pays for themselves and chips in to cover the guest of honor.

"Number five—Don't invite people not invited to the wedding.

"Number six—Don't plan something the bride or groom won't enjoy. Bridesmaids, if you love to gamble but the bride doesn't, no card night. Groomsmen, if you love to golf but the groom hates it, plan something else. This is their day, not yours.

"And last but not least, number seven—No videos! No one needs video of themselves dancing while tipsy, and things can be taken out of context."

I looked back up at the camera. "I'm going to open up the chat now and take a two-minute water break while you all start typing. I'll be right back!"

I hit the mute button, slipped off my headset, and stepped away from the desk. Wilder's eyes were so dark and his smirk so dirty, I was a little scared. I held up a finger in warning. "I only have two minutes."

He buried his face in my neck. "I can be quick."

"Oh my God!" I giggled and made a lame attempt to escape from his arms. "Definitely not. I'll be done in fifteen minutes, and then we can take our time."

Wilder stroked my face with his thumb. "Give me this mouth first. I've missed you."

Our teeth clanked together because I couldn't stop smiling while we kissed. The man made me melt. We made out like two teenagers for longer than two minutes. When I begrudgingly pulled back, my lips were swollen. I wiped lipstick from Wilder's mouth. "I missed you, too. But I gotta finish up. Why don't you get changed and get comfy?"

"Alright . . ."

The way he said it told me he had something up his sleeve, but I needed to get back on camera. I took my seat and turned the audio back on. Comments were already pouring in.

"Oh boy," I said. "I see we have a lot of thoughts on the subject." I scrolled for the first comment to read. Almost every viewer had something to say about rule number two—no strippers. I picked out a comment and read aloud. "JuneBride says her fiancé is watching with her right now, and he disagrees on the no-strippers rule. He thinks it's a tradition—the last hurrah and all in good fun. He says there's nothing wrong with looking; you just can't touch."

I didn't have to dig very far into the comments to find an opposing viewpoint. But I made the mistake of glancing *past* my computer screen when I went to speak. And found Wilder undressing—on the subject of strippers, he looked better than any I'd ever seen. I salivated at every carved indentation on his perfect chest. It was impossible to tear my eyes away. Especially when he got down to his boxer briefs, hooked two thumbs into the sides, and slid the material over his muscular thighs.

Oh.

My.

God.

I was live on freaking camera. I needed to say something—anything. But my mouth was dry, and swallowing wasn't easy. Eventually I cleared my throat and managed. "MariaBenz disagrees with your fiancé, JuneBride. She thinks having strippers at a bachelor or bachelorette party is juvenile and unnecessary. She says people who are ready to commit to one another should be celebrating their upcoming nuptials. Not . . ."

I again got sidetracked. This time it was because of the *slapping* noise—the one Wilder's dick made every time it hit his belly. He was naked, gyrating his hips like he was keeping an invisible hula hoop in place, and every time he thrust forward, his big penis slapped into his abs. It would've been hilarious to behold, if I wasn't totally turned on by the sight of him naked and semihard.

I really hoped none of my bosses were watching this episode, because this was about to be the quickest wrap-up in the history of wrap-ups. I forced my eyes away from Wilder and looked straight at the camera. "Well, as you can see, this is a hot topic, and one I think might be a personal choice for each couple. However, it's definitely something to discuss before heading out to plan those bachelor and bachelorette parties. We'll pick back up with these rules next time. That's it for today. Have a great week, everyone, and happy wedding planning!"

I clicked to end the show and fell back into my chair. "I can't believe you did that while I was live."

"You told me to get changed and make myself comfortable." He stalked over to my desk, pulled out my chair, and straddled my lap, still naked. "I was just doing what I was told."

"Oh yeah? Will you do whatever I tell you?"

His eyes darkened. "Fuck yeah. I'll do whatever you want."

I bit my lip shyly. "Alright. How about you . . ." I leaned to his ear and whispered, *"do the dishes."*

"Funny." I was quickly hoisted out of the chair and into the air. Wilder tossed me over his shoulder, fireman style. I couldn't stop giggling. He swatted my ass. "Just for that little tease, you're *not* getting whatever you want. I'm gonna *take* whatever I want." He dumped me unceremoniously in the middle of the bed. I bounced as he joined me and climbed on top.

Wilder kissed the underside of my chin. "You ended your show a little abruptly."

"I was distracted because of *your* show."

"For the record, you can't have strippers at your bachelorette party."

"Why not?"

"Because the thought of you looking at another man's junk makes me feel violent."

"Aww . . . That's oddly sweet. But that means you wouldn't be allowed to have strippers, either."

Wilder shrugged. "Why would I need to look at another woman, if I have you?"

My belly fluttered. It felt like I was falling down a rabbit hole with this man—one I was pretty sure I'd never climb out of if things didn't work out.

Wilder brushed his knuckles along my cheek. "Being with you is like waking up to Christmas morning every day."

My heart skipped a beat. "You scare me, Wilder."

"Likewise, sweetheart. But you're worth the risk."

"Oh my God!" my niece Olivia shrieked from the other room.

I ran into the kitchen and found her covering her eyes. Wilder stood in his boxer briefs, frozen, with a coffee mug in his hand. I gestured for him to go into the bedroom. Once the coast was clear, I spoke to my niece. "You can uncover your eyes now."

"Yes, but I think my retinas might be permanently scarred."

I cracked a smile. "I think what you got a peek at is pretty spectacular."

"He's like sixty." She took her hands away and promptly rolled her eyes. "Is Wilder your boyfriend or something?"

"Umm . . . It's new. Sorry. I should've locked the door."

Wilder strolled back into the room wearing jeans and a T-shirt. He picked up the coffeepot and nodded at Olivia. "Good to see you, kid. Don't you knock?"

"Don't you wear clothes?"

He poured a cup of coffee and leaned a hip against the counter. "Not when I sleep. Your aunt was kind enough to let me crash on her couch last night because I got in late."

She wasn't buying it. "Uh-huh, sure."

"Shouldn't you be at school?" he asked.

"I was just leaving, but Dad forgot to leave me lunch money."

Wilder pulled his wallet from his pocket and slipped out a bill, extending it to my niece. "Here you go."

"She doesn't need a *fifty*, Wilder."

"It's the only American bill I have."

Olivia smirked. "I'll bring him change."

I shook my head. "Like I haven't heard that a hundred times."

She tucked the fifty into her pocket. "I thought Lucas was coming in tonight?"

"He is." Wilder sipped his coffee. "I have a meeting, so I came a day early. I'm picking him up from the airport later. You two gonna hang out?"

"We want to."

"That can be arranged. *If* . . ." He tipped his mug to her. "You're not late to school."

"Whatever." She rolled her eyes again, but waved. "See you later, Aunt Sloane."

"I'll walk you out."

I pulled the door closed behind me. "I'm sorry you had to see Wilder half-dressed."

She shrugged. "I gotta go."

"Alright. Have a good day."

Olivia stopped two steps down and turned back. "Do you think his brother looks like that with no shirt on?"

Oh Jesus. "I don't know. And I hope you don't find out for another twenty years—when you're old enough. Now get to school."

I was still shaking my head when I walked back into my apartment. Wilder poured a second cup of coffee and added half and half before passing it to me.

"I think we might have a problem," I said.

"What's that?"

"She's hot for your brother."

He nodded. "I think the feeling is mutual. But I'll talk to him when I pick him up tonight, make sure he's not an ass to her."

"Thank you."

He sipped and looked at me over the brim of his mug. "I overheard you talking when I was getting changed. What's with the answer you gave when she asked if I was your boyfriend?"

"What do you mean?"

"You skirted the question. That's why I threw out that I'd slept on the couch. Do you think she's too young to know?"

"She's fourteen. Half the girls in her grade have had boyfriends already, unfortunately."

"So why the vague answer?"

"Because . . . I wasn't sure how to respond."

Wilder held my eyes for a few heartbeats before setting his coffee on the counter next to him. He closed the distance between us and locked his hands around my waist.

"We are, sweetheart." He ducked down so we were eye to eye. "Boyfriend and girlfriend, or whatever you want to call it."

My pulse raced like I was back in ninth grade and Eddie Anderman had asked me to the spring dance. I smiled. "Okay."

He pressed a kiss to my lips. "I have a meeting at ten. But I'm going to go visit Coach after. You want to meet him?"

I nodded. "I'd like that, boyfriend."

He chuckled and kissed my forehead. "My girlfriend is a goofball."

⟋

"Hey, Wilder." A nurse with a Caribbean accent and long, beaded braids smiled. "He made me do it."

"Do what?"

She chuckled. "You'll see."

Wilder took my hand, tugging me with him down the hall. "That's Lucinda. She's great. She's been here as long as Coach has. He has a big crush on her. The more his disease progresses, the less he hides it. She's a really good sport."

Coach's room was at the end of a long hall. On our way to the nursing home, he'd filled me in a little more about his old coach's dementia battle, so I walked in expecting to find an old man in hospital pajamas, hunched in a chair with his eyes glazed over. But I wasn't even close.

Coach wore a Hawaiian shirt and basketball shorts, blasted reggae music, and was dancing all by himself. He also had a full head of gray, beaded braids.

Wilder shook his head. "Now that's a new look . . ."

Coach grinned and patted his hair. "You like it? Lucinda's last boyfriend had braids. I thought it would help my chances."

"I think you've got a better shot at finding rhythm at seventy-five than you do with Luce, and that's saying something." He hugged his coach. "How are you, old man?"

Coach noticed me for the first time. His eyes perked up. "Now that's much better than the shitty pastries you usually bring me."

Wilder held up his pointer in warning. "Easy. No hitting on my girlfriend. This is Sloane."

Coach opened his arms for a hug. I was happy to oblige. "It's nice to meet you. Wilder told me all about you. You're the only thing he talks about when he calls lately."

Wilder shook his head. "Don't believe anything he says. It's all lies."

"She must be someone special," Coach noted. "Never brought anyone with you for your visit before."

Wilder caught my eye. "She is."

"Well, come sit." Coach turned down the radio. "Patty can bring us some lunch on the patio."

Wilder whispered, "Patty was his wife. She died ten years ago."

He'd told me Coach often slipped in and out of current and past time, but I didn't realize he would seem so lucid doing it. I thought Patty was someone who worked here, the way he'd said it.

"You feeling up for a walk before Patty brings us lunch?" Wilder asked.

"Yeah. Sure."

Wilder helped Coach put on sneakers, and then the three of us took a walk. On the way out, Wilder let the front desk know what we were doing.

"Did you see I signed Santiago?" Wilder asked.

"Who?"

"Left flanker from California. We talked about him when I called last week."

"Oh. Yeah, right." Coach nodded, but I wasn't sure he remembered anything.

We walked around the building on a path for the next hour. At times, conversation flowed and there was no doubt Coach's memory was there, but there were other moments when Coach would trail off midsentence, like he'd forgotten he was even talking. One thing clear as day, though, was the bond between these men. Eventually, Coach's steps became more of a shuffle, so we went back inside.

Wilder was down on a knee, unlacing a shoe when Coach yanked at the top of his hair. "You still using that girly yellow blow-dryer to make your hair fancy?"

Wilder shook his head with a smile. "Not anymore, Coach. Pretty sure you spend more time fixing those braids than I do on my hair these days." Wilder's eyes slanted to me.

I lifted a brow. "So the girly habits Lucas told us about aren't new then?"

He smiled and turned back to Coach. "I'm going to get going. You want me to help you into bed?"

"Yeah. Why not? Then I'll be ready when Lucinda finally comes around."

Coach's eyes fell to me briefly as Wilder pulled the covers up.

"I'll call you next week. Take care, alright?"

Coach put a hand on Wilder's bicep. "She's a nice girl. I'm glad you finally moved on."

I waited until we got to the car before poking around. "Was Coach referring to your high school girlfriend when he said he was glad you moved on?"

Wilder started the car, looking straight ahead. "No. He's just confused."

24

WILDER

TEN YEARS AGO

"I'm so bored." Whitney sighed.

She'd been swiping through social media reels for the last hour, starting and stopping catchy little tunes as I tried to study, so it was on the tip of my tongue to say something snarky. But then I looked over at her propped-up feet and swollen ankles and felt bad. I closed my textbook. "What do you feel like doing?"

Her eyes lit up. "Let's go shopping."

"Again?"

She rubbed her swollen belly and pouted. "We need a lot of things."

It would be easier to finish studying when she went home later anyway. The sounds from her phone were too distracting to concentrate.

I offered my hand to help her up, then pulled her against me once she was standing and wiggled my brows. "Unless you'd rather do something else . . ."

She frowned. "It's hard to be in the mood when you're fat."

"You're not fat. You're five months pregnant." I squeezed her ass. "And I think you're sexy this way."

She rolled her eyes. "Let's just go to the mall."

Whatever. We hadn't had sex or even fooled around in at least a month, but she was going through a lot with hormone and body changes—changes I didn't have to go through, so I didn't complain. Though her excuse that she felt fat or ugly felt flimsy when she liked herself enough to buy a new wardrobe and makeup every week. But maybe I was just cranky from studying and listening to the player announcements for the England rugby team—announcements that would no longer include my name for next season.

Two hours later, my mood wasn't much better as I carried a half-dozen department store bags through the mall, trailing behind Whitney. At least her spirits seemed higher. We stopped in the food court, and I got us each a big pretzel. I suggested she brush off the salt since her ankles were swollen, but that didn't go over well. When Whit and I had first gotten together, everything was easy. We'd seemed to agree on most things. We had sex all the time and didn't argue. She almost always had a smile on her face. But that had changed over the last few months, and I was beginning to wonder if it was the pregnancy or if we didn't get to know each other well enough and hadn't made it past the honeymoon phase in our relationship until now.

Whitney finished her pretzel and crumpled up the wax paper it had been served on. "Let's go to Sephora and then Baby Gap."

We'd just gone to the makeup store a week ago, and I couldn't remember the last time she'd even worn makeup. Yet I bit my tongue again and stood. "Sure."

The line at the cash register was a mile long, so I got in it while she finished shopping. On our way out, I noticed a guy standing in front of the store, directly across the way. He looked familiar, and it seemed like he was watching us. I'd noticed him earlier, too, when we were at the food court. But I chalked it up to a guy checking out Whitney. Pregnant or not, she turned heads. I lifted my chin, gesturing across the way.

"Do you know that guy?"

She looked over, but the guy had already started walking. "No. But let's go."

"I thought you wanted to go to Baby Gap?"

"My feet are too swollen."

I wasn't about to complain. I hated the damn mall. Though in hindsight, maybe her *not* wanting to finish maxing out my card at the mall again should've been a hint that something was off.

"Will you rub my feet before you go?"

I needed to get home and study, but ten minutes more wouldn't kill me. Whitney's studio apartment wasn't much bigger than my dorm room, and it was packed with crap, piles everywhere. I took a box of shoes and some unopened mail from the couch and patted the seat next to me. Her head drooped as I lifted her feet onto my lap and dug my thumbs into the ball of her right foot.

"Did you talk to your parents about dinner next week yet?" I asked.

She sighed. "My dad's too sick for that."

"I thought you said he was feeling better?"

"He was for a little while, but he's not now."

"Maybe he'll feel better by next weekend?"

"I doubt it."

My father was coming into town and wanted to meet Whitney's family. She'd already met my family twice, and they weren't the ones who lived locally. I hadn't met either of her parents or her brother yet. Come to think of it, the only friend I'd met of hers was Ashley, who we'd run into at the mall.

"I'd like to meet them before the baby comes . . ."

She pushed my hand from her feet. "I can't help it if he doesn't feel well. Chemotherapy isn't easy, you know."

My brows knitted. "I thought you said he'd finished his treatment."

"I didn't say that."

I was pretty certain she had, because she'd said it the day after *my* mother's last round of chemo. And I remembered commenting about the timing. "Are you sure?"

"Of course I'm sure." She stood. "Can we not talk about cancer? It's upsetting for me to think about."

I'd learned a lot about Whitney these last few months, the most important tidbit being that she had a *tell* when she lied. She talked faster than usual and tried to change the subject or walk away as quickly as possible—exactly like she was doing now. I was just about to call her on it, when she grabbed her stomach.

"Oh my God."

I jumped up. "What?"

She smiled. "I felt the baby move."

"Really?"

She reached for my hand and set it on the lower part of her belly. "Here. Let's see if it happens again."

We were both quiet for a few minutes, but I didn't feel anything. Then all of a sudden, I did—a subtle shift beneath my fingers— almost like a small ball rolling, pushing against her skin. My eyes widened. "I felt it!"

"Isn't it wild?"

I'd had five months for it to sink in that Whitney was carrying my child, and I was going to be a father. I thought it had. But something changed in that moment—and it hit me hard. *I'm going to be a dad. Soon.*

I looked down at my hand on her belly with a sense of wonderment. "That's our baby."

She laughed. "No shit, Sherlock."

I swallowed. "We need to find a place to live. A house with a yard."

"Us? You mean move in together?"

I nodded. "Shouldn't we? We're going to be a family."

Whitney smiled. "I'll start looking tomorrow."

25

SLOANE

"What time is your flight tonight?" I leaned closer to the mirror, brushing on mascara.

"Eight." Wilder came up behind me. He reached around and tugged the belt to my bathrobe. It fell open, revealing that I hadn't put on my bra yet, only my panties. He cupped a breast in each hand and squeezed, burying his head in my neck for a kiss. It felt good, but I was going to be late if I didn't hurry.

"Don't even think about it, Mr. Hayes. I have to get to work. I have a packed day, starting with a department meeting at nine."

"Mr. Hayes, huh?" He nipped at my earlobe. "I like it. I vote you stay home from work and we play asshole boss/naughty employee."

I turned to face him. Wilder didn't budge an inch, so we were practically nose to nose. "Another day. But I'm the boss, and you're the employee."

He grinned. "Yes, ma'am."

"I really need to get ready for work. And it's Wednesday, so tonight I have to relieve my dad at the bar at six."

"How about I call my dad and tell him you need the day off and we stay in bed all day instead?"

"I don't think so."

He pouted. It was adorable, but I still needed to get to work. So I ducked under his arm and went to my closet. "What are you going to do all day?" I yelled from inside.

"I have a meeting with an agent I can't stand at ten. He tried to get me to sign with him a dozen years ago. Now he's representing a player I want and being difficult. I think he's doing it on purpose because I turned him down."

I slipped on a navy dress and a pair of cream wedges and stepped out of the closet. "That's unprofessional."

He shrugged. "It is what it is. I'm meeting my dad for lunch after, probably about one o'clock. Why don't you come with us?"

I blinked a few times. "I can't do that."

"Why not?"

"Because then he would know."

Wilder's forehead wrinkled. "Know what?"

"About us."

"So?"

"It's where I work. I don't want anyone to know."

"For how long?"

"I don't know."

Wilder got quiet. I walked over and rested my palms against his chest. "If people at work know that I'm dating the boss's son, they're going to make assumptions and talk. That type of stuff sticks. They'll look at me funny even when we aren't seeing each other anymore."

Wilder pulled his neck back. "You're planning for the fallout from our breakup already?"

"No, that's not what I'm doing, but—"

He shook his head with a frown. "Whatever. You should get going. I wouldn't want you to be late for work."

"Wilder . . ."

"It's fine."

I sighed. "I didn't mean it like that."

"Whatever."

"I don't want to fight with you before you go back to London tonight."

"Who's fighting?" He kissed my forehead, the same as he had *before* we were a couple. "It's no big deal."

Still, I could see in his eyes that I'd hurt him. But I was going to miss my meeting if I didn't hurry. So I nodded. "Okay. I'll talk to you tomorrow?"

"Yep. I'll lock up behind me."

Ten hours later, I still hadn't shaken the uneasy feeling after leaving things the way I had with Wilder. We'd had such a great week, too—spending time alone, hanging out and playing board games with Olivia and Lucas, and we'd even had dinner with both my brothers. And here I wouldn't even go to lunch with his dad. I felt like such an idiot for the way I'd handled things this morning. I walked into Carrick's, stuffed my purse under the bar, and wrapped an apron around my waist.

"Hey, Dad."

"Hey, sweetheart. Everything okay?"

"Why do you ask?"

He shrugged. "Your smile isn't reaching your eyes."

"Just tired."

A group of regulars came in, firemen from the twenty-third. I walked over and helped them while Dad went back to watching a horse race with his old partner. He hollered when one of them won, and Frank made a face and passed cash over the bar. The two of them would've bet on an ant race if they could see things that small anymore.

Sometime later, I went to the back and grabbed a rack of clean glasses to stock behind the bar. Frank called it a night, so Dad walked over to help me. His tremors were really bad lately.

"When's your next doctor's appointment?" I asked, sliding a stemmed glass into the rack over my head.

"Soon. When's your eye exam?"

"Huh?"

He pointed down at the glasses. "Those aren't clean."

I did a double take. "Oh."

Dad leaned on the bar. "You usually put half of them back even when they *are* clean because they aren't clean *enough* for your liking. You want to tell me what's going on? Because I'm not going to leave my pretty daughter alone in a bar full of men when she's not on her game."

I put the dirty glass back into the crate. "I'm fine. Just a little distracted, I guess."

"That have anything to do with a certain rugby player I saw coming out of the building again this morning?"

I sighed. "I made Wilder feel bad earlier. He asked me to go to lunch with his dad, and I said I didn't want people at work to know I'm dating the big boss's son. Which I think is reasonable, but it came out wrong, and it seemed more like I was concerned about how people would view me after we split up—like I expected we would. Wilder said he wasn't mad, but I could tell it upset him. And he's at the airport by now, on his way back to England, so it's not like I can take the subway and apologize in person."

"Sometimes we say what we mean, even when we don't mean to, honey."

I nodded. "Honestly, that's exactly what I did. I think I just expect things to not work out, based on my past experiences. And that's not fair to put on Wilder."

"We all bring baggage to a relationship. The important thing is what you do with it. You can carry it with you forever, or you can unpack it. The choice is yours."

I nodded. "That's a really good analogy. Would you mind staying for a few minutes more, Dad? I'm going to go in the back and call Wilder, see if I can catch him before he takes off."

"Take all the time you need, sweetheart."

But the phone rang three times and went to voicemail. Wilder should still have had a while before he took off, so I hoped he wasn't ignoring my call. When voicemail picked up, I decided to leave him a message.

"Hey. It's me. I was hoping I'd catch you before you boarded. I wanted to apologize again for what I said this morning. It's been bugging me all day." I took a deep breath. "I'd like to get to know your dad better. Maybe next time you're back in New York we can have that lunch? Or maybe I can make you both dinner at my place?" I paused. "Anyway . . . give me a call if you have time before you take off, okay? Talk to you soon."

I swiped to end the call and tucked my cell into the pocket of my apron. I hoped I hadn't screwed things up with Wilder because of my experience with Josh. That man had really left his mark. Maybe I should call the jerk back after all and give him a piece of my mind.

Though when I walked back out to the bar, I realized a call wouldn't be necessary. Because my ex-fiancé had just walked through the front door.

Not surprisingly, Dad spotted him first. He'd been putting on his jacket and stilled. I wasn't sure where to go first, but I ended up waving to Dad to tell him everything was okay and walking over to Josh.

"What are you doing here?"

He smiled. "Hey. I took a chance that you still worked Wednesday nights."

"I see that. But *why* did you come?"

"I want to talk to you, and you won't return my calls or messages."

"That's because I don't have anything to say to you."

Josh frowned. "Can we just talk for a few minutes?"

I glanced over at Dad. Josh did the same and waved, but Dad didn't return the sentiment.

"He's still pissed, huh?"

"Did you ever really know my father at all? There's no coming back from leaving his daughter standing at the altar. You're lucky Will and Travis aren't here tonight."

Josh looked down. "Yeah, of course. Should I go over and apologize again?"

"No. I think you should say what you came to say and leave before he chases you out."

He nodded. "Can we sit for a minute?"

I sighed. "Fine. Go sit in a booth. I need to talk to my dad first."

"Okay."

Dad already had the baseball bat on top of the bar. I shook my head. "You don't need that."

"Jury is still out on that one. What's he doing here?"

"I'm not sure. He said he wants to talk to me."

Dad clapped the bat to his hand. "He can talk to me instead."

I smiled sadly. "It's fine. I'll talk to him. Why don't you go home?"

"I'll leave after he does."

I knew there was no point in arguing with my father about that. But his tremors got worse when he was stressed, so I needed to make it fast. "I won't be long."

Josh was seated in a booth with his hands folded. I took the seat across from him.

"What's going on that you needed to speak to me?"

"Do you know what today is?"

"Wednesday?"

"The date?"

I had to think about it. "July thirt—" Halfway through, I realized this was the day we'd met and the day he'd proposed two years later. But it no longer meant anything, and I was proud of myself that I hadn't even noticed. I shook my head. "Is that why you're here? To remind me of the date? Because my dad's tremors get worse with stress, and him seeing you sitting here is not helping. So why don't you get to the point?"

"I'm sorry." He looked down. "I've been trying to figure out what to say to you for a long time, so you would think I'd have something more eloquent planned, but the only thing that sums it up is . . ." He looked up and met my eyes. "I miss you, Sloane."

I felt my face twist. *"What?"*

"I do. More than anything. I made a giant mistake leaving the church that day. I was immature and scared, worried I was making the wrong choice like my parents did, and I couldn't see that it didn't matter what else was out there because the best thing in the world was right in front of me all along."

Turmoil flared inside of me. Not that long ago, I would've given anything to hear those words. But now I just felt anger. He had no damn clue how much damage he'd done. I'd almost missed out on the best thing to happen to me because of how scarred I was, and here he was worried about himself.

"What happened to Monica?" I asked.

"We broke up."

And there it was. I folded my arms across my chest. "Oh. So she dumped you and now you don't want to be alone?"

Josh shook his head. "It's not like that at all. I broke up with her. It was four months ago, actually. But I didn't want to come to you until I got my head straight and was sure. I know how much I hurt you, Sloane. I didn't want to risk doing it again." He paused. "I started seeing a therapist."

I didn't reply. I just stared into his face blankly. After everything he'd said, I felt . . . nothing. Though that wasn't completely true. Maybe I felt a little appreciation. Because if Josh hadn't been a complete jerk, I would be married to him right now, and then I wouldn't have met Wilder.

But Josh must've taken my silence as contemplation, because he leaned closer. "We can start slow, Sloane. I know I'll have to win your trust back. But if you give me another chance, I promise you won't regret it."

Just then, the front door opened and a big group of familiar faces walked in—there had to be eight or ten of them, all cops. "I have to go."

"I'll wait for you."

I stood. I was about to tell him to go home, not to bother waiting—not today or for me—but when I opened my mouth, I realized one of the guys who'd come in with the group was not a cop. And that man was currently staring right at me.

Wilder.

I walked to him without saying anything more to Josh. "What are you doing here?"

"I didn't want to leave things the way they were this morning. So I took Lucas to the airport and made sure someone could pick him up on the other side. Then I grabbed a cab here." Wilder looked to the table where I'd been seated, a few feet away. He lifted his chin. "Who's that?"

I swallowed. "Josh."

"Josh, your ex?"

I nodded. "He just stopped by. I had no idea he was coming."

Wilder's jaw flexed.

The crowd that had just come in was rowdy. I needed to go help

Dad. "Could you—would you give me two minutes? I need to help behind the bar."

Wilder nodded and pointed to the seating area with booths, where Josh was seated. "I'll wait over there."

I hesitated, but he couldn't possibly mean he was going to wait *with* Josh. He meant the seating area in general . . .

"Go help your dad," he said. "I'll be fine."

I nodded, but by the time I'd made my way across the room and taken my position behind the bar, Wilder was sliding into the seat across from Josh. *"Oh shit."*

Dad heard me and looked over. He grinned. "Guess I won't have to take out the trash after all. Wilder will do it for me."

A heavy, sinking dread formed in the pit of my stomach as I took orders and mixed drinks. I poured half a beer from the tap onto my hand, because I couldn't stop looking over at the two men in the booth long enough to see what I was doing. Wilder's face was stern as he spoke. I couldn't see Josh, but I knew I needed to get back over there. A few minutes later, everyone who'd just come in had their first drink.

Dad looked at me. "Go. I got it."

"Thanks, Dad."

As I approached the table, Josh stood. He looked like someone had run over his dog. The smile he attempted failed miserably, and his eyes went briefly to Wilder before returning to me. "I'm going to head out. Call me if you want to talk, okay?"

I nodded, feeling bad, though I knew I shouldn't at all. "Take care, Josh." My mind was jumbled, my nerves still a tangled mess as I slid into the seat my ex-fiancé had vacated.

Wilder studied me for a moment. "He came to tell you he wants you back."

The words were a statement, not a question, though I felt the need to confirm and nodded. "I had no idea he was coming."

"He's been calling and texting you, and you never answered."

"That's because I'm not interested in what he has to say."

Wilder took a deep breath before looking into my eyes. "You sure of that?"

"Very." I reached across the table and held out my hand. I was grateful Wilder didn't hesitate to take it. "I'm sorry about this morning," I said. "I called you and left a message, but even if you already listened to it, I want to say it again in person. I'd like to spend time with you and your dad."

"You don't have to, if you're not ready."

"I am, and I want to. This morning had nothing to do with how I feel about you and our relationship, and everything to do with my own insecurities, which was wrong. Again."

Wilder smiled and squeezed my hand. "Okay."

"Are we good? You believe me that I had no idea Josh was going to show up, right?"

"Of course I do. Why wouldn't I?"

"I thought I was going to have a heart attack when you sat down across from him. What were you guys talking about anyway?"

"I told him politely that I'd break every bone in his body if you didn't want to talk to him and he harassed you."

"Oh boy. What did Josh say?"

"I have to give him credit, the guy has balls. He asked what I would do if you did want to talk."

Wow, yeah. That was ballsy. Josh wasn't small, but he was no match for Wilder. "How did you respond do that?"

Wilder shrugged. "I told him you make your own choices, and if that's what you want, then that's what you want. But if he ever hurt you again, I'd be back to break every bone in his body."

My heart fluttered. This was the type of man I wanted—one who put my choices first, even when my decision wasn't his first choice. It reminded me of how my dad had always treated my mom, and that meant the world to me. I got up and went around to the other side of the booth, parking my ass on Wilder's lap with my arms locked around his neck. "I don't want to talk to Josh. Being with you is like having Christmas every day."

"Are you stealing my lines, Cupcake?"

I laughed. "I am."

He pressed his lips to mine. "I guess that's fair, love. Because you've stolen my heart."

26

WILDER

No . . . don't do it.

A devilish voice played inside my head. *Why not? You'll make her feel good. Do it. Do it, you pussy.*

My eyes rose from Sloane's exposed tits to her face. She looked so peaceful sleeping. And it was only five in the morning here in New York. My internal clock had me up extra early on a Saturday because I'd only flown back in last night. I'd always racked up a lot of frequent-flier points going between London and the States, but the last few months had been nonstop. This time it had been a little over a week, but I couldn't seem to spend more than a few days away from Sloane unless business forced me elsewhere. Each trip back home became shorter and shorter so I could get here faster.

I looked over at my sleeping beauty again. God, I wanted to be selfish. Climb on top, sink deep inside, and return to my happy place. But she liked her sleep. And she was the kind of woman who made you want to do the right thing—day in, day out, every day. Even when I wasn't with her or she was sleeping with her tits calling my name. So instead of waking her, I snuggled in and tried to fall back asleep.

I was just about knocked out when an alarm went off—a high-pitched chirping. I jumped out of bed, thinking it was some sort of fire alarm and I needed to get us the hell out of here. When Sloane's eyes opened, she sat up calmly and reached over to her nightstand. "Sorry."

"You set an alarm?"

She shook her head. "It's my insulin pump. It has an alarm."

"Is everything okay?"

She pushed a bunch of buttons and fell back into bed. "Yeah, it's been happening every once in a while, and I have to reset it."

I raked a hand through my hair. "Shit. Okay."

"Sorry it woke you."

I climbed back into bed, smiling at my girl. "It's alright. I almost woke you, so we're even."

She laughed and turned on her side, tucking two hands under her cheek. "Why did you almost wake me?"

"Because I woke up wanting to do very bad things to you."

Sloane bit her lip. "Like what?"

"Like spread your legs and feast."

"Oh my." She giggled. "That doesn't sound very bad to me."

I guided her onto her back and climbed on top, dropping a kiss on her chin. "Just like Christmas morning . . ."

I spent the next hour opening my gift and playing with my favorite toy.

—

Later that morning, Sloane was in the shower while I sat at the kitchen table with my second cup of coffee, sorting through emails on my phone. Since I was just visiting for the weekend, I hadn't brought my laptop. Andrew had sent me a forty-seven-page contract to review, and the thought of reading it on my little device gave me a headache. I wondered if Sloane would mind if I left a laptop here? Maybe some shoes and a shaving kit, too. On my last trip, I'd been rushing to catch an earlier flight from London and only packed one dress shoe to wear with my suit. I wound up having to put on sneakers—a look I didn't particularly like, but it was popular with athletes so at least no one looked at me too strangely. Maybe she could leave some things at my place, too, make it convenient until we moved in together.

My finger froze on my phone screen when I realized what I'd just thought—*until we moved in together. Holy shit.* Six months ago, if a woman left her *umbrella* at my place, it freaked me out. It meant I had an obligation to see her again, if only to return it. And now, I wanted Sloane's shit in my place. Was I nuts that I wanted her

self-help books piled on my nightstand, wanted her wedding magazines strewn all over the counters, wanted her gentle snore to be
the first sound I heard each day when I woke up, even wanted her—

Thump.

A sound echoed from down the hall.

"Sloane?" I stood and started toward the bathroom. "Babe? Was
that you?"

No answer. A sick feeling formed in the pit of my stomach. I
didn't like it. Didn't like it one bit. When I got to the door, I knocked.

"Sloane? Are you okay?"

But that feeling in my belly didn't have much patience, and I
didn't wait more than two seconds for an answer before I busted in
the door. My heart stopped.

"Sloane!" She was on the floor, slumped into a ball, eyes rolled
back into her head as her body twitched—short, jerky movements
like someone kept shocking her with bursts of electricity. I ran into
the shower, water pouring down on both of us, and lifted her. It
dawned on me as I stepped over the lip of the tub that maybe I
shouldn't have moved her. Was a seizure like a fall, and you should
leave the person exactly where they are? I had no fucking idea, but
she was in my arms already so I kept moving—out of the bathroom
and into the bedroom. Setting her on the bed, I didn't want to take
my hands off of her but I needed to call 911.

Thirty seconds into talking to the operator, the twitches stopped.
"She's not seizing anymore!"

"That's good. Medical attention is on its way. Has your girlfriend ever had a seizure before?"

"Not when I was with her."

"Do you know if she hit her head recently?"

Fuck. Was I too rough this morning and it smacked against the
headboard? "Maybe? I'm not sure."

"Is she a diabetic?"

Oh shit. *The alarm!* In my panic, I'd forgotten all about it. I
hadn't even led with that information when the 911 operator asked
me if I knew what happened. "Yes! And her pump alarm went off
this morning."

Sloane's eyes fluttered open. I held my breath while she stared into space for a solid minute. Eventually her vision came into focus, and she tried to lift her head. "What happened?"

I held my hand up. "Don't move. You had a seizure."

"Where am I?"

"Home. You were in the shower when it happened. You fell."

She reached up and rubbed her wet hair. "My head hurts."

"You probably banged it on the tile when you went down."

"My cell. Can you get my cell?"

"I don't want to leave you."

"It controls my pump."

I'd completely forgotten I was still on the phone with 911 until the woman on the other end spoke. "Sir, the paramedics are pulling up now. Why don't you stay with your girlfriend? You can grab her cell when they get to you."

"Okay, yeah."

A minute later, there was a knock at the door. I was glad the paramedics let themselves in because I wasn't leaving Sloane's side.

"We're back here," I yelled. "In the bedroom."

As footsteps approached, I realized for the first time that Sloane was still completely naked. *"Shit."* I ripped the sheet from the bed and wrapped it around her just as two paramedics walked in, followed by a half-dozen firefighters. I was confused as to why there were so many people, until one of the firemen knelt next to the bed.

"You're Will's little sister?"

Sloane nodded.

"You're going to be fine. Your brother's on a call, so we didn't let him know because we don't want his head elsewhere when he's fighting a fire. But we got you now."

One of the two paramedics working on her tore open the Velcro blood-pressure cuff. "Low but stable."

The other guy pricked Sloane's finger and tapped a dot of blood onto a testing strip before sticking it into a handheld machine. The number fourteen came up. I had no idea if that was good or bad, until the guy frowned. "Let's give her a gel pack orally now. We'll start an IV with fifty-percent dextrose in the bus on the way to the hospital."

Less than a minute later, they were carrying Sloane down three flights of stairs on a stretcher and loading her into the back of an ambulance. I went to climb in with them, but one of the guys held his hand out. "You'll have to follow to the hospital in a car or taxi."

The older fireman rolled his eyes. "It's the captain's little sister, jackass."

"Oh . . . okay." He put his hand down. "Right. Come on in."

The older guy smiled as I hopped in. "You should've seen your face. I should've let you kick his ass just for fun."

The hospital was a ten-minute drive with lights and sirens blaring. They took Sloane in through the ER, but wouldn't let me go into the treatment area with her. So I found myself a seat in the waiting room and waited.

The nurse at the desk had told me they'd call me after the initial exam, but that was forty-five minutes ago now, and I was freaking out. I went up to ask if I could see Sloane for a third time.

"Sir, I still don't have an update for you."

I held up Sloane's cell phone. "Could you at least give her this? It reads her insulin pump, and the doctors might need the history."

The woman sighed, but slid the glass window open and took it. A few minutes later, she opened the actual door. "Mr. Hayes?"

I practically ran over.

"Follow me. Your friend is in bed eight."

The emergency room was a big, open space with a nursing station in the middle and glass rooms around the perimeter with numbers on top. I spotted Sloane's hair as we walked. The muscles in my neck loosened slightly, seeing her sitting up in bed. She was hooked up to an IV and a bunch of monitors, and she looked a little pale, but she was alive. I rushed to her side and took her hand.

The grumpy admitting clerk smiled and shut the door behind her.

"Are you okay?"

Sloane nodded. "My blood sugar went low. But I'm fine. I'm sorry if I scared you."

"Is that why the alarm went off this morning?"

"I guess I shouldn't have ignored it. But I've gotten so many false alarms lately, and it always just needs to be reset."

I frowned. "Until it doesn't."

"Sorry."

I lifted her hand and kissed it. "You scared the crap out of me. How's your head?"

"It feels a little better. But they're making me get X-rays and a CAT scan since I lost consciousness and don't know how hard I hit my head. But the headache can be from the seizure itself, too."

"Have you had seizures before?"

"A few times. But not in years."

"I had no idea what to do. I felt so damn helpless."

She smiled. "You did fine. You found me and got medical help. That's always the safest bet."

"I sort of broke your bathroom door lock."

Her smile widened. "It's okay."

While Sloane seemed to think everything was back to normal, I couldn't shake my worry. What if I hadn't been there? She could've been in the bathtub instead of the shower and drowned.

I dragged a hand through my hair. "I can't stay in London."

"You mean when you go back on Monday?"

I shook my head. "No. I don't want to be that far away from you."

Sloane's eyes went soft. "That's really sweet. But I'm fine, really."

"I don't care. Maybe—"

Whatever I was about to say was interrupted by a half-dozen firemen in full gear marching through the ER. Her brother Will was leading the charge. His face was black with soot, as were a few of the others.

"You alright, Peaty?" he asked from the doorway.

"I'm good. You didn't have to come. I told the other guys before they left."

"That crew is going to be running ten miles every morning and every night for not telling me you were brought in."

"They didn't want you to worry while you were busy."

"Don't care." Will seemed to notice me for the first time. He nodded. "What's up, man?"

"Just recovering from the heart attack your sister gave me when I found her passed out on the ground having a seizure."

Will shook his head. "What happened to your pump?"

"I reset it when the alarm went off."

"And didn't check your sugar?"

"I thought it was a false alarm. It's been happening a lot lately."

Will pointed two fingers spread into a V at his sister. "You and I are going to talk when you got out of here. That was dumb."

I smiled.

Sloane caught it out of the corner of her eye and squinted. "What are you happy about?"

I pointed. "I'm glad he's around. Because I feel the same way, but I'm a little afraid of you."

Will smirked. The nurse stepped in. "Umm . . . we love seeing all you boys, but I'm going to have to ask some of you to wait outside."

Will nodded. "You got it, Renee. How's my sister?"

"She's going to be just fine, Captain." The nurse thumbed at me. "Pretty sure this one is going to wrap her in bubble wrap when they leave, so I predict she'll be well taken care of."

I wished I *could* wrap her in bubble wrap after today. Maybe carry her with me everywhere I went, too.

Will laid a hand on my shoulder. "I gotta get the truck back to the house. You staying?"

"I'm not going anywhere anytime soon."

He leaned over and kissed his sister's cheek. "Check in within an hour or I send the entire house here."

"Yes, *Dad*."

The guys were barely gone before the nurse, Renee, came back in. "We're going to take Miss Sloane down to get a head scan in a few minutes. The admitting desk just called to tell me her dad is here. You won't be able to wait in the treatment area while she goes to CT, so maybe you can update her father out in the waiting room?"

I nodded. "Yeah, sure. How long will the scan take?"

"Probably an hour or less, depending on how backed up they are."

"Okay, thanks."

I kissed Sloane and walked out of the glass examination room with the nurse.

"You'll call me when she's back?"

She smirked. "Yes, I will."

"Alright. Take good care of her."

Out in the lobby, I found Harry standing at the desk. I walked over and gave him the details. He pointed to the exit. "It sounds like she's going to be a little while. Why don't we get some fresh air? You're looking a little green, son."

"That sounds good."

Outside, I bent over with my hands on my knees, gulping air.

Sloane's dad smiled. "You care about her a lot. I can see by how worried you are."

"I do. It was scary as hell finding her like that."

He nodded. "Sloane's mother, Lily, was diabetic. Only had a seizure once, but it was something I'll never forget. Saw plenty of medical emergencies in my years on the job. It's not the same when it's someone you love."

I blinked a few times. "Holy crap. I do love her."

"You sound like you're just figuring that out now." Harry chuckled. "Haven't you ever been in love before? I could have told you that two months ago, dumbass."

27

WILDER

TEN YEARS AGO

"Who the hell are all these women?" Andrew sat with me on the back deck of the new house I'd rented.

I shrugged. "I don't have a clue. Whitney and I have been together for more than seven months, and I've never seen ninety percent of them. Yet she introduced them all as her *bestie*."

"No offense, but there's a lot of tits and ass spilling out in there. It looks more like the pregame for a night out clubbing in Miami than a baby shower. I don't know where the hell to look when I'm inside without getting myself into trouble."

I chuckled. "I know. Why do you think I'm out here with your ugly ass?"

My buddy held up a bottle of beer. "Made a batch of cosmos and poured it in here for old times' sake. Got two shot glasses in my pocket, too. You in?"

"Definitely."

He poured two overflowing shots and passed me one. "To tits and ass."

I chuckled. "To having a healthy baby might be more appropriate. But yeah, let's go with that."

We sucked back the sweet shots, and Andrew gestured toward the house. "When my sister had her baby shower, the place was filled with aunts, moms, and grandmas. Half the guests were over fifty."

I nodded. "My mom was going to come with my aunt Lena, but she wasn't feeling up to traveling at the last minute."

"How's Charlotte doing?"

"She just started a second round of chemo, so not great. I'm going to visit next week before school starts back up and the baby comes."

"I'm sorry, man. She's too damn young to be sick. You got a lot on your plate right now." He looked around the yard. "This place is nice. Big. Must be costing you a fortune to rent."

I shrugged. "Whitney picked it out. I don't know why we need four bedrooms when it's just the two of us and a baby, but it made her happy."

"Any of her family here?"

I shook my head. "Her parents are divorced. Her dad's sick, and her mom lives in New Jersey. She said it was too far of a drive for a baby shower."

"Yet Charlotte was going to fly from England with cancer, and my sister drove in from Philly."

I frowned. "Yeah, I know."

"What's the deal with—"

The sliding door behind us glided open, stopping Andrew midsentence. His sister, Ella, stepped out onto the back deck. I hadn't seen her in a year, not since her graduation party. She'd just finished her first year of law school at UPenn.

"There you are," she said. "What are you two huddled up talking about?"

"Not much."

She sat on the arm of Andrew's chair. "Did you eat? The food is really good."

My buddy patted his belly, which was new. He'd put on a few pounds. The guy had always been able to eat whatever the hell he wanted and stay stick thin. "Two plates full."

"Did someone make all that food?" Ella asked.

"Nah. Whitney ordered it from a restaurant in Boston."

"*She* ordered it? Not whoever threw the party?"

"Her friends are all broke students, so I picked up the bill for the party."

"What about her family? Are they here?"

I side-eyed Andrew. "No, they couldn't make it."

"How do they feel about her being pregnant?"

I shrugged. "Okay, I guess."

"Do you like them?"

"I haven't met them yet."

"You haven't met them? Why not?"

I shook my head. "You're going to make a great lawyer. I feel like I'm being interrogated."

Ella leaned forward. "You mean *we're* going to make great lawyers."

My eyes shifted to Andrew. "You heard back from Yale?"

He smiled. "Yeah. I got in. Found out yesterday."

"Why didn't you tell me?"

He shrugged. "I don't know. We started talking about Charlotte's health and Whitney's dad being sick. It didn't feel like the right time to celebrate."

"That's crazy. It should've been the first thing you said when you walked in. Congratulations, man. I'm proud of you."

"Thanks."

Ella stood. "I'm going to get some wine. You guys want anything?"

I lifted my beer, which had been sitting on the ground, and swirled it. It was almost empty. "I'll take another. Thanks."

Andrew nodded. "Me, too. Thanks, Ella."

I leaned back in my deck chair with a sigh. "Who would've thought our lives would turn out like this? I'm old and practically married, and you're single these days."

Andrew smirked. "That I am."

I laughed. "Good for you. I'm happy for you. On all fronts."

"What about you?" He pointed with his beer toward the house. "Are you happy?"

"I'll be happier when I hear my name called in the draft in a few months."

He nodded. "It'll happen. But what about with the situation you got going on here? Are you happy with Whitney?"

I thought about it. "I'll be honest. I wasn't exactly thrilled when I found out she was pregnant. That wasn't part of my five-year plan. Hell, I'm not sure it was part of my ten-year plan. I had to make some hard decisions. But you know what?"

"What?"

I smiled. "I'm happy now. I talk to my kid every night. Sometimes I even sing to him."

"I've heard you sing. That's cruel."

"Shut up, knucklehead." I laughed. "But yeah, I'm excited to meet my kid soon."

"That's great. But you didn't answer my question."

"What was your question?"

"I asked if you were happy with Whitney?"

"I'm learning to be. We had some growing pains moving in together. Like, she's a slob and I like shit neat. But I'm happy she's having my baby." I paused. "I'm thinking about proposing."

"Really?"

"Why do you sound surprised? We're having a kid, for Christ's sake."

"I guess. But do me a favor and make sure you have a good prenup."

My skin prickled. "Seriously? I tell you I'm thinking about proposing and that's your reaction?"

"I'm just looking out for you. You guys come from two different worlds, man."

"So do we."

"Yeah. But I'm not entitled to half your assets if our friendship ends."

28

~

SLOANE

Dr. Connolly, the ER doctor who'd examined me when I first came in, knocked on the open glass door. "I think you're in trouble when you get home," she said.

My brows knitted.

She smiled and walked in. "Will called. He said you were supposed to call him with an update but hadn't."

"Shoot. I forgot. He's worse than an overprotective father, and I have one of those already."

"It's sweet."

"Not when you're sixteen and fifteen minutes late getting home, and he's waiting at the door with an axe."

"An axe is pretty intimidating. My brother just took off his shirt and flexed. He went to the gym every day, so he thought he was a tough guy. But in reality he was five-foot-eight and pretty scrawny. So my dates only humored him. I would imagine Fireman Will with an axe is a lot scarier. Smart of you to pick a boyfriend who looks like he could go toe to toe with him."

I smiled. "Wilder played rugby."

"I know. The nurses were all gossiping about a celebrity in the house. I don't follow sports, so I wasn't aware, but they tell me he's a big deal."

"That's what I've heard. Though I didn't know who he was when we met, either."

She pulled up a stool and sat next to me. "So, before we take you down to get your CAT scan, I wanted to talk about your blood test results." She shuffled some papers. "Your glucose concentration was where it should be by the time we tested here at the hospital since they did dextrose at fifty percent in the field. Which is good."

I nodded. "This is all my fault. My monitor alarm went off, and I ignored it. It's given me a few false alarms recently, and I was sleeping, so I didn't double-check my sugar. I should've. I know better. Though I've been eating well, so it shouldn't have gone so low."

Dr. Connolly nodded. "I know the reason your body is acting out of sorts."

"What do you mean?"

"Sloane, you're pregnant."

"Wha . . . what?"

"It's standard procedure, when a female patient comes in with diabetes, to do a full workup to see what's going on in the body. One of the tests is a pregnancy test. Yours came back positive." She offered a hesitant smile. "I figured it would come as a surprise since your intake sheet said your last menstrual period was only a month ago and you answered no when asked if you were pregnant."

"But . . . but . . . we used protection. Every time."

"No birth control is a hundred percent effective."

My head started to spin, and I thought I might pass out again. "Oh my God."

Dr. Connolly stood and pulled up the guard rail on the bed. "Take a deep breath, Sloane. Take a few deep breaths."

"Did you tell Will?" I wasn't sure why I'd asked that. Will was the least of my problems.

"No, of course not. I would never reveal your private medical information to anyone without your consent."

I shook my head, looking down. "I'm sorry. That was a stupid question."

"It's fine. Your privacy is both of our concern. Would you like to talk about it? We can discuss your options, or I can answer any medical questions you might have about diabetes and pregnancy. Or . . ." She paused and waited until I looked up. "Or we can talk about how you feel right now. I'm not just a doctor. I'm a woman, too."

I looked at her, tears welling in my eyes. "Wilder and I haven't been together that long. Less than a year ago, I was engaged to another man."

"I haven't been with anyone else since my ex." My heart pounded. "Oh God, how am I going to tell him? I already gave him a heart attack today. He was the one who found me seizing in the shower."

"Well, you don't have to tell him today. Maybe you need some time to absorb it yourself. You're entitled to that, Sloane."

I took a deep breath and nodded. "Yeah. That's true."

"You just experienced a major medical trauma—a seizure and possibly a concussion. That alone is a lot for anyone to handle. Things aren't going to change if you give yourself a few days—or a few weeks—however long you need to heal before you deal with this new medical condition."

I'd forgotten all about the possible concussion. "Is a CAT scan okay when you're pregnant?"

"Studies have consistently shown that the amount of radiation used in CT imaging does not cause any harm to a child. And only your head will be scanned, not your abdomen. But of course, the choice is yours."

I felt so lost. "What would you do?"

"You have a nice lump on your head, so we know you likely hit it when you lost consciousness. You're not having blurred vision, vomiting, or experiencing ringing in your ears, which are positive signs when considering the chances of internal bleeding. But I would have the CAT scan, to be safe. Cranial bleeding can be treated in its early stages, but it's dangerous if left untreated."

I nodded. "Okay. Let's do the CAT scan."

"Alright." Dr. Connolly stood. "I'll have the nurse bring you down, and I'll come check on you when you get back."

"Thank you."

She rested her hand on my arm. "You're going to get through this. I promise."

I wasn't sure she was right, yet I nodded. "Thanks, Dr. Connolly."

Over the next hour, I went through the motions of getting the scan. Thankfully, the technicians guided me on and off the table, because while I might've been looking at them while they spoke, I wasn't hearing a word.

Pregnant. I kept repeating it over and over in my head. *I. Am. Pregnant.*

I'd never even had a scare before. Not even when I was on the pill and messed up taking them once. *Thank God* this didn't happen when I was with Josh. I couldn't imagine having his baby. Would he have married me, and I'd be stuck in a marriage where my husband felt trapped and had questioned whether he was still in love with another woman? Or would I be raising a child alone?

Why the hell was I wasting time thinking about this when I needed to figure out how to tell the *actual* father of my child?

Wilder.

Oh God. How was he going to take the news? The man hadn't had a relationship of more than two months in over a decade. *Two months!* That's not even the first trimester! What if he left me and I was alone the rest of the time? I didn't want Will or my father in the delivery room with me. Would I be alone? Me and some nurse I'd just met in an understaffed hospital? She probably wouldn't even be able to hold my hand because she'd be too busy.

I started to hyperventilate as I waited in the little room for whoever was going to wheel me back to the ER. *The ER where Wilder is waiting!*

The technician who had done the scan walked back over. She started to say something, but when she got a look at me, she sprung to action, pushing a red button on the wall. "What's going on, Miss Carrick? Can you speak to me?"

I couldn't. I clutched my chest and took deep, painful breaths. A few seconds later, a team of people burst in.

"What happened?" someone demanded.

"I don't know. She was fine when I took her out of the machine. I went to call the transporter, and when I came back, she was hyperventilating."

"Let's get her on a monitor." I was suddenly flying down the hall on a gurney, back toward the ER. Dr. Connolly was in another patient's room as we passed, but she jumped out and followed.

"What happened?" she yelled.

The nurse kept moving. "I think it might be a panic attack, but I want to get her on the monitor to be sure."

Fifteen minutes later, after guided belly breathing and an oxygen mask, my breaths finally returned to normal. I lay back in the bed, feeling exhausted—like I'd run a marathon without a day of training.

Dr. Connolly smiled. "Well, you certainly know how to make an entrance."

"I'm so embarrassed." I shook my head.

"You have nothing to be embarrassed about. This has been a lot. I didn't have a seizure and a head injury this morning, and I'm pretty sure if someone told me I was pregnant right now, I'd be on the stretcher next to you, swiping your oxygen mask."

I was sure she was just being kind, but I appreciated it. "Thank you."

"The good news is, you scared the CAT scan department, so they read your images quickly. Everything looks clear. But I'm going to admit you, to be on the safe side. A night of observation after a head injury is never a bad thing. Plus, I'd like to get a tech to look at your monitor. With all the changes going on in your body, I want to make sure your pump is working properly." She typed into an iPad. "It might also give you some time to think, since they won't let visitors stay too long when you're on concussion protocol. You need your rest."

Being in the hospital did seem less scary than going home and having to face Wilder. I nodded. "Okay."

She typed more into her iPad and hugged it to her chest. "I hear there are two very anxious men bugging the desk clerk."

Oh God—my dad is here! I completely forgot they'd said that earlier. What was *he* going to say when he found out I was pregnant?

"Would you like me to let your visitors know everything is fine and it's going to be a bit longer before they can come back? I can tell them things are backed up, which is never a lie around here. That way you can rest a little more before seeing them?"

I shook my head. "Thank you. But I'm sure my dad is worried. I don't want to keep them waiting any longer than I have to."

"How about if we let them in for a bit to see you're okay with their own eyes? They won't be able to go up with you when you're being admitted to the floor, so if you want, I'll see if we can get a rush on that."

I let out a loud sigh of relief. "That would be great. Thank you."

"No problem. I'll give you a few minutes, then tell the nurse to bring them back."

Not long after, Wilder and Dad walked in. Each went to a different side of my bed.

"Are you okay?" Wilder took my hand. "Did you get the scan results yet?"

"How's your blood sugar?" Dad asked. "And why didn't the damn alarm go off? I'm going to get on the horn with that company and—"

I lifted a hand. "Dad, it was my fault. The alarm did go off, and I reset it."

My dad looked to Wilder. He nodded. "I didn't know any better. Now I do. Trust me, she won't be ignoring it again." Wilder turned to me. "What about the scan?"

"Everything came back clear."

He blew out a relieved breath, but I was one breath away from freaking out and blurting out words I wasn't ready to say.

"Are they discharging you?" Wilder asked.

"No. They're going to keep me overnight for observation."

"Good." He leaned down and kissed my forehead. "Better safe than sorry."

The two of them tag-teamed me with medical questions until Dad's phone buzzed. He held it up. "It's Will. I'm going to step out and take this, give him an update."

"Okay."

When it was just Wilder and me alone, he stroked my hair. "You scared the shit out of me, Cupcake."

"I'm sorry."

"It made me realize something."

"What?"

He looked into my eyes. "I . . . I . . . ." For a second I thought he was going to tell me he loved me. But then he cleared his throat. "I need to take a refresher first-aid class, CPR and stuff. The last time I took it was in high school."

"That's sweet. But I won't ignore the alarm again, so it's not necessary."

"Maybe not. But you never know what life's going to throw at you, and I want to be able to take care of you."

My heart melted. His concern also made me feel absolutely awful for not telling him I was pregnant. But the doctor was right, I needed a moment. Maybe two.

Dad came back, snapping his flip phone shut. He refused to upgrade to anything more. It made me smile. "Will's gonna come by after his shift ends."

"I'm fine. Tell him he doesn't have to. You should go, too, Dad. The bar must be opening soon."

Dad waved me off. "Eh. Frank lets himself in when I'm late."

My head was so jumbled and my heart was so heavy from keeping a secret that I found it difficult to talk. Luckily, a few minutes later, Dr. Connolly came into the room.

"We're going to be bringing Ms. Carrick up to the floor to admit her shortly," she said. "Visiting hours are eleven to eight, but visitors aren't permitted during transfers, so the doctors and nurses can get the patient settled in."

"How long will that take?" Wilder asked.

"Probably an hour or two. But I think Ms. Carrick really needs to get some rest. So maybe hold off coming back until this evening?"

Wilder frowned, but nodded. "Okay."

Dr. Connolly caught my eye before walking out. "I'll give you a few minutes to say goodbye."

"I'll come back later," Dad said. "Bring you something to eat." He kissed my cheek and nodded to Wilder. "I'll meet you outside."

Wilder looked stressed. "You gonna be okay? I hate to leave you."

I smiled. "I'll be fine."

He searched my eyes. "I don't know what I would've done if something had happened to you."

"I'm sorry I scared you."

"I'm just glad you're okay." He brushed his lips against mine. "I'll be back later."

"What time is your flight tomorrow?"

"Already changed it. I'm not going anywhere for a while."

God, I hoped that held true even *after* I told him the news.

⸺

"Hi." That evening, Dr. Connolly popped her head into my room upstairs. "Thought I'd check on you before I left. My shift just ended."

"Thank you." I sat up a little taller in bed. "I'm doing good. Blood sugar has been stable."

"Great." She walked in and pulled over the chair that sat in the corner. "But I was less worried about your glucose levels and more worried about your stress levels."

I sighed. "I didn't tell Wilder yet. He came back to visit and stayed until they kicked him out. But I couldn't bring myself to say the words."

"Have you been together a long time?"

I shook my head. "It's really new. We only met a few months ago."

"Do you love him?"

I nodded. "I think I loved him before I finally agreed to go out with him."

She smiled. "Played hard to get, huh?"

"In my case, it was more scared to get hurt, but yeah . . . it took me a while."

"I don't usually share personal information with patients, but I'm a single mom."

"Really?"

She nodded. "Long story, but my daughter's father is a good friend. We were residents together, and we quickly realized we were better off as friends."

"Is he involved with her?"

"He is. He recently got married, and his new wife is great. I look at it like my daughter's lucky. She gets three parents. Hopefully four someday, if I ever meet Mr. Right." She shrugged. "Anyway, after you left today, I was thinking a lot about how I felt when I found out, and I figured I'd come see if you wanted to talk. You may have already called a friend or spoken to someone, but just in case, I thought I'd pop in."

"I appreciate it. I was going to call my best friend earlier, but it didn't feel right telling anyone before Wilder."

She smiled. "I felt the same way. It took me about a week to tell Mark, and I think I might've only told him because I was going to explode if I didn't."

"Yeah, I'm not sure I'll make a week. I felt so guilty when Wilder was visiting tonight. Plus, he kept asking me what was wrong, and I hated lying to him. I'm in the hospital, so when I'm quiet, he thinks I'm in pain and not telling him so he won't worry, and that just makes him worry."

"He seems like a doting boyfriend."

"He is. He's the exact opposite of what I expected when we met." I sighed. "Do you have any advice for how to tell him?"

"I do, actually. Two pieces of advice. One, figure out what *you* want before you tell him. Did you see yourself having children?"

I nodded immediately. "Definitely. I want a family."

"So it's more about timing and circumstances then?"

"Yes."

"Do you have a good support team of family and friends?"

I thought of my brother raising a teenage girl alone, how we'd all rallied around him and moved into the brownstone to pitch in. That was my family. My eyes filled with tears—happy ones this time. "I have the best family support."

She smiled. "That's great. Well, it sounds like you want a family, and even if your boyfriend winds up not being in the picture, you could handle it. Those are two important things. Timing and circumstances—those are often out of our control, even with the best-laid plans."

I thought about my parents, how they'd done everything the right way—engaged, married, children. They'd had the timing and circumstances they wanted, yet look what happened. My mother didn't have the time she thought, and my dad wound up with different circumstances than they'd planned—as a single father of three. So really, sometimes the best-laid plans brought you to a different place anyway.

"Thank you," I told her. "I was definitely focusing on the wrong thing. I was so worried about what Wilder was going to want, I never stopped to ask myself what *I* want."

Dr. Connolly smiled. "I'll let you rest. You should get some sleep. Your body needs it after today."

"Thank you."

She stood. "Take care, Sloane. It was nice meeting you."

"You, too."

Dr. Connolly was halfway out the door when I realized something. "Hey, wait!"

She turned.

"You said you had two pieces of advice. What was the other thing?"

She smiled. "Don't tell him after you've just finished doing a colonoscopy together. He'll be white as a ghost, and then the poor patient will burst into tears, certain you're about to tell her she has cancer."

29

SLOANE

I looked in the mirror, turning sideways, and put my hand on my belly.

A week had gone by since my trip to the emergency room, and I still couldn't believe I was pregnant. Then again, it was easy to pretend I wasn't when no one knew—not even Wilder. I'd promised myself I'd tell him before he went back to England three days ago, but I'd chickened out at the last minute. It was eating me alive to keep such a life-changing secret, so I'd decided I was telling him tomorrow. I even wrote up what I was going to say and practiced it in front of the mirror. I just needed to get through the wedding to-night, let him enjoy the evening with his friends, and then it would be time.

Wilder and I were supposed to go the wedding together. I usu-ally traveled with Elijah, but his grandma had died unexpectedly three days ago. So he was back home in Utah until Sunday, and a substitute photographer was filling in. Then Wilder's flight had been delayed, so I was going by myself. It might've been the first time I was relieved he wasn't with me. The wedding would keep him busy, what with groomsmen duties and all, and it would be one less lie I'd have to tell when he inevitably asked why I was quiet. The excuse of a concussion and being tired was wearing thin. He was already asking if I should go see the doctor again, and I hated to make him worry.

I took one last look in the mirror. To settle my nerves today, I'd kept myself busy—doing my hair in loose curls, applying a full face of makeup that included sultry cat eyes, and painting my finger-nails and toes. My dress was gorgeous—green, as Wilder preferred, low cut, and with a slit higher than I'd normally wear. I looked good—really good even. Now if only the way I looked on the outside could seep into how I felt on the inside.

I took one last look down at my belly and wondered how much longer I'd fit into my stock of dresses. Heaving a deep sigh, I grabbed my silver clutch and headed for the door.

Tonight's wedding was at a venue I'd covered before for the magazine. It would've been my choice for my own wedding, if the price had been anywhere near what Josh and I could've afforded. I loved it so much that not even my nerves put a damper on the excitement I felt as we pulled up to the New York Public Library.

It was a magical building, especially at night with a red carpet rolled out on the grand marble staircase and twinkling lights adorning the handrails. I snapped a few pictures for the magazine's social media, then made my way inside.

"Hey, Sloane." Aiden, the groom from the very first wedding I'd attended for this project, stood in the rotunda. He was a nice guy, unlike his other half, Piper.

"Hi, Aiden. How are you?"

"Good." He pointed down a hall and smiled. "Just waiting for my lovely bride."

Lovely? To each his own, I guess. "How is Piper?"

He slipped his hands into his pockets and rocked from heel to toe. "Pregnant."

My jaw dropped, but I somehow managed to recover with a smile. "Wow. That's . . . well, fast. But great news. Congratulations."

He beamed. "Piper wanted to start a family right away. It happened the first month we tried."

"That's amazing."

Piper came down the hall. She had on a barely off-white dress—*at a wedding.* Yet she looked me up and down.

"Green." She pursed her lips in a judgy smile. "Again."

It was difficult to not roll my eyes. Instead, I forced an over-the-top smile. "Hello, Piper. How are you?"

"Pregnant."

"Yes. Congratulations." I pointed to her husband. "Aiden just told me the good news."

"I would've liked to have waited, but I didn't want to be pregnant at the same time as half of Aiden's friends. It was bad enough we all got married the same year. I'd like to at least have the limelight for myself and my baby instead of sharing it again."

That might be the first positive thing I'd felt about being pregnant . . . It would annoy Piper when she found out.

"I hear you and Wilder are still a thing?" she said, narrowing her eyes.

I nodded. "We're together, yes."

"Then I guess congratulations are in order for you, too. You've held on to him longer than the rest of them."

This woman was really something. I couldn't even muster a good fake smile—she got the plastic one. "I should get going to the bridal suite."

I was thankful she wasn't one of the bridesmaids, so I didn't have to be around her anymore. Though when I walked into the bridal suite and saw *a sea* of the same blue dresses, I wondered if she was the *only* guest who wasn't part of the bridal party. The room also smelled like the Sephora perfume department the week before Christmas. It made me a little nauseous.

"Hi." I looked around and spoke to an attendant. "I'm a writer for *Bride* magazine. I'm covering the wedding tonight for a feature. Is the bride here?"

"She's in the next room with the rest of the bridal party."

"The *rest* of the bridal party? How many are there exactly?"

The woman laughed. "Twenty-two bridesmaids. Apparently that's the bride's lucky number. Counting the groomsmen and the bride and groom, there are forty-six in the wedding."

"Wow." *Note to self for a future YouTube episode: How many brides-maids is enough?* I'd have to text that to myself so I wouldn't forget. "Did you happen to see a photographer from the magazine?" I asked her. "I'm meeting someone, and I'm not sure what they look like."

"I think he's already in with the bride. But to be honest, I've lost track of where everyone is because there are so many people."

With a nod, I took a deep breath and went in search myself. I'd been expecting the worst—a bride with twenty-two bridesmaids must be a diva—but I was pleasantly surprised. Marley seemed lovely. It turned out her family was a foster-care host, and most of the bridal party were her foster siblings from the last two decades. She didn't want to leave anyone out since she considered them all family. I'd misjudged that one. The hour I spent getting to know everyone and working with the substitute photographer was pretty fun.

As the bridal party lined up for the ceremony, I realized I hadn't even thought about the fact that I was pregnant. At least until a hand wrapped around my stomach. Wilder hauled me against him. "There's my girl." His hot breath against my neck sent chills across my body.

I turned. "Hey. You made it."

He pressed his lips to mine. "I missed you."

I smiled. "It's only been three days."

"Three days too long."

The music playing in the chapel stopped, and I thought they might be getting ready to start the wedding march. "I'd better take my seat."

"See you after the ceremony."

I always tried to sit toward the back of the crowd, not wanting to take a better seat than a real guest. But I'd lingered in the bridal suite too long, and now there were only seats left toward the front. Mine had a clear view straight to Wilder once everyone had taken their places, and I felt him watching me throughout the ceremony. There was a warmth in his gaze that I hadn't noticed before, and it made me think maybe . . . just maybe he might not be upset with my news.

That was a dangerous thought to have. I'd readied myself for the worst response—that he wanted nothing to do with me or the baby. Because I could handle being happily surprised. But I wasn't sure I could handle allowing myself to believe things could work out and then being disappointed.

Though the seed had been planted now. And all I could do for the next forty-five minutes of stolen glances and exchanged smiles was water it and watch it bloom.

Maybe he would be happy.

Maybe he felt the same way about me as I felt about him.

The length of time you're with someone wasn't really important. When you know, you know.

Then I started to picture it—all the dreams I'd had as a young girl and had given up after Josh.

A wedding. My niece as a junior bridesmaid. Lucas as a junior usher. Flowers. A new dress. Maybe a honeymoon somewhere tropical. A house—a picket fence. A yard. A dog, maybe two. Doctor's appointments together where we'd hold hands and stare at the sonogram screen in awe together.

Maybe . . .

Just maybe.

I was still daydreaming when the ceremony ended. I didn't even snap out of it during the post-ceremony bridal pictures. At one point, I caught Wilder watching the bride and groom. His eyes slanted to mine as if to say, *You'll be my bride one day.*

Apparently the seed I'd planted was ivy—because it just kept growing and growing. And I allowed it. This had been the most stressful week of my life, and I needed a little breather. Wilder made it easy. He seemed to be in a particularly playful mood tonight, all lovey-dovey.

Once wedding-party duties were done and the reception was underway, Wilder led me out to the dance floor. He took one of my hands in his and the other wrapped around my waist and tugged me close.

"I love you in green. You look beautiful," he said.

I smiled as we swayed to the music. There had to be three hundred people in the room, but the way Wilder looked at me made me feel like it was just the two of us. "Thank you. And you look handsome. With most men, a tuxedo wears them, but you wear the tuxedo."

"I have no idea what that means, but I'll take it as a compliment."

I laughed. "It was meant that way."

Usually when I was this close to Wilder, what I saw in his eyes was heat—not that I faulted him for that. My body lit on fire when the man stepped into the room. But tonight, something was different. I saw more.

Wilder shook his head. "I really don't know what I would've done if anything had happened to you."

I smiled. "Well, you're not going to have to find out, because I'm fine."

"Maybe. But it was a wake-up call, a reminder that life is short, and I don't want to have regrets."

"What would you regret?"

He looked into my eyes. "Not telling you I was in love with you."

My heart raced. "You love me?"

"I've felt it for a long time, but I was too afraid to say the words. But I'm done being a chickenshit. I love you, Sloane Carrick."

Tears filled my eyes, happy ones. And that ivy grew a little taller. "I love you, too."

Wilder closed his eyes. When he opened them, it looked like he was on the verge of tears as well.

My heart was so full.

He loves me.

Wilder loves me.

So many emotions bubbled up, it was difficult to contain them all. It hit me that I didn't want this moment to be marred by a secret. I hadn't been planning on telling him until tomorrow, but it felt right.

Wilder loves me.

It would be okay.

So I took a deep breath and swallowed. "I'm . . . pregnant."

The change was immediate. Wilder's face fell, and he took a step back. He *let go of me.* "What did you say?"

"I . . . I'm pregnant."

30

WILDER

TEN YEARS AGO

"Thank you for everything."

My dad patted my leg. "I'm glad she let me help out at the end."

We'd just boarded our flight back to New York after the most horrible week of my life. My mom had died eight days ago. It felt like I was leaving a piece of my heart behind in England. Up ahead, the flight attendant closed the cabin door, and I suddenly felt claustrophobic. Leaving seemed so *final*. But I had a baby coming in a few weeks, so it wasn't like I had a choice.

Two days after Whitney's baby shower, my mom had called to tell me she'd stopped the chemo months ago. She hadn't wanted to give me the news while I was waiting for a child, so she'd been lying and telling me she was still in treatment. She'd hoped to make it until after the baby was born, but it wasn't in the cards. My dad flew out the following day to help take care of her. That didn't go over too well with wife number three, especially when he stayed for over a month, but nothing could have dragged him back home. My divorced parents had a strange relationship. They couldn't make it work married, yet they never stopped loving or caring for each other.

"I should call Madison and let her know we caught the red-eye," Dad said. "They're going to tell us to turn off all devices any minute."

"Shit. Yeah. Let me call Whitney, too. She sleeps late. I don't want to scare her when we get in tomorrow morning. She's not expecting me until this time tomorrow night. But my phone is in my bag in the overhead." I was in the window seat, so I slid in front of my dad, stepped into the aisle, and reached up to unzip my duffle.

"Sir," the flight attendant said, "you're going to need to take your seat. We're going to start moving any minute."

I felt around inside my bag and pulled out my cell before shoving my bag back in. But when I closed the overhead compartment, my phone slipped from my hand. It landed with a loud clank on the armrest of my father's aisle seat and tumbled to the floor an aisle up.

The flight attendant wasn't happy when I bent to get it. "Sorry."

Back in my seat, I tried to turn my phone on. But when I flipped it over, I found a big crack through the middle of the screen. Usually that just meant a hundred bucks for new glass, but when I pressed the button, the only thing that illuminated was a fat yellow stripe down one side.

"Crap."

"What happened? It broke?"

I turned the screen to show my dad. He had his wife's name called up on his own cell, about to push the call button, but he held his phone out to me. "Here, use mine. I'm in the doghouse with Madison anyway."

I smiled sadly. "Thanks. But I don't know Whitney's number. I don't know anyone's number anymore because of these things."

Dad nodded. "Me neither."

In the end, it didn't matter. Neither of us got to call anyone, because the flight attendant came on the overhead speakers and said all cell phones had to be switched to airplane mode or turned off.

Dad shrugged. "Oh well."

A half hour later, we hit cruising altitude. Dad conked out, but I was too wired to even shut my eyes. I tried putting the airline's complimentary headphones on and listening to music to relax, but the inside of my head felt like a merry-go-round.

Brown horse up. What should I do about Lucas? I wasn't sure his father could handle a six-year-old. Especially one who was whip-smart and already a bit of a troublemaker. *Brown horse down.*

White horse up. What about Mom's business? She and my dad had split up the magazines and newspapers they owned when they divorced. She had a good staff, a lot of trustworthy people, but someone had to keep an eye on things. *White horse down.*

Gray horse up. Could I still play for England? The manager of the team I'd planned to join before Whitney got pregnant had reached out to give his condolences, and we'd had breakfast this morning. He'd pretty much told me I had an open invitation to train and play with the team. But would Whitney consider moving? *Gray horse down.*

Black horse up. Whitney . . . Should I propose? I'd been considering it before all hell broke loose with Mom. And now I even had a ring.

I pulled the letter my mom had left me, along with the ring box, from my pocket. Unfolding the note I'd already read a dozen times, my eyes dropped to the last lines at the bottom.

The day your father gave me this ring was the happiest day of my life. I know that might be hard to understand now, since we haven't been together in so long. But your father was and still is the love of my life. It was your grandmother's ring, and her mother's ring before that, and now it should belong to the love of your life.

I tasted salt when I swallowed. It was difficult to see my mother's handwriting. *Black horse down.*

So much to think about . . .

I closed my eyes and tried to sort through some of it. But hours later, the only thing I'd decided was that it wasn't a good time to make decisions. Dad stirred while I was staring out the window into the dark night sky. I'd forgotten Mom's ring was still in my hand.

"I wondered what happened to that," he said.

I sighed. "She left it for me with a letter."

Dad nodded. We hadn't talked much about Whitney or the baby. Considering the first thing he'd said to me when I told him my girlfriend was pregnant was that I should get a paternity test, he wasn't the sounding board I was looking for.

"You thinking about giving it to your girl?"

I shrugged. "I don't know. Mom told me to give it to the love of my life. I'm not sure that's Whitney. But the baby she's carrying already is. So is that enough?"

"Well, I'm not the best person to give marriage advice with my track record. But I can tell you it's hard enough to make a marriage work when she *is* the love of your life. It's nearly impossible without that bond. Trust me—wife number two was a bad idea. And the jury is still out on number three." Dad chuckled.

"What happened with your marriages?"

"We're only flying to New York, kid. China wouldn't be enough time to unpack that bag."

I smiled. "How about what happened with Mom?"

Dad sighed. "I was young and stupid. Arrogant, too. I put my life and my business before her and you. We had different priorities. Hers were right. Mine weren't. I regret that now, not changing my life to be who she needed. I thought building an empire was the most important thing. Turned out, none of it ever meant shit without your mother. You know, I asked her to marry me again a few weeks ago. But she turned me down. It was too late for us."

"You're also married to wife number three, so there's that . . ."

We both laughed.

Dad rested his hand on my shoulder. "You'll figure things out with your girl. No one else can but you."

The cab pulled up to the rented house in Boston at 8 a.m. I looked it over like it was my first time seeing it—white picket fence, big yard, nice house. The neighbor next door waved as I grabbed my bag from the trunk. She was walking her little girl, who was about seven or eight, to the bus stop.

I stood in the street for a minute, even after the cab pulled away.

I had a good life. A beautiful girlfriend, a baby on the way, a promising career—even if it wasn't in England. So why was I holding back? Maybe Whitney wasn't the love of my life, but I did love her and the baby . . . Well, at least I cared for her deeply. They deserved commitment. It didn't have to be Mom's ring. I bet Whit would like to pick out her own anyway.

I took a deep breath and decided. *Fuck it.* I'm asking her to marry me. And if she says yes, we'll do it before the baby's born. My kid should have a family. If I waited for things to be perfect, my kid would grow up shuttling between two houses like I had. Whitney and I would just have to work on it, that's all.

Blood pumped through my veins as I went up to the house. I unlocked the door and tiptoed inside, not wanting to wake her—but maybe I should. Maybe I should propose right now. We didn't have much time left before the baby came. Hell, it could be today.

Setting down my bags, I slipped off my shoes and walked down the hallway toward the bedroom. It sounded like maybe Whitney was up anyway. Or if not, she'd fallen asleep with the TV on. The door was shut, and as I opened it, I heard what sounded like grunting.

Nice. Was she watching porn? It had been a while since we'd had sex, so that was a welcome surprise. Maybe my proposal could wait an hour or two . . . And if she was sleeping with that on, I was most definitely waking her.

I walked in feeling more upbeat than I had in a week. And then I froze.

I was definitely not going to have to wake Whitney. Because she was up on all fours on the edge of the bed while some guy plowed into her from behind. The two were so busy, they didn't even notice someone had walked in—not until my phone hit the mirror above the dresser a few feet away. It cracked again, shattering into a million pieces. *Just like my life.*

"What the fuck?" I roared.

The guy jumped back. Whitney grabbed for a sheet, pulling it up over her chest like being naked was her biggest problem.

The guy took one look at my face, one look at the size of me, and very wisely backed away. He held his hands up. "I don't want any trouble."

"Well, you fucking found it anyway!"

But . . . why did the guy look so familiar? It took a few seconds of staring, while debating which leg I was gonna break first, for it to come to me. *The guy from the mall.* And I wasn't sure how I hadn't recognized him when we saw him again, but he was also the guy who'd been watching Whitney the night we met.

It felt like my blood was boiling, I was so filled with hot rage.

The guy grabbed his clothes. The motherfucker was lucky as shit that I was so surprised, or he'd be pounded into the ground by now. He ran past me, looking like he was going to piss his pants.

And that—*that's* what Whitney was focused on. She screamed after the guy. "You freaking wimp! Running away like a damn coward!"

Un-freaking-real.

I shook my head. "You're lucky you're a woman." I pointed to her, then to the door. "Get your goddamned clothes on and get the fuck out of my house."

"Gladly!"

This woman had some set of balls. No apology. Not even an attempt at faking embarrassed or ashamed. She acted like I'd done something wrong. I needed to put some distance between us so I didn't explode. So I stormed into the living room and waited for her to get dressed.

A few minutes later, Whitney stomped out—the Louis Vuitton duffle bag she'd talked me into buying as her hospital bag on her shoulder. Her face was indignant. "*You're* the one who should leave," she spat. "*I'm* the one who's pregnant."

My eyes dropped to her belly. I swallowed. "Yeah? With whose baby?"

31

WILDER

"Whatever you did, we'll fix it." Andrew slid onto the stool next to me.

I raised my hand to order another drink, though I'd already had one too many, and shook my head. "I don't think even you can get me out of this mess."

"Well, you got me out of bed at three in the morning. So why don't you clue me in on what we're talking about and let me be the judge of that."

I deadpanned at my friend. "I told Sloane I loved her earlier tonight."

"So? How the hell does that equate to . . ." He dug his cell from his pocket and swiped to open, reading the text I'd sent him an hour ago. "'*I fucked up. I royally fucked up.*' Does that mean you don't love her? Did it come out during sex? I've done that before. Some orgasms affect our brain, man."

I sucked back the rest of my whiskey. "No, we were on the dance floor at a wedding, and I love her. I love her more than anything I've ever loved."

"More than that ratty purple bear you carried around until you were like seven and I know you still have somewhere, even though you deny it?"

I sighed. "Way more than Mr. Bongo."

"So what's the problem?"

"Didn't you hear me? I fell in love."

"So? It's not a deadly virus. It won't kill you."

"It almost did last time."

"When were you ever in love?"

"I loved my high school girlfriend and my mother—both of whom died. And then there's Whitney."

"You never loved Whitney."

"I loved our baby."

Andrew smiled sadly. "I know you did, man. But this is different."

"No, it's not." I met his eyes. "Sloane's pregnant."

My friend's shoulders slumped. "Oh fuck."

The bartender walked over. I ordered a refill, and Andrew ordered a vodka seltzer. Neither of us said a word until we had our drinks and were a few sips in.

Eventually, it was Andrew who spoke. "What did you say when she told you?"

"Nothing. I took off like a fucking coward. Last night was another wedding. I left her standing on the damn dance floor. Didn't even say goodbye to the bride or groom."

"Dick move, but okay. You'll apologize. Grovel. Do you think she loves you back?"

"She said she did."

"Then she'll forgive you. Look at me—I did something much worse to Camille, and she's giving me another chance. You acted like an idiot. Sloane will get over it." He smirked. "She should probably get used to it if she's going to be around a while."

I shook my head. "I'm not sure I can do it."

"You gotta trust someone again sometime, Wilder."

I sucked back my drink. It burned going down. I'd never liked liquor much. "Who says?"

"Well, I suppose you don't. But then you stand to lose the woman you love and your child. I guess you have to make a decision. What's scarier—the thought of taking a chance and maybe being let down again, or the thought of losing Sloane and the baby?"

32

SLOANE

I couldn't believe two weeks had gone by. I still hadn't told anyone I was pregnant, except for Wilder. His reaction had devastated me, made me recoil and turn inward. But I needed to talk to someone. I could have gone to Elijah. He would've been supportive, but instead, I'd decided to go to my brother Will.

It was early Saturday afternoon, and I knew the bar would be empty. So I picked up a pie from our favorite pizza place and went to pay him a visit.

Will was wiping down the counters, but he stopped when I walked in. "Uh-oh. When do you need off?"

I smiled. "I don't need off."

He squinted. "Does the pie have pepper and onions?"

"It does."

He resumed wiping the counter. "Then you want something."

I laughed. "Can't I just want to spend time with my big brother?"

He took out his wallet. "How much do you need?"

I swiped the rag he was using from his hands and threw it at him. "Jerk."

He smiled. "What's going on, Peaty?"

I climbed up on a stool and flipped open the pizza box, grabbing a slice. A few droplets of grease dripped on the bar as I brought the tip up for a bite. "Sorry."

Will shook his head and reached under the bar for a roll of paper towels. "Some shit never changes." He positioned the top of the open box under where I was eating. "Here. Use this."

There wasn't an easy way to start this conversation, so I decided to just come out with it. "So . . . I'm pregnant."

Unfortunately, Will had just bitten into his slice, and he started to choke, *really* choke. I stood on my seat and climbed over the bar, ready to do the Heimlich maneuver. But he held his hand out, stopping me. His face was red and his voice hoarse, but at least he was able to chirp out words. "No." He coughed. "I'm good."

I grabbed a glass and poured seltzer from the tap. Will chugged half of it down, then bent with hands on his knees and took a few deep breaths.

"Are you okay?"

"No. You just fucking told me you're pregnant. Of course I'm not okay. You're my little sister."

"I'm twenty-six, not twelve."

"You're not married."

"Thanks for pointing that out. I wasn't aware. Come to think of it, I also didn't realize it was 1952 and you had to be married to be pregnant."

"You know what I mean . . ." Will kept shaking his head. But he seemed to be able to breathe, so I walked back around to the other side of the bar.

"Whose head am I busting open? Wilder's, I assume?"

I frowned. "There will be no busting anything. But yes, Wilder is the father. I came to you because I need someone to talk to, Will. Do you think you can put all your dumb masculinity and archaic opinions aside for a few minutes?"

My brother was quiet as he stared down at the bar. He took a deep breath before looking up. "Are you happy?"

"I was pretty shocked when I found out, but I'm warming up to happy. I always wanted a family. I just didn't expect it so soon."

Will shook his head. "Doesn't matter if you plan it. You're never ready for it. It's like a punch; you take it as it comes."

"Poetic."

"Not that I give a shit, but it affects you—how did Wilder take the news?"

I knew my brothers. If I told them the full truth—that he'd walked out on me after I told him and had sent me only a few one-sentence texts in the last two weeks—they'd hold a grudge against him forever. I wasn't sure how Wilder was going to be in my life, but we were going to have a baby together, so it probably wasn't smart to turn the entire family against him.

"He was even more shocked than I was."

Will's jaw flexed. "So he's not going to be a father to this kid?"

"He'll be involved in some way. We're . . . still figuring it out."

"Sending a check isn't being a parent."

"I know."

"Raising a kid alone isn't easy."

"I know that, too. I've watched you do it. But Olivia turned out great."

Will let out a big sigh. "You won't be doing it alone. I got your back. You've always had mine. And Olivia's."

The choice to speak to Will, of all people, seemed a little insane. He was the toughest critic of the family. Yet I'd wanted to tell him first. Now I realized why. I'd needed to hear those words. *"I got your back."*

I fought tears. "I'm scared, Will."

He smiled half-heartedly. "Welcome to parenthood. What you're feeling right now? It never goes away. The things you're scared about just change. You go from being terrified about whether you're ready to have a baby, to being terrified about whether you're holding the kid's head right. Eventually you settle in and think, *maybe I got this.* Then the terrible twos start, and don't even get me going on the shit I worry about with a fourteen-year-old girl."

"Anne would be proud of how you've raised Olivia."

"She'd be proud of how you stepped up, too. I'm not sure who would've been more traumatized if I'd had to have that period conversation with her six months ago, me or Olivia."

"Considering you came home with a bag of incontinence products instead of period stuff, I'm pretty sure it would've been her."

Will chuckled. "How the hell was I supposed to know?"

I picked up my slice of pizza and bit into it again. My appetite had been nonexistent lately, but suddenly I was starving.

"Does Dad know yet?" Will asked.

I shook my head and finished chewing. "You're the only person who knows besides Wilder. I'd appreciate it if you kept it to yourself until I'm ready to tell everyone else."

"Of course. It's your business. Are you waiting until the end of the first trimester to tell people?"

I'd been waiting to have a real conversation with Wilder. His occasional text asking how I felt left me in limbo. I'd hoped to have a more concrete plan on how Wilder and I were going to handle things before talking to Dad, but the last few days I'd lost faith that was going to happen anytime in the near future.

"No, I'm going to tell him soon."

Will nodded. A few minutes later, a couple of early customers wandered in, effectively bringing our conversation to an end. It was just as well, since I didn't have much more to say. After I finished two slices, I stuck around for another half hour, helping stock behind the bar and getting things ready for the weekend crowd.

Will walked over as I put my jacket on. "You getting out of here?"

"I have a bunch of errands to run. I'll stop back and do the books tomorrow."

His eyes shifted to the customers at the other end of the bar. They were too busy yelling at a horse race on one of the TVs to pay us any mind. Though my brother lowered his voice anyway. "I think most of parenting you learn as you go, and most advice people give isn't worth shit because every situation is different. But there is one important thing I learned that's worth sharing."

"What's that?"

"You can't make someone else happy unless you're happy yourself. After Anne died, I spent years pretending I was happy for Olivia's sake. But she knew the truth—kids always do. Once I allowed myself to feel happiness again, I saw a change in my daughter. She was lighter, laughed more. Of course that was before the teen years set in, but I think you get what I'm saying. I hope things work out with Wilder, if that's what you want. But if they don't, focus on finding happiness for yourself. The best gift you can give your kid is showing them not to dwell on the things we can't change and live life to the fullest, even if it's not the one you planned."

I kissed my brother's cheek. "Thanks, Will."

"Congratulations, Peaty. You're going to be a great mom."

Later that night, I climbed into bed exhausted at nine o'clock. I'd spent yet another day rushing around, trying to outrun my thoughts. What I needed was some mindless TV and a good night's rest. So I flicked on the television and went directly to one of the channels that was always good for reality TV. Except *Say Yes to the Dress* was on, and the bridal boutique they were in reminded me of the morning Wilder had shown up unexpectedly to help me keep my appointment to sell my old wedding gown.

I sighed and flicked to another channel. *Love Island* was on that one—and the guy currently flirting with a curvy blonde was *British*. I jabbed my thumb at the remote a third time and a movie flickered on—where *the woman was pregnant*. That was it for my attempt at *mindless* relaxation. I turned the TV off, forcing my eyes shut.

But a few minutes later, my phone buzzed from my nightstand. Wilder's name flashed on the screen. Just seeing it made my heart beat faster. It had been a few days since his last uninspired text, so I was certain this would just be another four-word letdown—*how are you feeling?* or whatever. Taking a deep breath, I steadied myself for disappointment yet again.

Wilder: Could we talk?

I sat up in bed. *Could we talk?* It didn't sound very promising. But at this point, any outcome was better than the unknown. So I texted back.

Sloane: Of course. When?
Wilder: Are you busy now?

Oh God. My stomach rolled. As much as I needed to know where he stood, I was also terrified. I reached for the lamp and switched on the light. We usually FaceTimed, but I considered suggesting a call so he wouldn't see me get upset. But screw it, I had every right to cry. Served him right. Though I should be prepared with some tissues.

Sloane: No, just give me a minute and I'll FaceTime you.

He typed back before my feet had even hit the floor.

Wilder: Would it be okay if we talked in person?

My brows furrowed.

Sloane: You're in New York?
Wilder: I'm downstairs. I came straight from the airport and took a chance you'd be home.

My eyes widened. I jumped to look out my bedroom window. Sure enough, Wilder was standing on the sidewalk. I watched him pace back and forth a few times, emotions twisting a knot inside me.

Two weeks of four-word texts and he just shows up with no advance notice?

He *took a chance* I'd be home? What else does a pregnant woman do on a Saturday night?

He's come to tell me in person that he wants nothing to do with us.

Us.

My heart squeezed. I wasn't a *me* anymore. I was an *us*.

I was so busy worrying about a dozen things that *could* happen, that I forgot what was *actually* happening and didn't respond right away. Eventually, my phone buzzed again.

Wilder: I should've called. I'm sorry for showing up unannounced. I can come back tomorrow, if you want.

I might not be able to focus enough to respond to a text, but I knew for damn sure that I wouldn't sleep a wink if I turned him away. There was no point in prolonging things any more.

Sloane: I'll buzz you in.

Living on the fourth floor of a walk-up at least gave me a minute or two of lead time. I went to the bathroom, ran my fingers through my unwashed hair, and swiped at what I thought was day-old smeared mascara under my eyes. But it turned out it wasn't makeup; it was dark circles from lack of sleep.

My nerves were at an all-time high as I went to the door and un-locked it. Wilder was already coming up the last flight of stairs as I stepped into the hall. He carried two big duffles, one in each hand. I hadn't noticed any bags from the window, so my focus narrowed to them and what they might mean. *Is he planning on staying over? Will I let him if he wants to? Did I leave stuff at his apartment and he's returning it?* Momentarily lost in my head, I didn't look up to see the face of the man carrying the bags. When I did, my heart stuttered.

Wilder looked awful. Probably about as good as I felt. His hair was a mess, his eyes were puffy and rimmed with darker rings than mine, and it looked like he'd slept in his clothes. My instinct was to open my arms, give him a hug, and tell him everything would be okay, but I forced myself to remember what I'd been struggling through the last few weeks. *Alone.*

Instead, I folded my arms across my chest. "You couldn't have called before you boarded your flight? Or even after you landed? Give me a little notice?"

Wilder raked a hand through his hair. It looked like he'd been doing that for hours. "I'm sorry. I was afraid you might tell me not to come after the way I've acted for the last couple of weeks."

If he thought that, he had *no clue* how I felt about him. Pissed off or not, hurt or not, I was crazy about this man. I shook my head and opened the door, stepping aside for him to come in.

Wilder slowed as he passed, looking into my eyes and speaking softly. "Thank you." He set the bags on the floor in the kitchen and swallowed, looking down at my belly. "How are you feeling?"

"Physically fine."

"Your blood sugar?"

"Right where it should be."

We were both silent for a long time. I hadn't realized I wasn't looking at him until he called my name.

"Sloane?"

My eyes met his.

"I'm so fucking sorry." His eyes filled with tears, so I thought he might have meant for the way he'd acted.

But I was afraid to get my hopes up since he could also be apologizing for not wanting to be involved in our life. "For what?"

"For running away. For acting like a coward. For not being the man you deserve."

I tasted salt in my throat as I swallowed.

"I know there's no excuse for running away, but I want to tell you why I acted the way I did."

"Okay . . ."

"Do you think we can go sit on the couch or something?"

I hesitated before nodding.

Once we were seated in the living room, Wilder took my hand and squeezed. "Do you remember when you asked me about my past relationships? I told you I had a relationship in high school and another one in college, but I didn't go into detail about Whitney."

I nodded. "You said she destroyed you."

Wilder nodded. "That's true. But it's not the whole story. I met Whitney in one of the bars near Harvard. She'd taken the semester off because of some financial-aid issues and her dad being sick—at least that's what she told me. We started hanging out. It was when my mom was sick, so we had that in common. I liked her well enough, though not enough to say she was someone I wanted to spend the rest of my life with. But then Whitney got pregnant. She told me it was mine, but it wasn't."

"Wilder, I would never—"

He held up his hand. "Shit—no, that's not what I meant. This is coming out all wrong. I wasn't insinuating you would ever—" Wilder shook his head. "I know you would never do something like that."

"Okay . . ."

"But . . . I thought that baby was mine for nine months. I talked to him. We had names picked out. I might not have been in love with Whitney, but I fell in love with our baby. It threw a big wrench in my life that I hadn't been expecting, but Whitney and I moved in together, and I accepted that I wasn't going to play for a UK rugby team, like I'd always dreamed. I needed to be around to help raise my child. Two weeks before the baby was due, my mom died. I flew to England alone for the wake. Whitney was too far along to travel. And when I came home earlier than expected, I walked in on her and another guy. I'd been nothing more than their mark from the beginning. Whitney wasn't ever a student at Harvard. She'd never been to college. Her father wasn't sick, and she was twenty-nine years old, not nineteen. She also already had two children with the guy I caught her with. Both kids were bringing in child support from guys like me who had no clue they were being scammed. Whitney and her partner did their homework, found young, stupid guys with deep pockets, and made up relatable stories to help create a bond. A year or so after each kid was born, Whitney broke things off with the current schmuck, but the child support would keep coming for eighteen years."

"Oh my God. That's terrible. I'm so sorry."

"I never even saw the kid who was born a few weeks later. And I thought I was long past all that, but I . . . I got scared." Wilder looked down in silence for a long time. When he met my eyes again, tears streamed down his face. "I never doubted that you were carrying my baby, I swear. I just . . . I know this might sound stupid, but I loved that little boy. And it felt like I lost him after. Maybe it was because I'd just lost my mom and the lines were blurred, but it hurt just the same. I lost three people I loved—my high school sweetheart, my mom, and my baby. Whitney was the last real relationship I had, and it wasn't real at all. I'm so afraid I'm going to lose you or fuck something up with you. And my dad is on his fourth wife, and I was just . . . a fucking chickenshit. I'm so sorry, Sloane. I acted like a coward when you deserved so much more."

I pulled Wilder into my arms. "It's okay. Please don't cry. You're here now."

We held each other for a long time. Eventually, he stepped back.

"I know this is going to be hard for you to believe because of the way I've acted, but I'm happy you're pregnant."

Hope bloomed in my chest. I wanted to believe him, but he was right. A part of me was also afraid. "Happy? Are you sure?"

He nodded. "I need to show you something."

"Okay . . ."

Wilder went to the kitchen and unzipped one of the duffle bags. He pulled something out—bunches of white fabric. At first I thought it was a christening outfit, maybe his own from when he was a baby? But too much material spilled out of the bag. He shook it out, holding it up as he returned to the living room.

My jaw dropped. "Is that . . . ?"

He nodded. "The dress you loved at the shop the day we sold your old wedding dress. I went back after I dropped you off and bought it."

"But . . . we weren't even dating yet."

"Do you remember what you said when I suggested you buy it?"

"No?"

"You said you loved it, but you weren't buying a dress for a fantasy that didn't exist." Wilder looked me in the eyes. "So I bought it. Because since the day I met you, you've made *me* believe the fantasy exists. And I wanted to give this to you, if I was lucky enough to ever make you mine."

"Oh my God." I jumped into his arms. "I can't believe you did that."

Wilder stroked my hair. "I'm so sorry, Cupcake. If you give me another chance, I promise not to let you down."

My answer was to crush my lips against his. This wasn't the fantasy I'd dreamed of, but maybe my reality was better than anything I could ever imagine. We stayed in the living room a long time, kissing and saying *I love you* over and over. The two of us must've looked like loons—tear-streaked cheeks, dark circles under our puffy eyes, and yet the biggest smiles spread across our faces.

"I almost forgot. I brought you something else."

"What?"

Wilder set me on my feet and lifted the second duffle bag to the coffee table. "Go ahead. You unzip this one."

I pulled the zipper back and was surprised to find . . . books. There had to be twenty inside. "What are all these?" I slipped out a few and read the titles aloud. *"It's Not You, It's the Pregnancy; The Self-Love Workbook for First-Time Mums; There's No Right Way to Raise a Child; Your Pregnant Brain."*

Wilder smiled when I paused. "I figured you would need a new crop of self-help books."

"I thought you said my self-help books were dumb."

"That was before I found this one . . ." He riffled around inside the duffle. "Here we go. This is the one that changed my mind."

He turned the cover to face me. *Forty New Positions for Forty Weeks of Pregnancy: The Couple's Guide to Orgasming Through Full Term.*

I laughed. "Figures that's what it would take."

Wilder tossed the book on the table and wrapped his arms around my waist. "I missed a few weeks. We'll have to play catch-up."

33

SLOANE

A rude streak of sunlight cut across my face, waking me the next morning. The first thing that popped into my head was the memory of Wilder in my kitchen, holding the wedding dress he'd bought. I smiled as I turned to say good morning, but the spot next to me on the bed was empty, and the sheet was cold. So I wrapped the blanket around myself and went searching for Wilder. I found him at the kitchen table, shirtless with a cup of coffee, nose buried in a book.

"Let me guess which one you're reading."

He grinned. "I might've dog-eared a few pages."

I chuckled. "What time is it?"

"Almost ten."

"Wow. I had my alarm set for nine. I must've slept right through it."

"I turned it off. You didn't get enough sleep last night."

"I think it's more like you kept me up half the night."

Wilder pulled me onto his lap. "You didn't seem to object."

"I couldn't. Your tongue was in my mouth."

He buried his face in my neck. "My tongue was a lot of other places, too."

That it was. My belly fluttered, thinking about the way he'd made me feel last night. "How long have you been up?"

"A few hours. I went to the grocery store to get some things for breakfast. Your fridge was pretty bleak."

"I haven't been hungry lately."

Wilder ran his nose up and down my neck. "I'm starving."

I got the feeling we'd just changed subjects. "Is that so?"

I would've been happy to go back to bed. Surprisingly, it was

Wilder who put the brakes on things. He kissed the tip of my nose. "I saw your brother this morning."

Uh-oh. "Which one?"

"Will."

"Sorry." I closed my eyes. "I should've warned you that I told him. How did that conversation go?"

"Same way it would've if I had a little sister who got knocked up by a guy with a reputation, and he didn't do the right thing off the bat."

"Shit." My shoulders slumped. "That well, huh?"

Wilder brushed hair from my face and smiled. "It's all good. He'll come around when he's ready. I'm glad he's protective of you. I wouldn't want it any other way."

I guessed I should be happy no one had a black eye. "I need to tell Travis and my dad still. And Olivia."

"I'd like to tell my dad when you're ready, too."

"Oh God." I had completely forgotten that Wilder's dad was *Mr. Hayes*—the CEO of the company I worked for. "My job. I wasn't even thinking of that."

"There's no rush." Wilder ran his hands up and down my arms. "But I would like to go with you when you tell your father, if that's alright."

"He likes you, but I'm not sure how he'll take the news. He and my brothers still treat me like I'm twelve in a lot of ways."

"They need to see that I'm going to be here for you. Telling them isn't enough."

I nodded and let out an audible breath. "Okay. We'll tell him together. He works at the bar on Sundays, and it's usually pretty busy because of games and races. How long are you staying?"

Wilder looked me in the eyes. "Forever."

My pulse picked up. "What do you mean? Aren't you going back to England?"

"I'll keep an office there, but my life is here. I think it's time I moved back."

"Wow. Okay."

"I think I might have found the perfect place, too."

"Really? Where?"

He patted my ass. "How about you get dressed while I make breakfast, and I'll show you. I have an appointment to see the place at eleven."

I couldn't believe the last twenty-four hours. After weeks of dragging, I felt like I was floating. I was still scared, nervous that things might turn sour, but at least those feelings were balanced with excitement and happiness. Only time would tell how things would turn out. But I had hope again.

I took a quick shower and got dressed, then stuffed my face with the ridiculous feast Wilder had cooked for breakfast.

"Do we need to get going?" I piled my dish in the sink. "You said your appointment was at eleven. Are we taking the train? The subway has reduced service on the weekends."

Wilder smiled. "You'll see."

A few minutes later, we were out the door. On the street, we turned left, so I assumed we were heading to the C train up the block.

But Wilder stopped a few steps into our walk. "We're here."

I squinted. "Here where?"

He pointed to the brownstone next door to my brother's. I'd noticed the small FOR SALE sign a few weeks ago, but didn't pay it much attention. A real estate agent opened the front door and smiled.

Wilder laced his fingers with mine. "I need a place to live other than a hotel, and I want to be near you. Eventually, we'll need more space for the baby. I figured you wouldn't want to move too far from Olivia." He shrugged. "Saw the sign this morning, and it seemed like the perfect solution. I know you're probably not ready to move in with me. I have a lot to do to earn back your trust. Until then, I'll be close enough to be there when you need me, but you'll still have your space."

"You're really going to move here from London? Your home has been there for ten years. I don't want you to make any rash decisions."

"My home is where you are, Sloane. And this decision isn't rash for me. I've wanted nothing but to be with you since the day I met you."

I looked over at the brownstone. It was as big or bigger than my brother's. "What would you do with this much house? Rent the floors?"

Wilder shook his head. "The real estate agent said it needs some fixing up. But I'd make it into one big house. Between the baby and Lucas, who will probably visit more often than we'd like, we're going to need space. Plus, I'm hoping we'll fill some of the extra rooms with more kids someday. I'd love a family like you have, with everyone close in age. Lucas is sixteen years younger than me, so I pretty much grew up an only child—bouncing from one parent's house to the other. I like what you guys have. It feels right."

My chest filled with warmth. Yet there were still those nerves. A part of me was afraid to believe this was real.

Wilder must've seen the doubt in my face, though I'd thought I'd hid it well. He pulled me in tight. "Eventually it won't be so scary. I promise." He nodded toward the brownstone. "Come on. Let's go see where I'm going to live."

—————

Later that night, I was lying in bed while Wilder finished up a call.

"Thanks, buddy." He tossed his cell on the end table and slipped into bed next to me. "They accepted my counteroffer."

"Oh my God. So that's it? The house is yours?"

He nodded. "After a shitload of paperwork, but Andrew will take care of that."

"Wow. I can't believe how fast that happened."

"Sometimes you get lucky and something perfect falls into your lap." He ran his thumb over my bottom lip. "Like you."

"I didn't quite fall into your lap. More like you pulled me into the coat closet."

He smiled. "Semantics."

"Well, congratulations."

"Thank you. Back at ya."

"Me? I didn't just buy a house."

"Actually you did. I told Andrew to put the house in both our names."

"What? No. You can't do that."

"Of course I can."

"I didn't mean you can't—I meant you shouldn't do that."

"Why not?"

"Because . . . this is still new, Wilder."

"What's new?"

I motioned between us. "Us. The pregnancy. Things can happen."

Wilder's face fell. "Are you afraid to be tied to me?"

"No. That's not it at all."

"Then let me do this. I don't want this to be my house. I want it to be *our* house. I know what I did made you have doubts. But what I was scared of was never you, Sloane. I was afraid *I* wasn't enough for *you*."

"You are enough . . ."

Wilder brushed his lips with mine. "Then let me make this commitment. To us. To our family. Please."

"It's still so early in the pregnancy. What happens if . . ."

"I loved you before I knew you were pregnant. Whatever happens happens. But we'll always have each other."

I inhaled deeply, blowing out with a nod. "Okay."

He flashed a cocky smile, like he knew all along he'd win. "Thank you."

This man was dangerous. I was pretty sure he could get me to do anything he asked with a little begging and that grin. "You know, I'm not always going to be that easy."

"No?" He reached over and took my hand, bringing it between his legs. "I'll always be this hard for you."

We both laughed. "I walked right into that one, didn't I?"

Wilder climbed on top of me, hovering. "I love you, Cupcake."

My heart felt so full. "I love you, too."

EPILOGUE

SLOANE

SIX MONTHS LATER

Slam!

Lucas came in from outside with Olivia trailing behind. My niece stopped short when she got a look at Wilder lying on the couch—with a mud mask on his face and cucumber slices over his eyes.

"What the heck are you doing?"

Lucas rolled his eyes. "That's just one of his beauty treatments."

Olivia chuckled, and the two of them disappeared up the stairs.

"Door open!" I yelled after them.

Wilder sat up, removing the vegetables from his face. "Do we still need that rule? They're kind of related now, aren't they?"

"Not by blood. Would it have stopped you if my aunt had married your brother?"

"Good point." Wilder cupped his hand around his mouth and yelled up the stairs. "If I catch it shut, it comes off the hinges."

I smiled and sat down on the other end of the couch, lifting my feet onto Wilder's lap. "Rub, Mr. Hayes."

"Yes, *Mrs.* Hayes."

Wilder and I had gotten married a few days ago in England. It was the wedding I'd never dreamed of that turned out to be everything I ever wanted. We'd decided to do it before the baby was born, but I no longer had the desire for a big, lavish affair. Turned out, when I finally found true love, looking into each other's eyes and committing to spend the rest of our lives together was all the fairy tale I needed. Being somewhere special with our family around us was more than enough. We married at St. Dunstan in the East, the park Wilder had taken me to when I first went to visit him in London. Not only was it beautiful, but what it represented felt right—it was a place of hope, a place people had attempted to destroy so many times, yet it had never fallen.

The ceremony was short and the guest list small—only our dads, our brothers, Olivia, Andrew, and Elijah. But today we were having a party at Carrick's to celebrate. I couldn't imagine now why that hadn't always been my first choice of venues.

Wilder finished rubbing my feet and tugged me down onto the couch at his side. "Come here, wife."

I smiled. "I like the sound of that."

He cupped a hand at the back of my neck. "And I like the sound you make when I stick my cock in you. Let's go upstairs."

"First of all, I can't take you seriously when you're wearing a mud mask. But more importantly, we have to leave in a little while."

He rubbed his muddy nose with mine. "I'll be fast."

"You're getting mud on me." I laughed.

"Yeah, wait till you see where else I spread this stuff . . ." Wilder pressed his lips to mine. As usual, the kiss grew heated quickly. Luckily, the moment was interrupted by Lucas and Olivia stomping back down the stairs.

"Ugh," Lucas said. "Get a room."

"This is a room," Wilder noted. "A room in *my* house. Maybe you should go somewhere else."

Lucas shook his head. "I can't even look at you with that crap on your face."

"Yet another reason you should be elsewhere."

I smiled and stood. "Liv, why don't you go next door and get dressed? We're going to leave for Carrick's soon."

"That's where I was going."

Wilder lifted his chin to his brother. "And where do you think you're going?"

"With her."

He shook his head. "Wrong answer. Olivia doesn't need help dressing. But Harry wants to move some furniture around. I told him you'd stop over. Why don't you go do that next door before we leave?"

Lucas rolled his eyes. "Fine."

A few seconds later there was another slam!

"Why can't they shut that door without making the house shake?" I asked.

"I have no damn clue." Wilder reached for my face. "But where were we?"

I put a hand on his chest. "*You* were just about to get in the shower and wash that mud off. I'm going to attempt to fit into the dress I bought."

He pouted. "Fine. But I have something I want to give you after I get out of the shower."

"We really don't have time, Wilder."

He smiled. "I meant an *actual* gift."

"Oh." I laughed. "Okay."

A little while later, I'd just put my new dress on when Wilder came into the bedroom dressed and clean-shaven.

"Can you zip me?" I stood in front of the mirror while my husband went behind me and pulled the zipper up. When he got to the top, the dress was pretty snug. "God, I tried this on a week ago when you bought it, and it wasn't this tight."

He reached around and pulled the material against my belly. It looked like I was hiding a basketball. "My little boy is growing. He's going to be big and strong, just like his old man."

I turned in his arms. "I hope he has your eyes."

"I hope he has your everything else. Except maybe height and shoulders."

Two months ago, we'd found out we were having a boy. Wilder had said he didn't care about the sex of the baby, but I knew he was secretly happy to have the first member of his future rugby team.

"I don't think I ever asked you, what did you weigh when you were born?"

He met my eyes. "You don't want to know."

"Oh Jesus. You were big?"

He bent and kissed my belly. "Your mother scares easily, so we're going to keep that info to ourselves." Wilder stood and kissed my lips. "Come on. I want to give you something."

I sat on the edge of the bed, and Wilder slipped a manila envelope from his nightstand. "This is only a proof. I wanted you to see it before it goes to print on Monday."

"Print? What is it?"

"Open it and see."

I unfastened the metal closure and reached inside, pulling out a magazine. It was upside down and backward, so I flipped it over. My heart stopped when I saw the cover.

"Oh my God. Is this real?"

Wilder smiled. "There's a six-page spread inside, too."

A photo from our wedding was on the cover of *Bride* magazine. Wilder was dipping me for a kiss in front of one of the stone archways of St. Dunstan. It looked even more magical than I remembered.

"It's the last wedding in the series," he said.

"How did you do this so fast? We only got home two days ago."

"I had a lot of help from Elijah, and the art department at the magazine was on alert, waiting for the photos to come in. I'd already given them all the details to draft the article."

"I can't believe you did this."

Wilder lifted his chin. "The spread starts on page thirty-three."

I flipped, anxious to read the article and see what other photos were included. My eyes jumped around the pages—photos of the venue, the cake, my dress, the small restaurant where we all went to dinner after the ceremony. A photo of Wilder holding my hand, displaying what had been his mom's engagement ring but now adorned my finger, a photo of us walking down the aisle at Piper and Aiden's wedding, only a few minutes after we'd met—there had to be twenty different photos on the six pages. I covered my mouth as I turned to the one at the very end. Wilder had snapped it the night of our wedding. It was taken from the back, and I was looking over my shoulder with a flirty smile. I wore only his old rugby jersey, with nothing underneath, but you couldn't tell that since it hung to my knees.

"Oh my God. I can't believe you included this."

"If you don't like it, we can use a different one. But I love that picture of you smiling with my name on your back."

"It's actually perfect—the perfect ending to our love story."

"No, sweetheart. It's not the ending; it's only the beginning. And this story will last a lifetime."

ACKNOWLEDGMENTS

Thank you to Monique Patterson and her publishing team for bringing my very first, brand-new romance novel to stores! And to Hannah Wann and Becky West for bringing *Jilted* to the UK.

To my agent, Kimberly Brower—thank you for always being there to support me and guide me to new adventures.

Behind every woman who succeeds is a tribe of successful women who cheer her on, have her back, and encourage her to do scary things. Thank you to my tribe leader, Penelope Ward, who is always by my side, and to Cheri, Luna, Julie, Elaine, Jessica, and the twenty-six thousand smart ladies in my amazing Facebook Group, Vi's Violets.

To my family—Chris, Jake, Gracie, Sarah, Kennedy, and Kylie (who better have a ring by the time this book comes out!), all of whom never complain when my head is stuck in a book or I'm working long hours.

To you—*the readers*. Thank you for your support and excitement. Whether we are meeting for the first time, or you've been with me for more than a decade reading my novels, I hope Wilder and Sloane's story allowed you to escape for a short while and you'll come back soon to see who you might meet next!

ABOUT THE AUTHOR

Irene Bello of Irene Bello Photography

VI KEELAND is a #1 *New York Times,* #1 *Wall Street Journal,* and *USA Today* bestselling author. With millions of books sold, her titles have been translated in twenty-six languages and have appeared on bestseller lists in the United States, Germany, Brazil, Bulgaria, Israel, and Hungary. Three of her short stories have been turned into films by Passionflix, and two of her books are currently optioned for movies. She resides in New York with her husband and their three children, where she is living out her own happily ever after with the boy she met at age six.